A GUIDE TO CHILDREN'S BOOKS ABOUT
ASIAN AMERICANS

A Guide to Children's Books about Asian Americans

Barbara Blake

SCOLAR PRESS

© Barbara Blake, 1995

All rights reserved. No part of this publication may be reproduced, stored in a retrieval system, or transmitted in any form or by any means, electronic, mechanical, photocopying, recording, or otherwise without the prior permission of the publisher.

Published by
SCOLAR PRESS
Gower House
Croft Road
Aldershot
Hants GU11 3HR
England

Ashgate Publishing Company
Old Post Road
Brookfield
Vermont 05036
USA

British Library Cataloguing in Publication Data

Guide to Children's Books About Asian Americans
  I. Blake, Barbara
  011.62

Library of Congress Cataloging-in-Publication Data

Blake, Barbara.
  A Guide to Children's Books About Asian Americans / Barbara Blake.
    p.   cm.
  ISBN 1–85928–014–5
  1. Asian Americans—Juvenile literature—Bibliography. 2. Asian Americans—Juvenile fiction—Bibliography. I. Title.
Z1361.07857   1995 E184.08
016.973'0495—dc20   94–36078
                  CIP

ISBN 1 85928 014 5

Typeset in Palatino by Poole Typesetting (Wessex) Ltd, Bournemouth and printed in Great Britain by Hartnolls Ltd, Bodmin

Dedicated to my mother, Mary Ellen Ethridge, who taught me to be an individual and to not give up. Thanks, Mom.

Barbara Blake

CONTENTS

Acknowledgements	ix
Purpose and organization of the book	xi
Part One	**1**
1 East Asia	3
2 Southeast Asia	16
3 South Asia	25
Part Two	**29**
Fiction – preschool through third grade	31
Fiction – fourth through sixth grade	97
Nonfiction – preschool through third grade	128
Nonfiction – fourth through sixth grade	145
Appendices	**179**
Alphabetical listing by author	181
Alphabetical listing by title	192
Listings by culture, category and grade:	203
Fiction – preschool through third grade	203
Fiction – fourth through sixth grade	209
Nonfiction – preschool through third grade	213
Nonfiction – fourth through sixth grade	216
Select list of sources of Asian children's books	221

ACKNOWLEDGEMENTS

The author wishes to recognize Managing Editor Sue McNaughton and Ellen Keeling of Scolar Press, Ashgate Publishing Limited, for their assistance in the production of this book. Thank you Sue, for your support, constant encouragement and for being available at all times throughout the project. Ellen, thank you for your patience during the final stages of production.

A special thanks to Kathryn Connell, Rita Henry and Sharon Sturns for encouragement when the project seemed overwhelming. To Jack Key, thanks for being there. To Dr Larry Muirhead, thanks Larry for ten years of constantly interesting interactions!

Finally, any discrepancies, errors or oversights are the sole responsibility of the author.

Barbara Blake
Rowlett, Texas
October 1994

PURPOSE AND ORGANIZATION OF THE BOOK

The purpose of this book is to provide the reader with specific titles of children's books to be used at home, in the classroom, in story times and in the library to help children better understand Asians and Asian Americans. This book is divided into two parts. Part One provides an introduction to the main groups of Asians covered in Part Two. It provides brief information about each immigrant or refugee group covered; about that group's country of origin and about the culture. Part Two contains entries of children's books written by or about members of the groups covered. The books listed are for preschool through sixth grade and include nonfiction as well as fiction.

The books selected for inclusion were published between 1970 and 1993. Most have received a favorable review in a review journal such as *School Library Journal, Publishers' Weekly, Library Journal, Kirkus, Booklist* or *Wilson's Bulletin*. Other books have been included that have not been reviewed in the professional journals or for which reviews were unknown.

Each entry provides bibliographic information on the book. A short synopsis is given as well as information on awards or unique features of the book or story. Sources of reviews of the book are included when known. The main subjects for the book are given. Suggestions on the types of programs the book would support are provided in the synopsis for each entry.

The books in Part Two are divided into two sections. Section one covers those for preschool through third grade. Section two, those for fourth through sixth grade children.

The East Asian nations of China, Taiwan, Japan, North and South Korea and the colony of Hong Kong are covered. For South Asia, the nations of India, Pakistan, Bangladesh, Nepal and Sri Lanka are included. The Philippines, Cambodia, Laos, Vietnam, Thailand and Indonesia are the Southeast Asian nations covered.

Appendices include: listings of the books in alphabetical order by author; by title; by culture and a select list of sources of Asian or Asian American children's books.

Introduction

Based on information gathered for the 1990 Census, the fastest growing minority in the United States is Asians and Pacific Islanders. (The demographic information and statistics on the following pages are based on data from the US Bureau of the Census, *Statistical Abstract of the United States: 1992*, 112th edition, Washington, DC, 1992.) Half of all admissions to the United States are Asians and Pacific Islanders. Filipinos (Southeast Asians) are the largest Asian immigrant group to the United States and the second largest of legal immigrant groups (Mexicans are the largest). An average of 40,000 Filipinos a year enter the United States. According to the 1990 Census, there are 1.4 million Filipinos living in the US. They are the second largest Asian American group. (Chinese Americans are the largest.) They constitute nearly 20 per cent of the Asian and Pacific Islander population in this country with two thirds concentrated in the West (over 50 per cent of the total number live in California) and another 12 per cent in Hawaii. Illinois, New York, New Jersey and Washington are other areas of concentration. They are among the highest ranked Asian American groups socially and economically and have a relatively high educational level.

Asian immigrants and refugees to the United States come primarily from three geographic areas: East Asia; South Asia and Southeast Asia. Immigrants and refugees from East Asia come primarily from China (including Taiwan), Japan, North and South Korea and the British Colony of Hong Kong. Immigrants and refugees from South Asia come mainly from India, Pakistan and Bangladesh. Immigrants and refugees from the geographic region of Southeast Asia come primarily from the Philippines, Cambodia, Laos, Vietnam, Thailand and Indonesia (based on data from the US Bureau of the Census, *Statistical Abstract of the United States: 1992*, 112th edition, Washington, DC, 1992).

Demographic overview

In ten years the number of Asians in the United States more than doubled from three and a half million in 1980 to seven million two hundred and seventy-four thousand in 1990. This represented a 107.8 per cent increase. By the year 2000, the Asian American population is expected to be around ten million. Part of this increase is due to immigration and part to the

PURPOSE AND ORGANIZATION OF THE BOOK *xiii*

higher than average birth rate of Asians. Southeast Asians have a particularly high birth rate, nearly double that of the national average.

Within the Asian category, the following six groups showed the largest increase from 1980 to 1990:

Group	1980	1990	% Increase
Chinese	806,000	1,645,000	104.1
Filipino	775,000	1,407,000	81.6
Japanese	701,000	848,000	20.9
Asian Indian	362,000	815,000	125.6
Korean	355,000	799,000	125.3
Vietnamese	262,000	615,000	134.8

In addition, the 1990 Census provides interesting data on the geographic distribution of these immigrants and refugees in the United States (expressed in numbers):

Group	Total	Northeast	Midwest	South	West
Chinese	1,645,000	445,000	133,000	204,000	863,000
Filipino	1,407,000	143,000	113,000	159,000	991,000
Japanese	848,000	74,000	63,000	67,000	643,000
Asian Indian	815,000	285,000	146,000	196,000	189,000
Korean	799,000	182,000	109,000	153,000	355,000
Vietnamese	615,000	61,000	52,000	169,000	334,000

(expressed in percentages):

Group	Northeast	Midwest	South	West
Chinese	27.0	8.1	12.4	52.4
Filipino	10.2	8.1	11.3	70.5
Japanese	8.8	7.5	7.9	75.9
Asian Indian	35.0	17.9	24.0	23.1
Korean	22.8	13.7	19.2	44.4
Vietnamese	9.8	8.5	27.4	54.3

Other pertinent data gives information about the age distribution of 7,023,000 Asians for 1991:

Under five	606,000	(8.6%)
Five to fourteen	1,170,000	(16.7%)
Fifteen to forty-four	3,494,000	(49.8%)
Forty-five to sixty-four	1,240,000	(17.6%)
Sixty-five and older	514,000	(7.3%)

For all races in the United States, the age distribution for the total given of 248,886,000 in 1991 are as follows:

Under five	19,299,000	(7.8%)
Five to fourteen	36,067,000	(14.5%)
Fifteen to forty-four	116,395,000	(46.8%)

| Forty-five to sixty-four | 47,031,000 | (18.9%) |
| Sixty-five and older | 30,093,000 | (12.0%) |

Asians as a whole have obtained a higher income and educational level when compared with other groups. For all races in the United States, the median income in 1991 was $35,353. For Asians, the median annual income for 1991 was $42,245 with 40.7 per cent having an annual income of $50,000 or more.

The following statistics on levels of education are for those aged twenty-five and older who completed four or more years of college:

Asian	39.0%
White	22.2%
Black	11.5%
Hispanic	9.7%
Native American	(not given)

Asians in the work force are comparable with other groups. Statistics of people sixteen and older in the work force are as follows:

Asian	59.6%
White	62.6%
Black	54.9%
Hispanic	59.6%
Native American	(not given)

Fewer Asians live below the poverty level. The statistics are:

Asian	12.2%
White	10.7%
Black	31.9%
Hispanic	28.1%
Native American	(not given)

Family make up of Asian groups are more like those of Whites than of other groups. The statistics are:

Married couples:

Asian	80.1%
White	82.8%
Black	47.8%
Hispanic	69.3%
Native American	48.0%

Single parent family with female head of household:

Asian	12.7%
White	13.2%
Black	45.9%
Hispanic	23.8%
Native American	20.5%

Single parent family with male head of household:
Asian	7.3%
White	4.0%
Black	6.3%
Hispanic	6.9%
Native American	6.3%

The above information provides a statistical overview of census data available on Asian immigrants and refugees in the United States.

PART ONE

1 EAST ASIA

This section focuses on immigrants and refugees from the East Asian countries of China (including Taiwan), Japan, North and South Korea and Hong Kong.

China

Chinese Americans form the largest group of Asian Americans with the Chinese having a long history of immigration to the United States compared to other Asian groups. During the 1820s one Chinese immigrant was admitted to the United States. During the 1830s two entered the country. After gold was discovered in California during the 1840s, large numbers of Chinese immigrated to the United States with California as their destination. Most early Chinese immigrants were young single men, or men who left their families behind in China, to seek their fortune in the New World. They intended to return to China once they accomplished their goal. These immigrants came primarily from Guangdong (Canton) province. Their two major occupations were mining and building railroads. Others left the mines and moved to towns where they established laundries, grocery stores and restaurants. Eventually Chinatowns formed within the cities where they settled and traditional structures such as clans and family associations formed that promoted traditional Chinese culture.

In 1869 the transcontinental railroad was completed and Chinese workers began to find other kinds of work. White workers resented the Chinese moving into jobs previously held by whites and in 1877 the Workingmen's Party was founded. This organization lobbied for legislation to prevent Chinese from immigrating to the United States. As a result of the Workingmen's Party efforts, the Chinese Exclusion Act was passed in 1882. At that time there were about 100,000 Chinese in the United States. In 1892 the act was extended and again in 1902. During this period many Chinese left the United States.

The Chinese Exclusion Act was repealed in 1943, after China became an ally of the United States during World War II. At that time a quota system of immigration was adopted. From 1943 until 1965 the quota for Chinese immigrants was 105 a year, half of which had to be professionals.

This quota system remained in effect until the Immigration and Nationality Act Amendments of 1965 were passed. This act allowed 20,000 immigrants per country from the Eastern Hemisphere, which resulted in a second wave of Chinese immigrants. These new immigrants (or San Yi Man) included significant numbers of professionals from urban areas in the People's Republic of China. They mainly spoke Mandarin or Cantonese, arrived as families rather than single men, and were settlers rather than temporary laborers. The majority settled in California and New York.

The third wave, consisting of ethnic Chinese living in Southeast Asia, began in 1978 and has continued into the 1990s. These recent Chinese immigrants came primarily from Cantonese speaking provinces of Vietnam and other Southeast Asian countries. Primarily members of the business class, they were discriminated against by the Communist régimes then in power. Many fled their country of origin to escape discrimination and death. The number of Chinese immigrants and refugees from China, Taiwan, Hong Kong and other Southeast Asian countries has continued to increase and more are expected to arrive over the next few years.

According to 1990 census data, in 1980 there were 286,000 Chinese foreign born residents in the United States. This increased to 543,000 in 1990. In all there were 5,412,000 Asians (or 25 per cent) foreign born residents in the US in 1990 with Chinese making up 2.5 of the 25 per cent (p. 42, no. 46, Foreign-Born Population, by Place of Birth: 1980 and 1990, US Bureau of the Census, *Statistical Abstract of the United States: 1992*, 112th edition, Washington, DC, 1992). There were 1,645,000 Chinese in the resident population for 1990. Of these, 445,000 lived in the Northeast; 133,000 in the Midwest; 204,000 in the South and 863,000 in the West (p. 32, no. 33, Resident Population, by Region, Race and Hispanic Origin: 1990, US Bureau of the Census, *Statistical Abstract of the United States: 1993*, 113th edition, Washington, DC, 1993).

Due to the various successive waves of immigration, the Chinese American population covers a wide range of cultural backgrounds. It ranges from monolingual, less educated and semiskilled individuals to middle class to affluent, highly educated, city and suburban residents.

Culturally the Chinese are also varied. Over the past 2,000 years the Chinese have been primarily influenced by Confucianism, Taoism and Buddhism. Known as the three teachings, they form the basis of Chinese religious and philosophical systems. The three teachings consist of complementary teachings that enable Asians to integrate and be guided by a complex mix of beliefs.

Confucianism was founded by Confucius (551–479 BC). He had no systematic doctrine. His goal was not salvation, but the realization of human potential for wisdom and virtue in this life. He promoted a way of life based on developing certain individual virtues and on observing a system of social obligations based on what became known as the Five Virtues: Ren (or jen) which is benevolence and humanism; Yi which is righteousness; Li which is proper conduct; Zhi (or chih) which is wisdom and Xin which is trustworthiness. Filial piety, or Xiao, is the essence of the five virtues. Xiao requires unquestioning obedience to parents. It includes reverence for ancestors and extends to all authority figures.

Lao Tzu (604–? BC) is credited with promoting Taoism. Tao literally means the way or path. Taoism promotes inner strength, selflessness, spontaneity and harmony with nature and man. Taoism stresses the need to transcend man made society. It encourages training, asceticism, meditation and discipline. The benefits to be derived from following Taoism include good health and long life. Taoism is based on the concepts of Yang and Yin. All things can be explained by these two counterbalancing forces. Yang (characterized as male and heaven) is the creative, forward, dominating and manifest force. Yin (characterized as female and earth) is the receptive, recessive, submissive and hidden background force. Taoism eventually evolved into a collection of practises associated with superstition, magic, divination and sorcery.

Buddhism, founded by Prince Siddharta Gautama (560–480 BC) began in India and was carried to China. The Four Noble Truths form the basis of Buddhist philosophy: all life is suffering; suffering is caused by attachment to the world; suffering can be eliminated by overcoming desire and worldly attachments and to eliminate desire, follow the eight fold path. The eight fold path consists of: right views, right thought, right speech, right conduct, right livelihood, right effort, right mindfulness and right meditation.

Reincarnation is another component of Buddhism. Reincarnation occurs because of one's actions (karma) in the previous life. The cycle of birth, death, rebirth is known as the Wheel of Life. The goal of a Buddhist is to be released from the Wheel of Life and reach nirvana, which is a state where one's soul is merged into the cosmic unity. This cosmic unity is the one reality, the world as we know it is only an illusion. Clinging to the illusion of reality is what produces suffering and leads to being trapped on the wheel of life. To escape the Wheel of Life, one must obtain enlightenment through dharma, the doctrine of the life of Buddha.

Chinese Buddhism blended the philosophy of Xiao (filial piety) with Buddhism. Mahayana Buddhism, one form of Buddhism, became the dominant form in China. The Chan (Zen in Japan) form was also widely practiced. It emphasized meditation and self discipline and became almost indistinguishable from philosophical Taoism. Eventually it spread from China to Korea and from Korea to Japan.

Ancestor worship is another component of Chinese religious beliefs. The three basic premises concerning ancestor worship are that our fortunes or misfortunes depend on our ancestors; departed ancestors have needs just as the living do; departed ancestors can help their descendants and their descendants can help them. One way descendants can help their ancestors is to provide them with food and possessions through offerings. In return, our ancestors can improve our fortune. In this way a social tie remains between departed ancestors and living descendants.

There are numerous dialects in the Chinese language. Putonghua (Mandarin) is spoken by more than 70 per cent of the people in the People's Republic of China and is the national language or common speech. Mandarin, which is spoken in the north, northwest, west and southwest regions of China, has more than one dialect. Wu dialects are spoken in the east and in the southeast Cantonese, Min and Hakka are spoken. Toishanese, another popular dialect, originated in the Taishan province in the People's Republic of China. Fukienese and Mandarin are frequently spoken by Taiwanese immigrants.

Chinese has many monosyllabic words with each syllable having a distinctive pitch known as a tone. There are four basic tones in Mandarin and ten in Cantonese. They convey different meanings for the syllables they are assigned to, and the meaning of a word changes depending on the tone used. The linguistic structure of Chinese is significantly different from English. Intonations rise at the end of a sentence rather than fall as they do in English. There are no digraphs in Chinese, no gender pronouns, tenses, plural endings or verb conjugations.

The written language for all dialects of spoken Chinese is the same. This has helped preserve Chinese culture and history and has bound the diverse peoples of China together. It has also helped establish ties with neighboring countries such as Korea and Vietnam since these countries used classical Chinese as their written language for official government documents and literature. There are about 40,000 ideographs, or characters, that represent an object or idea in the Chinese written language but basic literacy can be achieved with a knowledge of about 1,500 to 3,000 characters.

Taiwan

The number of Taiwanese immigrants to the United States has increased significantly between 1980 to 1990. In 1980 there were 75,000 foreign born Taiwanese in the United States and that increased to 244,000 in 1990 (p. 50, no. 55, Foreign-Born Population, by Place of Birth: 1980 and 1990, US Bureau of the Census, *Statistical Abstract of the United States: 1993*, 113th edition, Washington, DC, 1993). For 1990 15,151 Taiwanese immigrants were admitted to the United States. Of these 6,806 listed California as their state of intended residence; 1,783 listed New York; 1,034 listed Texas; 456 listed Illinois; 267 listed Florida; 970 listed New Jersey; 284 listed Massachusetts; 123 listed Arizona and 308 listed Virginia (p. 12, no. 10, Immigrants Admitted, by Leading State of Intended Residence and Country of Birth: 1990, US Bureau of the Census, *Statistical Abstract of the United States: 1992*, 112th edition, Washington, DC, 1992).

Taiwan is officially known as the Republic of China and it has the world's second highest population density. (The Republic of China is actually made up of the islands of Taiwan, Quemoy, Matsu and the islands of the Pescadores chain with Taiwan being the largest island.) During the first half of the twentieth century its population tripled. Since then the population rate has steadily declined and the government promotes family planning and birth control.

The original inhabitants of Taiwan were of Malayo-Polynesian ancestry. In the 1100s large numbers of Chinese settled on the island. Another wave of Chinese migration took place in the 1700s and 1800s and Taiwan was under the rule of the Imperial Chinese government from the 1660s until 1895. About 84 per cent of the current population of Taiwan are descended from these waves of immigrants. After Japan defeated China in the Sino-Japanese War of 1894–95, Taiwan was ceded to Japan and was under Japanese rule until the Japanese were defeated in World War II. In 1949 about two million Chinese Nationalists fled to Taiwan to escape the Communist Chinese takeover of mainland China and members of this group (or their descendants) account for about 14 per cent of Taiwan's population. Until 1971 the Republic of China was the official representative of China in the United Nations. In 1971 the Communist ruled People's Republic of China (instead of the Republic of China) was granted official status as the United Nations representative for China. In 1979 the People's Republic of China was recognized as the legitimate government of China by the United States. Economically, until 1949 Taiwan was a relatively undeveloped agricultural area. Since that time it has become an industrial nation and is able to compete with Japan for world markets. Almost 75 per cent of Taiwanese live in cities or towns.

Confucianism, Taoism and Buddhism all made their way to Taiwan from China and about 95 per cent of Taiwanese practice these religions or a mixture of them. Around 5 per cent practice Christianity and there are a few Muslims. Confucianism has had the greatest impact on Taiwanese ethnics, morality and way of life. The family is the most important social unit and filial piety is the basis of family unity.

The official language of Taiwan is Mandarin Chinese. Taiwanese and Hakka are two other dialects that are spoken and many older Taiwanese also speak Japanese. Education is highly stressed and 94 per cent of Taiwanese are literate.

Japan

The first significant immigration of Japanese to the United States began in the late 1800s. Most of these were students and merchants. In 1882, when the Chinese Exclusion Act was passed, there were about 2,000 Japanese in the United States proper and many more in Hawaii, which was not a part of the US at that time. Business groups in California sought to have the Chinese Exclusion Act expanded to include Japanese but their efforts failed. This is one difference in the treatment of Chinese and Japanese immigrants. The Chinese government during this time was weak and could not provide protection for its nationals abroad. The Japanese government, however, was an emerging power and saw treatment of its nationals abroad as being a reflection on the prestige of the nation of Japan. Therefore the Japanese government made an effort to see that its nationals in the US were not included in the Chinese Exclusion Act of 1882.

Hawaii had a shortage of cheap labor, partly due to the passage of the Chinese Exclusion Act in 1882 and Japan had problems with political dissention and lack of land. To alleviate their problems, the Japanese government encouraged emigration. From 1886 to 1895 about 25,000 Japanese men and 5,000 Japanese women emigrated to Hawaii under labor contracts. These early Japanese immigrants, like the Chinese, worked primarily at difficult, low paying jobs in agriculture. Their passage was paid for by plantation owners. In return they were required to work for the plantation owner for three years. Before Congress could create the territory of Hawaii, planters brought an additional 26,000 Japanese contract laborers into Hawaii. The planters expected these workers to fulfil their three year contracts. However, when Hawaii was annexed by the US in 1889, the contracts were declared invalid and the laborers were free to leave. Many left Hawaii for the mainland United States in search of better jobs, moving primarily to California. These early immigrants were mainly from rural areas of Japan and the Ryukyu Islands and were mostly peasants.

In the census of 1890 2,039 Japanese were counted in the US. By the census of 1900 this figure had increased to 85,437 with 61,111 of those being in Hawaii and most of the remainder being on the West Coast. Other Japanese immigrants worked at jobs related to railroad maintenance. The 1920 census showed about 110,000 Japanese immigrants with about two thirds of them living in California.

In response to pressure from business groups in the US, President Teddy Roosevelt entered into the so called Gentlemen's Agreement with the Japanese government in 1907–1908. Under this agreement, the Japanese government stopped emigration of their laborers to the United States.

Between 1908, when the US entered into the Gentlemen's Agreement with Japan, and 1924 when all Japanese immigration to the US was banned, Japanese women immigrated as 'picture brides'. These women travelled to the US to become the brides of the Japanese men who had previously immigrated. The marriages were arranged and the couple usually had not met until the bride arrived in the US. The groom had only seen a picture of his bride to be, hence the name 'picture brides'.

During this time Japanese immigrants were ineligible for naturalization. Under the 1970 Immigration and Naturalization Act only free whites were eligible and Orientals were ruled to be nonwhite and therefore not eligible. However, the US laws granted citizenship to anyone born in the US. When the first generation Japanese, known as issei, began having children, these second generation Japanese were known as nisei and, until 1924, had dual citizenship. This changed after 1924 when, to have dual citizenship, a child had to be registered at a Japanese consulate within two weeks of birth to retain Japanese citizenship.

In the census of 1930 there were 138,834 Japanese in the US. The West Coast had the largest number and most had economically reached lower-middle-class status. However, during this period, Japanese Americans continued to experience prejudice based on race and existed in a society that was structurally separate with little integration with the dominant culture. In addition to limited employment opportunities due to racism, Japanese Americans experienced decreased opportunities due to the Great Depression.

Nisei during this period made an effort to distance themselves from the previous generation. They formed organizations that were hyperpatriotic, most requiring all members be citizens, which made it impossible for those born in Japan to join. This carried over into the 1940s. When Japan bombed Pearl Harbor on 7 December 1941, life for people of Japanese ancestry in America changed. Between 31 March and 7 August 1942, about 110,000 Japanese Americans were sent to concentration camps. The ones incarcerated were primarily Japanese Americans living on the West Coast. For about two and a half years they were confined to one of ten camps while the approximately 160,000 Japanese living in Hawaii were allowed to remain free (Japanese Americans at this time made up almost 40 per cent of Hawaii's population). The ten Japanese internment camps were located in Arizona, Arkansas, California, Colorado, Idaho, Utah and Wyoming. In December 1944 the camps were officially disbanded. These Japanese Americans had an experience which was different from all other immigrant ethnic groups. Some of these people left the US after their release, disillusioned and bitter. Others stayed in the country, with the majority of them returning to the West Coast.

During the 1940s three generations of Japanese Americans, the issei (first generation immigrants), the nisei (second generation) and the sansei (third generation) co-existed. More opportunities were available to members of the nisei after the end of World War II. Most remained on the West Coast although some moved to cities such as Denver, Chicago,

Cleveland and New York. Sansei were dependent children during this period.

In 1959 the US admitted Hawaii as the fiftieth state and this provided Japanese Americans with opportunities not available to them before, such as election to political office. During the 1960s discrimination decreased and many Japanese Americans achieved middle class status. During the 1970s they began to be portrayed as a model minority and this period could be characterized as the sansei era. Members of the nisei generation continued to keep a low profile while many of the isseiu passed away leaving the nisei as the mature generation. During the 1980s health issues, retirement and understanding the younger generation became more important issues. In the 1990s existence of fourth (yonsei) and fifth generation Japanese Americans has blurred clear cut generational differences. The mix of peoples of Japanese ancestry in the US is further confused by the influx of Japanese businessmen, students and tourists from Japan. The sansei and yonsei are the most Americanized of the groups and there is much interracial marriage between Japanese Americans and other Americans.

In 1990 there were 848,000 Japanese residents in the United States. Of these, 74,000 lived in the Northeast; 63,000 in the Midwest; 67,000 in the South; 643,000 in the West (p. 32, no. 33, Resident Population, by Region, Race and Hispanic Origin: 1990, US Bureau of the Census, *Statistical Abstract of the United States: 1993*, 113th edition, Washington, DC, 1993). From 1961 to 1970 38,500 Japanese immigrants were admitted to the US. This increased to 47,900 between 1971 and 1980 and dropped slightly to 43,200 between 1981 and 1990 (p. 11, no. 8, Immigrants, by Country of Birth: 1961 to 1991, US Bureau of the Census, *Statistical Abstract of the United States: 1993*, 113th edition, Washington, DC, 1993).

The major religions practiced by the Japanese are Shinto, Buddhism and Christianity. Shinto, the oldest native religion in Japan, is based on myths, legends and rituals. The word Shinto was coined (after Buddhism became popular in Japan) in order to identify native beliefs from Buddhism. During the eighth century AD, two books were written which became the oldest histories of myths and lore of the Japanese: the Kojiki (712 AD) and the Nihongi (720 AD); the chief documents of Shinto. Kami is the basis of Shinto. It recognizes numerous deities of heaven and earth, spirits of shrines, spirits of trees, mountains, the seas and of animals. Mixed in with this is ancestor worship. It is not uncommon for a Japanese home to have a tiny Shinto shrine called the kami-dana. The head of the family would use the kami-dana as a place to make offerings to the family ancestors. In addition, there are thousands of Shinto shrines in Japan. Shinto today mainly provides participants with opportunities to wear traditional clothes and celebrate various festivals. The second major religion practiced in Japan is Buddhism, which began in India and was carried to China then to Korea. In the sixth century AD it spread from

Korea to Japan. Zen Buddhism is the form widely practiced in Japan. Zen (Japanese for meditation) Buddhism places the responsibility for obtaining enlightenment on the individual through that person's practice of meditation and self discipline.

In addition to Shintoism and Buddhism, Christianity is an important religion in Japan. About 60 per cent of the approximately 1.5 million Japanese Christians are Protestant, the other 40 per cent being Catholic.

The official language of Japan is Japanese, and while the spoken language is not especially difficult to learn, the same cannot be said about the written language. Originally Japanese was a picture language. Soon, however, they began to borrow characters from written Chinese called kanji, which were used to represent the sounds of words and the pictures that were previously used. There are thousands of kanji and by the end of the sixth grade a student is expected to know about 900 of them. To read a typical newspaper or magazine one would need to know about 1,850 kanji. There is another group of 48 characters called hiraganas (used to represent parts of speech) with a second group of 48 characters called katakanas that are used to represent foreign words. Japanese words represented in the Roman alphabet are called Romajis. It is common for Japanese to learn a system of Romajis and most students begin to learn English once they are in the seventh grade.

Korea

In ancient times Korea was known as the Kingdom of Choson. This kingdom was created about 2300 BC. Choson means Land of the Morning Calm. During the period 935–1492 AD the country was controlled by the Koryo Dynasty. The current name, Korea, was derived from the dynasty name Koryo. During the Yi Dynasty (1392–1910 AD), Korea closed itself off from the outside world and became known to Westerners as the Hermit Kingdom. During this time it was forbidden for Koreans to leave their country and to do so was punishable by death.

In 1910 Japan overran Korea, formally annexed it, and controlled it until 1945. It tried unsuccessfully to eradicate Korean culture. After the defeat of Japan in World War II, Korea was liberated from Japan. Soviet troops occupied North Korea and United Nations troops, primarily US soldiers, occupied South Korea. The Soviet Union refused to remove its troops and, in response, UN troops remained in South Korea. In 1948 the country was divided, North Korea becoming a communist ruled nation called the Democratic People's Republic of Korea. South Korea became a noncommunist nation, the Republic of Korea. War between the two nations erupted when North Korea attempted to unite the two countries under communist rule. Millions of Koreans died during the Korean War which lasted from 1950 to 1953. Most of the population became homeless refugees. It was one of the bloodiest wars in history effectively devastating the entire country.

The early isolationism of Korea is reflected in the Korean born population figures for the United States. There were only three Koreans listed in the US in 1885. In 1899 five were listed and in 1900 two entered Hawaii. It wasn't until 1902 that Koreans began to immigrate to the United States in substantial numbers. Korean immigration to the US can basically be separated into three waves. The first wave arrived between 1903 and 1905 and they were mainly farm laborers with families who were recruited to work in the sugar plantations of Hawaii. They came primarily from urban areas in Korea and from diverse occupational backgrounds. Immigration to Hawaii provided work for those who left Korea because of poverty, famine and drought. This group of early immigrants followed an immigration pattern of entering Hawaii then moving onward to California. From there they spread out to other parts of the country.

From 1910 to 1924 there was limited immigration. Some came fleeing Japanese rule after Japan annexed Korea in 1910. During this period about 1,000 young women entered the country as 'picture brides' to marry Korean men already in the US. From 1924 to the end of World War II practically no Koreans immigrated to the United States as a result of the 1924 Immigration Act.

The second wave arrived between 1945 and 1964. About 600 Koreans a year entered the US during the 1950s. Between 1950 and 1953 the majority were war brides of American servicemen who had been serving there during the Korean War or young children who were war orphans. Most of these war orphans were girls under the age of 4 who were adopted by Americans. The number of immigrants increased during the 1960s to about 3,000 a year. About a third of these were students.

Second generation Korean Americans frequently found it difficult to relate to their parents' continued interest in the affairs of Korea. They saw their future as being tied to America, not to Korea. This caused conflict between the two generations and many of the younger generation chose to leave their parents' communities. Koreans during this period had an intermarriage rate higher than that of all other Asians.

The third wave began after the Immigration and Nationality Amendments Act of 1965 and led to a dramatic emergence of Koreans as a highly visible group in America. Since 1976 the number of Korean immigrants to the United States has exceeded 30,000 annually. Koreans have become one of the fastest growing ethnic minorities.

During the 1970s the number of Koreans entering the US increased by nearly 800 per cent. By 1980 81.8 per cent of all Koreans in the US were foreign born. These recent immigrants were the most widely dispersed relative to other recent Asian immigrants. Most settled in California, especially around Los Angeles. New York has the second largest population followed by Illinois. Some factors contributing to the relative geographic mobility of this group is their educational level, their adaptability, previous experience with rapid change and with an urban industrial environment.

From 1961 to 1970 35,800 Koreans entered the US as immigrants. This jumped to 272,000 between 1971 and 1980 and increased to 338,800 between 1981 and 1990 (p. 11, no. 8, Immigrants, by Country of Birth: 1961 to 1991, US Bureau of the Census, *Statistical Abstract of the United States: 1993*, 113th edition, Washington, DC, 1993). In 1980 Koreans accounted for 290,000 of the total 14,080,000 foreign-born people in the United States. This increased in 1990 to 568,000 of the total 19,767,000 (p. 50, no. 55, Foreign-Born Population, by Place of Birth: 1980 and 1990, US Bureau of the Census, *Statistical Abstract of the United States: 1993*, 113th edition, Washington, DC, 1993).

Culturally North and South Korea differed to some degree after the country was divided into two nations. After the war, China and the Soviet Union helped North Korea recover. Kim Il Sung was made the leader of the country when it was established in 1948 and the people of North Korea were taught to revere him. After his death in 1994 his son, Kim Jong Ill, assumed power. In North Korea the major religions traditionally were Buddhism and Confucianism. However, after the establishment of the Democratic People's Republic of Korea, all religions were suppressed, artistic pursuits were curtailed and family ties were weakened by governmental policies. Under Communist rule Christians were especially persecuted, which caused most to flee to South Korea.

In South Korea, the major religions are Confucianism, Buddhism, Christianity and Chondogyo. Confucianism, Taoism and Buddhism all made their way to Korea from China in the first century AD. Confucianism provided the foundation for the development of Korea's educational, social and political systems. During the Yi dynasty, Korea became the center of Confucian learning and continues to dominate life in South Korea. Ancestor worship and shamanism are also practiced. Shamanism, or spirit worship, is one of the earliest religions of Korea and is based on the principle of animism – the belief that all forms of life and all things in the universe maintain their existence by virtue of anima (soul). In addition, everything is interrelated by shamanistic laws of cause and effect. A person's life, death, happiness and misfortune are dependent on the spirits. The spirits are immortal and must be worshipped and served to promote good fortune and to prevent bad fortune. Shamanism is still practiced in rural areas as well as by many older Koreans.

Christianity was introduced to Korea in the late 1800s and resulted in a major social and cultural transition. Missionaries promoted modern education and a Western work ethic and thousands of Koreans converted to Christianity. These converts were encouraged to immigrate to America and about 40 per cent of all first wave Korean immigrants were Christians. Christianity increased after World War II and South Korea now has the largest Christian population of any Asian country (with the exception of the Philippines). In South Korea, about 16 per cent of the population is Christian.

Korean Christian immigrants usually organize their own churches. These serve as a center of worship and during the week as a school to teach children the Korean language as well as the history and culture of Korea. Between 60 and 70 per cent of Korean Americans today are affiliated with a Christian church.

Korean is the official language. In North Korea the Pyongyang regional dialect is the official spoken language and about 95 per cent of the people are literate. In South Korea the Seoul dialect is dominant and over 90 per cent of the people are literate.

About 50 per cent of the Korean vocabulary is derived from Chinese. The language consists of a single phonetic alphabet with 24 phonetic symbols or characters representing different sounds which are combined to form words. The Korean written language was invented in 1443, centuries before phonetics became a systematic discipline.

South Korea, whose official name is the Republic of Korea, has the third highest population density in the world, a factor which has caused overcrowding in the cities, widespread unemployment and underemployment.

From 1948 to 1960 the president of South Korea was Syngman Rhee. He was forced to step down and in 1961 Park Chung Hee took power after a successful military coup. He was assassinated in 1979. General Chun Doo Hwan took control and was succeeded in 1987 by General Roh Tae Woo. A new constitution adopted in 1988 provided for direct presidential and National Assembly elections as well as guaranteeing certain human rights such as freedom of expression.

South Korea chose to develop an export oriented economy. In the 1960s South Korea attracted foreign industries. Strikes were forbidden and workers typically worked 54 hour weeks at low wages. The country's exports increased by 40 per cent per year from 1962 to 1971. North and South Korea signed a nonaggression pact in 1991 and both became members of the United Nations.

Recent Korean immigrants share several common characteristics such as nationality, customs and language. The majority are Christians, mainly of Protestant denominations. They have attempted to preserve their culture and have continued to have an interest in the political affairs of their native country. A large number of recent immigrants are professionals, but usually are not able to practice immediately within their profession. Because of this, many have chosen to become self employed. Koreans have the highest rate of self employment compared to all other Asian American groups. Self owned small businesses are the most common form of self employment. These businesses are frequently located in inner city sections of large metropolitan areas.

Major family and generational conflicts exist. Over 90 per cent of first generation Korean parents speak Korean. Despite the fact that the majority of parents encourage their children to learn Korean, the children are mainly English speaking, which complicates family life. School age Korean born children are fast becoming a lost generation. They need several years to attain English proficiency and in the process they gradually lose their Korean language skills. They may also fail to develop a positive self identity with either the Korean or American culture. Often they reject traditional values in favor of peer group culture, which can include membership in youth gangs.

Hong Kong

In 1980 there were 80,000 Hong Kong born residents in the United States, a number which had increased to 147,000 by 1990. From 1961 to 1971 2,128 people from Hong Kong were admitted as permanent residents to the US under the Refugee Act. This number increased to 3,468 from 1971 to 1980 then dropped to 1,886 from 1981 to 1989 (p. 12, no. 9, Immigrants Admitted as Permanent Residents Under Refugee Act, by Country of Birth: 1961 to 1990, US Bureau of the Census, *Statistical Abstract of the United States: 1992*, 112th edition, Washington, DC, 1992). From 1961 to 1970, 25,600 immigrants from Hong Kong were in the United States, by 1980 there were 47,500 and by 1990 63,000 (p. 11, no. 8, Immigrants, by Country of Birth: 1961 to 1991, US Bureau of the Census, *Statistical Abstract of the United States: 1993*, 113th edition, Washington, DC, 1993).

The island of Hong Kong became a British colony in 1841. In 1898 Great Britain signed a 99 year lease for the New Territories which included Hong Kong Island, about 235 smaller islands and part of mainland China north from Kowloon Peninsula to the Chinese border. On 1 July 1997 Hong Kong will become a Special Administrative Region of the People's Republic of China when the British lease expires and Hong Kong comes under Chinese sovereignty. The agreement between the British and Chinese guarantees that Hong Kong's political, legal, economic and social systems will remain as they are for fifty years after the expiration of the lease. However, many Chinese in Hong Kong are uncertain if the agreement will be honored and a number of them have chosen to immigrate to the United States. It is expected that many more will do the same before July 1997.

Hong Kong's population is about 5,800,000 (as of 1990) with Cantonese and English as the official languages. It has a manufacturing based economy. About 98 per cent of the people are ethnic Chinese. The major religions are Buddhism, Confucianism, Taoism and Christianity. About 10 per cent of the population are Christians with the other 90 per cent following one of the other religions.

2 SOUTHEAST ASIA

Southeast Asia includes Myanmar, Thailand, Laos, Cambodia, Vietnam, Malaysia, Singapore, Indonesia, Brunei and the Philippines. Southeast Asian immigrants to the United States come primarily from the Philippines, Cambodia, Laos, Vietnam, Thailand and Indonesia.

More than half of Southeast Asians in the US are concentrated in California (about 40 per cent), Texas and Washington state. Vietnamese are especially concentrated in California. Mien people from Laos are concentrated in Seattle, Portland, Sacramento, Oakland, San Jose and Long Beach. Over half of the Hmong refugees from Laos are concentrated in California, especially in Fresno.

Buddhism is the most predominant influence in the Southeast Asian culture. In Vietnam, Mahayana (Great Vehicle) Buddhism is the most practiced. In Cambodia, Laos and Thailand, Hinayana (Little Vehicle) or Theravata is the form most practiced. In addition Hinduism and animism (spirit worship) have influenced the Cambodians and Laotians.

Philippines

There are three main periods of Filipino immigration to the United States: 1906–1945; 1946–1964 and 1965 to the present. The earliest known Filipino immigrants arrived in the 1830s and 1840s when some Filipino seamen settled in Louisiana. However, the first sizable group of Filipinos did not arrive until 1903 when the United States instituted a program to provide selected Filipino students with higher education opportunities. The first real wave of Filipino immigrants arrived in 1906 in response to changes in the United States immigration policy towards Chinese and Japanese nationals. In 1882 the United States had passed the Chinese Exclusion Act which prohibited immigration of Chinese to the US for ten years and this period was eventually extended. In addition, by 1907 the United States and Japan had signed a gentlemen's agreement which severely restricted the immigration of Japanese to the US. Because of these policies there was a shortage of cheap labor which especially made an impact on the agricultural industry. In 1903 Filipinos started being recruited to fill the need for cheap agricultural labor. Unlike other Asian immigrants, the Filipinos did not develop strong ethnic communities or neighborhoods during the early immigration period because of the mobility inherent in being migrant workers.

In 1934 the Tydings-McDuffie Act was passed which limited the number of Filipinos who could immigrate to the United States to 50 per year. This was in place until after 1941. The Immigration and Nationality Act of 1940 allowed Filipinos who had entered the country as immigrants to apply for naturalization.

In 1946 the Philippines became an independent country. The Nationality Act of 1946 was signed by President Truman and allowed Asians who were permanent residents of the United States and who met other requirements to apply for naturalization.

The Immigration and Nationality Act of 1965 provided impetus for sustained immigration of Filipinos. Immigrants after 1965 differed from the earlier ones in a number of significant ways. The early immigrants were generally uneducated, clannish and usually accepted low paying jobs; but after 1965 they were normally educated, more cosmopolitan and more aggressive in securing better paying positions.

In 1990 63,756 Filipino immigrants were admitted to the United States. Of these, 31,223 listed California as their intended destination; 5,525 listed New York; 1,691 listed Texas; 3,104 listed Illinois; 1,532 listed Florida; 3,560 listed New Jersey; 325 listed Massachusetts; 341 listed Arizona and 1,398 listed Virginia (p. 12, no. 10, Immigrants Admitted, by Leading States of Intended Residence and Country of Birth: 1990, US Bureau of the Census, *Statistical Abstract of the United States: 1992*, 112th edition, Washington, DC, 1992). In 1980 there were 501,000 Filipino born people in the US, which increased to 913,000 by 1990 (p. 50, no. 55, Foreign-Born Population, by Place of Birth: 1980 and 1990, US Bureau of the Census, *Statistical Abstract of the United States: 1993*, 113th edition, Washington, DC, 1993). In 1990 there were 1,451,000 people of Filipino ancestry in the US: 10 per cent lived in the Northeast; 9 per cent in the Midwest; 13 per cent in the South and 68 per cent in the West (p. 51, no. 56, Population, by Selected Ancestry Group and Region: 1990, US Bureau of the Census, *Statistical Abstract of the United States: 1993*, 113th edition, Washington, DC, 1993). From 1961 to 1970 101,500 Filipinos immigrated to the United States, increasing to 360,200 by 1980 and to 495,300 by 1990 (p. 11, no. 8, Immigrants, by Country of Birth: 1961 to 1991, US Bureau of the Census, *Statistical Abstract of the United States: 1993*, 113th edition, Washington, DC, 1993).

Filipinos are predominantly Christian with about 85 per cent of the population being Roman Catholic. Another 5 per cent are Muslims and a small percentage are Buddhist. There are around 87 languages and dialects spoken in the Philippines. Ilocano, Tagalog and Cebuano are the three major dialects. English is also taught in the public schools and the Philippines has the third largest English speaking population in the world.

Cambodia

Cambodia is bordered by Vietnam, Laos, Thailand and the Gulf of Siam. The country was originally Kambuja or Kampuchea until it became known by the European name Cambodia. The Khmer people are the predominant ethnic group and their civilization dates back almost 2,000 years.

Cambodia was dominated by Thailand for a number of years, then became a French protectorate in 1863. It was under France's rule until 1954 when Cambodia's king negotiated independence. This monarchy lasted for sixteen years. In 1965 the king allowed North Vietnamese Communist troops inside Cambodia's borders. In 1971 the king was deposed by General Lon Nol who established the Khmer Republic. The United States extended the Vietnam War into Cambodia, bombing North Vietnamese supply lines in that country. By the end of 1971 an estimated two million of the country's seven million population had been displaced. In April 1975 General Lon Nol was overthrown and, under Pol Pot, the Khmer Rouge took over Cambodia and renamed the country Kampuchea. The new government set out to eradicate all western influence. This was known as the Khmer Rouge era which lasted from 1975 to 1978 and was infamous for its atrocities. Over half of Cambodia's population was killed through torture, execution, disease, starvation, forced marches and compulsory labor. Large segments of the middle and upper middle classes were killed including nearly all the educated and professional people. In 1978 the Vietnamese invaded the country.

In 1980 there were 20,000 Cambodian born people in the US, increasing to 119,000 by 1990 (p. 50, no. 55, Foreign-Born Population, by Place of Birth: 1980 and 1990, US Bureau of the Census, *Statistical Abstract of the United States: 1993*, 113th edition, Washington, DC, 1993). From 1961 to 1970 1,200 Cambodians immigrated to the United States, increasing to 8,400 by 1980 and to 116,600 by 1990 (p. 11, no. 8, Immigrants, by Country of Birth: 1961 to 1991, US Bureau of the Census, *Statistical Abstract of the United States: 1993*, 113th edition, Washington, DC, 1993). Looking at the statistics for the numbers who were admitted as permanent residents under Refugee Acts is instructive. From 1961 to 1970 no Cambodian refugees were admitted to the US. From 1971 to 1980 7,739 Cambodians were admitted and by 1990 that jumped to 114,064 (p. 12, no. 9, Immigrants Admitted as Permanent Residents Under Refugee Acts, by Country of Birth: 1961 to 1991, US Bureau of the Census, *Statistical Abstract of the United States: 1993*, 113th edition, Washington, DC, 1993).

Khmer or Cambodian is the official language of Cambodia. Khmer people make up approximately 85 per cent of the country's population. Khmer has words derived from Sanskrit and some borrowed from Chinese, Thai and Vietnamese. It is monosyllabic and nontonal. There are no plurals, possessive or past tense endings. The written language has a total of 66 consonant and vowel symbols and its alphabet originated in southern India. It is very difficult, if not impossible, to make an exact transliteration of Khmer and English sounds. Khmer is written from left to right and from top to bottom.

Laos

Laos is the only landlocked country in Southeast Asia, being bordered by Thailand, Vietnam, Burma, China and Cambodia. There are nearly 70 different ethnic groups in Laos, the majority of whom are the lowland Lao, the Hmong (which means free) and the Mien (which means people). The Hmong are also known as Meo or Mia, the Lao of the mountain tops. Lan Xang is the ancient name of Laos and means Kingdom of a Million Elephants. It was founded in 1353. In 1893 Laos was colonized by the French. In 1954 the Geneva Accord established Laos as an independent state. For the next twenty years Laos was torn by internal conflict. By the 1960s the Vietnam War was expanded into Laos. The political group the Pathet Lao was supported by the North Vietnamese. The Royal Lao was supported by the United States. The Hmong and Mien were also supported by the United States. They were based in the highlands and were to interrupt the movement of Communist troops and military supplies. The Royal Lao collapsed in the spring of 1975. The Pathet Lao established the Lao People's Democratic Republic and instituted a campaign of reprisal. The Mien and Hmong people were killed by the thousands. Others starved and many more were taken to reeducation centers where they disappeared. Some 70,000 ethnic Lao, 10,000 Mien and 60,000 Hmong, sought sanctuary in America as refugees.

In 1990 10,446 Laos immigrants were admitted to the United States, of whom 4,851 listed California as their intended destination; 126 listed New York; 216 listed Texas; 175 listed Illinois; 102 listed Florida; 16 listed New Jersey; 267 listed Massachusetts; 38 listed Arizona and 91 listed Virginia (p. 12, no. 10, Immigrants Admitted, by Leading States of Intended Residence and Country of Birth: 1990, US Bureau of the Census, *Statistical Abstract of the United States: 1992*, 112th edition, Washington, DC, 1992). In 1980 there were 55,000 Laos born people in the US, which jumped to 172,000 by 1990 (p. 50, no. 55, Foreign-Born Population, by Place of Birth: 1980 and 1990, US Bureau of the Census, *Statistical Abstract of the United States: 1993*, 113th edition, Washington, DC, 1993). From 1971 to 1980 22,600 people from Laos immigrated to the United States. This jumped to 145,600 between 1981 and 1990 (p. 11, no. 8, Immigrants, by Country of Birth: 1961 to 1991, US Bureau of the Census, *Statistical Abstract of the United States: 1993*, 113th edition, Washington, DC, 1993). Looking at the statistics for the number of Laotians who were admitted as permanent residents under Refugee Acts is instructive. From 1961 to 1970 none was admitted to the US. From 1971 to 1980 21,690 were admitted increasing to 142,964 by 1990 (p. 12, no. 9, Immigrants Admitted as Permanent Residents Under Refugee Acts, by Country of Birth: 1961 to 1991, US Bureau of the Census, *Statistical Abstract of the United States: 1993*, 113th edition, Washington, DC, 1993).

The national and official language of Laos is Lao. There are minority languages such as Hmong, Mien and Thai-Dam. Lao is monosyllabic and tonal. Written Lao is based on Sanskrit and consists of 50 consonant and vowel symbols with four tone marks. It is written from left to right.

Vietnam

Vietnam is bordered by China on the north; Cambodia and Laos on the west and by the South China Sea on the south and east. Eighty-five per cent of the population are Vietnamese. The rest are several different ethnic minorities. Most of these ethnic groups left Vietnam in 1975.

Vietnam has a recorded history of 2,000 years and an unrecorded history of another 2,000 years. From 111 BC to 938 AD China ruled Vietnam. Chinese rule was eventually overthrown and the country was independent for 900 years. In 1883 the French conquered Vietnam and remained in control until 1954, and French became the most commonly spoken second language. During World War II the Japanese drove the French out of Indochina. Ho Chi Minh, a Communist leader, organized an independence movement called the Vietminh to fight the Japanese and oppose the French. After World War II the French occupied southern Vietnam. The Vietminh controlled the North and established the Democratic Republic of Vietnam. The Vietnamese in the north and south were against French rule. In 1954, after eight years of fighting, the French were defeated and, following the Geneva Accord, Vietnam was divided into two states along the 17th parallel. North Vietnam was controlled by Ho Chi Minh with a Communist government and South Vietnam was ruled by Premier Ngo Dinh Diem under a non Communist government. Civil war erupted, with the United States assisting South Vietnam and China and the Soviet Union assisting North Vietnam. A full scale war was underway by 1960. By 1969 there were over 500,000 US troops in Vietnam. A cease fire agreement was signed in 1973 and the US withdrew all its troops. In 1975 the North Vietnamese conquered South Vietnam and reunited the country under Communist rule.

An estimated two million Vietnamese died during the twenty year conflict. Millions of others were maimed, made homeless and forced to flee as refugees from the country. Eventually over one million Vietnamese left the country. Hundreds of thousands died at sea trying to escape.

In 1975 the first wave of Vietnamese refugees, over 200,000, left their country. They were predominantly well educated, urban, middle class professionals who spoke both English and French. About 130,000 of them were sent to four processing camps in the United States: Camp Pendleton in California, Fort Chafee in Arkansas, Elgin Air Force Base in Florida and Fort Indiantown Gap in Pennsylvania. From these camps the refugees were sent to various areas around the country. Within a few years many Vietnamese relocated and gathered in communities such as Orange County, California. In many of these communities Mutual Assistance Associations were formed to help new refugees.

Second wave refugees entered the US between 1975 and 1978 and were usually family of those in the first wave.

Third wave refugees entered the US between 1978 and 1980. Several hundred thousand people left Vietnam by escaping in boats and became known as the boat people. During this period the boat people were mainly ethnic Chinese fleeing Vietnam. Others were Vietnamese who feared being sent to reeducation centers and, finally, many were children whose parents arranged for the children's escape while they remained behind. Two thirds of their boats were attacked by pirates. Most boat people who survived landed in the countries of Thailand, Malaysia and the Philippines. There they were housed in prison like holding centers.

Third wave refugees were most often fishermen, farmers and people from rural areas and small coastal villages. They had little contact with Americans before fleeing their country and had more cultural shock when they arrived in the United States. An added problem was the lack of compassion many were met with once they entered the US. Although some people were sympathetic, others were hostile to the refugees because of the difference in lifestyles, culture and inability of the refugees to speak English. Many Americans resented the refugees because the Americans perceived them as being dependent on welfare and because some of the refugees threatened the work of some segments of American society. Fishermen especially felt in conflict with the refugees, who were also fishermen, because the newcomers were unaware of the methods employed and agreements that existed between local fishermen.

In 1990 48,792 Vietnamese immigrants were admitted to the United States, of whom 19,675 listed California as their intended destination; 2,254 listed New York; 4,343 listed Texas; 954 listed Illinois; 1,275 listed Florida; 500 listed New Jersey; 2,048 listed Massachusetts; 872 listed Arizona and 1,505 listed Virginia (p. 12, no. 10, Immigrants Admitted, by Leading States of Intended Residence and Country of Birth: 1990, US Bureau of the Census, *Statistical Abstract of the United States: 1992*, 112th edition, Washington, DC, 1992). In 1980 there were 231,000 Vietnamese born people in the US, increasing to 543,000 by 1990 (p. 50, no. 55, Foreign-Born Population, by Place of Birth: 1980 and 1990, US Bureau of the Census, *Statistical Abstract of the United States: 1993*, 113th edition, Washington, DC, 1993). In 1990 there were 536,000 people of Vietnamese ancestry in the US: 9 per cent living in the Northeast; 8 per cent in the

Midwest; 28 per cent in the South and 54 per cent in the West (p. 51, no. 56, Population, by Selected Ancestry Group and Region: 1990, US Bureau of the Census, *Statistical Abstract of the United States: 1993*, 113th edition, Washington, DC, 1993). From 1961 to 1970 4,600 Vietnamese immigrated to the United States, increasing to 179,700 by 1980 and to 401,400 by 1990 (p. 11, no. 8, Immigrants, by Country of Birth: 1961 to 1991, US Bureau of the Census, *Statistical Abstract of the United States: 1993*, 113th edition, Washington, DC, 1993). The statistics for the number of Vietnamese who were admitted as permanent residents under Refugee Acts are as follows. From 1961 to 1970, 7 Vietnamese refugees were admitted to the US. By 1980 that number jumped to 150,266 and increased again by 1990 to 324,453 (p. 12, no. 9, Immigrants Admitted as Permanent Residents Under Refugee Acts, by Country of Birth: 1961 to 1991, US Bureau of the Census, *Statistical Abstract of the United States: 1993*, 113th edition, Washington, DC, 1993).

Vietnamese have been influenced by Confucianism, Taoism and animism, but the majority are Buddhist. Ancestor worship is a common Vietnamese practice and underlies all other religions. About 10 per cent of Vietnamese in the United States are Catholic. Of the first wave of refugees who came to the US almost one third were Roman Catholic.

Vietnamese is the national language of Vietnam. It is not mutually intelligible with any other language spoken in Asia. There are three main regional dialects, northern, central and southern regions, and they differ somewhat in pronunciation and vocabulary. It is tonal, monosyllabic and contains many words of Chinese origin. It does not have plurals or past tenses. These are determined by context. The written language is based on the Roman alphabet and was devised by European missionaries in the sixteenth-century. It became the national writing system after World War I. The alphabet consists of about 32 consonant and vowel letters with five tone marks. There are high rising tones; low falling tones; low rising tones; high rising broken tones and low constricted tones.

Thailand

Thailand was known as the Kingdom of Siam until 1939. By 1991 the population was 56,814,000. Thai is the official language with English the most commonly taught second language. About 89 per cent of the population is considered literate. The official state religion is Buddhism, with Islam, Confucianism and Christianity the other three main religions. Thailand lies between Laos, Cambodia, the Gulf of Thailand, Malaysia, the Andaman Sea and Myanmar. It is the only southeast Asian country that has not been a European colony at any time. About 85 per cent of the people belong to one of four ethnic groups known collectively as the Core Thai. Of these four groups, the Central Thai makes up about 36 per cent of the population and the Northeastern (or Thai-Lao) Thai about 32 per cent. The other two Core Thai groups each account for a smaller per cent of the population. Over half the people are involved in agriculture; however, since the 1980s, the government has promoted industrial development. Thailand is the world's main exporter of tapioca and the world's second largest exporter of rubber.

In 1980 there were 55,000 Thailand born people in the United States, increasing to 107,000 by 1990 (p. 50, no. 55, Foreign-Born Population, by Place of Birth: 1980 and 1990, US Bureau of the Census, *Statistical Abstract of the United States: 1993*, 113th edition, Washington, DC, 1993). In 1990 there were 91,000 Thai residents in the United States: 12,000 living in the Northeast; 13,000 in the Midwest; 24,000 in the South and 43,000 in the West (p. 32, no. 33, Resident Population, by Region, Race and Hispanic Origin: 1990, US Bureau of the Census, *Statistical Abstract of the United States: 1993*, 113th edition, Washington, DC, 1993). Between 1961 and 1970 there were 5,000 immigrants from Thailand, increasing to 44,100 between by 1980 and to 64,400 by 1990 (p. 11, no. 8, Immigrants, by Country of Birth: 1961 to 1991, US Bureau of the Census, *Statistical Abstract of the United States: 1993*, 113th edition, Washington, DC, 1993).

Buddhism is the main religion with about 95 per cent of the people adhering to its teachings. Of the remaining, about 4 per cent are Muslims. The official spoken language is Thai. The phonetic language is related to Chinese but the written alphabet is based on Cambodian script.

Indonesia

Indonesia's official name is the Republic of Indonesia. Its population in 1990 was 191,216,000. It lies between Malaysia, Brunei, Papua New Guinea and the Indian Ocean. The official language is Bahasa Indonesia. English, Dutch and Javanese are the other major languages. It is the largest nation in Southeast Asia. Indonesia was under the control of the Dutch from the early 1600s till 1949 when it became independent. It is made up of over 13,500 islands with Java, Sumatra, Kalimantan, Borneo (the Indonesian part), Sulawesi and Irian Jaya (the Indonesian part of New Guinea) being the main islands. Java is the most important island and about 66 per cent of the inhabitants of Indonesia live on it.

From 1981 to 1990 14,300 Indonesians immigrated to the United States (p. 11, no. 8, Immigrants, by Country of Birth: 1961 to 1991, US Bureau of the Census, *Statistical Abstract of the United States: 1993*, 113th edition, Washington, DC, 1993). In 1980 30,000 Indonesian born people were in the United States. This increased to 48,000 in 1990 (p. 50, no. 55, Foreign-Born Population, by Place of Birth: 1980 to 1990, US Bureau of the Census, *Statistical Abstract of the United States: 1993*, 113th edition, Washington, DC, 1993).

Indonesia has a diverse population with around 300 distinct, although related, ethnic groups. The Javanese and Sundanese represent about 60 per cent of the population. They live on the island of Java. In addition there are about four million Chinese residents living in Indonesia. Islam is the main religion with Christianity and Hinduism being the other two primary religions. The largest Muslim population of any country in the world can be found in Indonesia where 90 per cent are Muslims, 9 per cent are Christian and 2 per cent are Hindu. Animism is practiced in some of the more isolated regions of the country.

3 SOUTH ASIA

Six main nations form South Asia: India, Pakistan, Sri Lanka, Bangladesh, Nepal and Bhutan. The majority of immigrants from South Asian countries are from India, Pakistan and Bangladesh.

India

The Republic of India, with a population in 1990 of 850,067,000, has nearly one sixth of the world's population. It is the world's seventh largest country in landmass and lies between China, Nepal, Bhutan, Myanmar, Bangladesh, the Indian Ocean, Pakistan and the Arabian Sea. Ethnically and culturally India has great diversity. There are 16 main languages and over 1,000 dialects. The language groups in the north include Hindi, Gujarati, Bengali, Marathi, Oriya, Assamese, Sindhi, Punjabi and Urdu. In southern India the main languages are Tamil, Telugu, Kannada (or Kanarese) and Malayalam. Of the population 80 per cent live in villages most of which have less than 1,000 inhabitants. The other 20 per cent live in towns and cities. There are a limited number of these, around 200, with the majority of the 20 per cent living in one of the large urban centers or in one of the major cities, Calcutta, Bombay and Delhi. Calcutta has over ten million residents; Bombay has nine million and Delhi has 7.5 million inhabitants. The main religions of India are Hindu (83 per cent); Muslim (11 per cent); Christian (2.5 per cent) and small groups of Buddhists, Jains, Sikhs and Jews. About 40 million tribal people are primarily believers of animism (spirit worship).

The practices and beliefs of Hinduism evolved over a period of 4,000 years and no one founder is identified. It covers a wide range of beliefs from those related to spirit worship to a belief in a single, personal God. The Vedas, sacred books of Hinduism, are believed to have been composed around 1500 BC. The four main principles of Hinduism are: the belief in God as the creator of the world; an eternal soul that is indestructible; moral responsibility for actions; and belief in reincarnation. Hindus believe that everyone must go through a series of births, deaths and rebirths and that the nature and form of our next life is determined by our actions in the present life.

Muslims believe in one God and worship in buildings called mosques. Mecca (Makkah) in Saudi Arabia is the holy city of Islam.

The caste, or class, system determines much of an individual's life. One's place in society is determined by one's caste and one belongs for life, normally, to the caste one is born into. Marriages are within one's caste and are usually arranged by the parents of the couple. There are four main categories of castes: the highest is called the Brahmans (priests), then the Kshatriyas (warriors), the Vaisyas (merchants and bankers) and the Sudras (farmers, artisans and laborers). There are believed to be around 3,000 caste divisions within these broad categories.

In 1990 30,667 immigrants from India were admitted to the United States, of whom 5,794 listed California as their intended destination; 4,931 listed New York; 1,956 listed Texas; 3,431 listed Illinois; 822 listed Florida; 3,927 listed New Jersey; 671 listed Massachusetts; 167 listed Arizona and 805 listed Virginia (p. 12, no. 10, Immigrants Admitted, by Leading States of Intended Residence and Country of Birth: 1990 US Bureau of the Census, *Statistical Abstract of the United States: 1992*, 112th edition, Washington, DC, 1992). In 1980 there were 206,000 Indian born people in the US. This increased to 450,000 by 1990 (p. 50, no. 55, Foreign-Born Population, by Place of Birth: 1980 and 1990, US Bureau of the Census, *Statistical Abstract of the United States: 1993*, 113th edition, Washington, DC, 1993). In 1990 there were 570,000 people of Asian Indian ancestry in the US, 32 per cent living in the Northeast; 19 per cent in the Midwest; 26 per cent in the South and 24 per cent in the West (p. 51, no. 56, Population, by Selected Ancestry Group and Region: 1990, US Bureau of the Census, *Statistical Abstract of the United States: 1993*, 113th edition, Washington, DC, 1993). From 1961 to 1970 31,200 Asian Indians immigrated to the United States, increasing to 176,800 by 1980 and to 261,900 by 1990 (p. 11, no. 8, Immigrants, by Country of Birth: 1961 to 1991, US Bureau of the Census, *Statistical Abstract of the United States: 1993*, 113th edition, Washington, DC, 1993).

Pakistan

The Islamic Republic of Pakistan was created in 1947, establishing a separate sovereign state carved out of India made up of primarily Muslims, and leaving India primarily Hindu. Pakistan lies between China in the north, Afghanistan in the northwest, Iran in the west, the Arabian Sea in the south and India to the east and southeast. There are four provinces in Pakistan: the Punjab, the Sind, the North-West Frontier and Baluchistan. There are three main regions in Pakistan: the northern highlands, the Baluchistan Plateau west of the Indus River and the Indus River plain on the eastern side of the river. The Indus is the most important river in Pakistan and is vital for agriculture since Pakistan is one of the few countries in the world with too little rainfall to grow crops. The water from the Indus River and its main tributaries form the basis of an elaborate irrigation system which makes it possible for farmers to grow their crops. Seventy per cent of the inhabitants of Pakistan live in the lowlands adjacent to the Indus River and its tributaries.

The majority ethnic group is the Punjabis. They make up between 60 to 70 per cent of the population. The second largest ethnic group is the Sindhi, then the Pathans, the Baluchi and the Muhajirs.

The population is 97 per cent Muslim. About 20 per cent belong to the Shi'ite branch of Islam with the other 77 per cent belonging to the Sunni branch.

Urdu is Pakistan's official language and is spoken as a first language by about 9 per cent of the population. Punjabi is spoken by 64 per cent and 12 per cent speak Sindhi. These languages belong to the Indo European language family.

About 25 per cent of the population is literate, with less than a third of these being women. Pakistan has the world's lowest women to men ratio with 91 females for every 100 men due to the high rate of death during pregnancy or childbirth and malnutrition and inadequate health care.

In 1990 9,729 Pakistani immigrants were admitted to the United States, of whom 1,532 listed California as their intended destination; 2,553 listed New York; 1,026 listed Texas; 934 listed Illinois; 444 listed Florida; 690 listed New Jersey; 112 listed Massachusetts; 44 listed Arizona and 582 listed Virginia (p. 12, no. 10, Immigrants Admitted, by Leading States of Intended Residence and Country of Birth: 1990, US Bureau of the Census, *Statistical Abstract of the United States: 1992*, 112th edition, Washington, DC, 1992). In 1980 there were 31,000 Pakistani born people in the US, increasing to 92,000 by 1990 (p. 50, no. 55, Foreign-Born Population, by Place of Birth: 1980 and 1990, US Bureau of the Census, *Statistical Abstract of the United States: 1993*, 113th edition, Washington, DC, 1993). From 1961 to 1970 4,900 Pakistani people immigrated to the United States, increasing to 31,200 by 1980 and to 61,300 by 1990 (p. 11, no. 8, Immigrants, by Country of Birth: 1961 to 1991, US Bureau of the Census, *Statistical Abstract of the United States: 1993*, 113th edition, Washington, DC, 1993).

Bangladesh

Bangladesh, previously called East Pakistan, lies between the Bay of Bengal, India and Myanmar and has a population of 117,930,000. It declared its independence from Pakistan in 1971. The official language is Bengali with English being the other major language. Islam and Hinduism are the main religions. The climate is rainy with annual monsoons and frequent tropical cyclones. Flooding is common due to the enormous amount of rainfall the country receives. It is one of the world's most densely populated nations with over 80 per cent of the population living in rural areas and it is also one of the world's poorest nations with an average annual per capita income of $150. The majority of the people, about 80 per cent, are involved in agriculture and Bangladesh is the world's leading producer of jute. Dhaka, one of the few large cities, is the country's capital. It has about 3.5 million inhabitants and has been continuously inhabited since the 400s. Ethnically, 98 per cent of the people are Bengalis, descendants of migrants to the country thousands of years ago from what is now Myanmar, Tibet and northern India. The majority of the people are Muslims and Islam is the state religion. However, other religions are freely practiced. Women marry early with the average lifespan being 49, two years less than the average lifespan for Bangladesh men. Literacy is low with about 39 per cent of men and 18 per cent of women being able to read and write.

Between 1981 and 1990 15,200 people from Bangladesh immigrated to the United States. More immigrants are expected during the 1990s. As an example, in 1991 alone 10,700 people from Bangladesh immigrated to the US (p. 11, no. 8, Immigrants, by Country of Birth: 1961 to 1991, US Bureau of the Census, *Statistical Abstract of the United States: 1993*, 113th edition, Washington, DC, 1993).

PART TWO

FICTION – PRESCHOOL THROUGH THIRD GRADE

Judy ALLEN

Panda
Illustrated by Tudor Humphries.
Candlewick, 1993.
ISBN: 1-56402-142-4, pp. 32.

Culture: Chinese

Twelve-year-old Jake accompanies his father, a botanist, on an expedition to China. He is visited by a panda while he is alone in the camp and has difficulty getting his father to believe the panda appeared when the camera he used to photograph the animal is broken. The story provides much information about pandas and their natural habitat and a fact sheet about pandas is included. Could be used in programs on pandas; China; botanists; camping; fathers and sons.

Reviewed in: *Booklist*
Main subjects: China; pandas; botany; camping

Jennifer ARMSTRONG

Chin Yu Min and The Ginger Cat
Illustrated by Mary Grandpre.
Crown, 1993.
ISBN: 517-58656-8, pp. 32.

Culture: Chinese

This dramatically illustrated folktale tells the story of Chin Yu Min and a ginger cat. Chin, a widow, learns about friendship, happiness and humility through her relationship with a ginger cat. This book could be used in programs about Chinese folktales; comparative folktales; friendship and cats.

Reviewed in: *School Library Journal*; *Horn Book*; *Publishers Weekly*
Main subjects: China; Chinese folktales; Asians; cats; friendship

Jose ARUEGO and Ariane DEWEY

Crocodile's Tale: A Philippine Folk Story, A
Scholastic, 1976.
ISBN: 0-590-09899-3.

Culture: Filipino

This story is about a smart young boy and a crocodile. The boy saves the crocodile's life, then must save himself from the crocodile. Could be used in programs on Philippine folklore; crocodiles; wisdom and comparative folklore.

Main subjects: Philippines; crocodile; wisdom; humor

Bernard ASHLEY

Cleversticks
Illustrated by Derek Brazell.
Crown, 1992.
ISBN: 517-58878-1, pp. 32.

Culture: Chinese

The story of Ling Sung, a young Chinese American boy, who searches for a special talent. He finds it; his skill in using chopsticks. Could be used in programs dealing with lifestyles; customs; Chinese Americans; eating utensils and chopsticks.

Reviewed in: *School Library Journal*
Main subjects: Chinese American; chopsticks

Asian Cultural Centre of UNESCO (eds)

Folk Tales from Asia for Children Everywhere: Book Three
Weatherhill, 1975.
ISBN: 0-8348-1034-4.

Culture: Asian

Nine folktales. Could be used in programs on comparative folklore; Asian folktales or Asian literature.

Main subjects: Asia; folklore

Jeannie BAKER

Where the Forest Meets the Sea
Illustrated by Jeannie Baker.
Greenwillow, 1988.
ISBN: 0-688-06364-0.

Culture: Australian

A young boy and his father spend a day in the Daintree Wilderness in North Queensland, Australia. Could be used in programs on Australia; rain forests; environmental conservation and Queensland.

Reviewed in: *Our Family, Our Friends, Our World* by Lyn Miller-Lachmann
Main subjects: Australia; rain forest; Queensland; environmental conservation

Keith BAKER

Magic Fan, The
Illustrated by Keith Baker.
Harcourt Brace Jovanovich, 1989.
ISBN: 0–15–250750–7, pp. 18.

Culture: Japanese

A village carpenter makes various things for the villagers. He finds a magic fan that enables him to come up with new ideas. They laugh at his new creations including a rainbow bridge he builds over the town. The bridge saves the villagers from a tidal wave and they change their minds. The carpenter loses the fan and realizes the magic was within him rather than the fan. Could be used in programs on Japan; self-esteem; talents; life styles; fans and occupations.

Special features: The fan is open on each double page spread with the text surrounding it.
Reviewed in: *School Library Journal*
Main subjects: Japanese; fans; magic; social life and customs

Molly Garrett BANG

Paper Crane, The
Greenwillow Books, 1985.
ISBN: 0–688–04109–4.

Culture: Japanese

Based on an ancient folktale, it tells the story of an old man who pays for his meal with a magic paper crane. The paper crane comes to life and dances for the owner of the restaurant. When others hear of the magic crane, they come to the restaurant to see it and to eat. Eventually the old man returns and leaves with the magic crane. Could be used in programs on origami; Japanese folktales; magic; cranes and kindness.

Special features: photographs of three dimensional paper cutouts.
Reviewed in: *Bulletin of the Center for Children's Books*; *Booklist*; *Horn Book*
Main subjects: Japanese folktale; magic; cranes; origami

Tye May and the Magic Brush
Series: A Greenwillow Read-alone book
Greenwillow Press, 1981.
ISBN: 0–688–84290–9, pp. 55.

Culture: Chinese

Retelling of a Chinese tale about a girl with no parents who dreams she has a brush which brings to life everything she paints. Could be used in programs on China; orphans; painting and magic.

Main subjects: China; magic; painting; orphans

David BIRCH

King's Chessboard, The
Illustrated by Davis Grebu.
Dial, 1988.
ISBN: 0–3087–0367–8.

Culture: Asian Indian

How a man's wisdom helps him to outsmart a vain king. Could be used in programs on India; vanity and wisdom.

Reviewed in: *Booklist; School Library Journal*
Main subjects: India; wisdom; vanity

Tom BIRDSEYE

Song of Stars, A
Illustrated by Ju-Hong Chen.
Holiday House, 1990.
ISBN: 0–8234–0790–X, pp. 32.

Culture: Chinese

The princess weaver and the herdsman were banished to opposite sides of the Milky Way for daring to love each other. They are reunited each year on the seventh day of the seventh month. Could be used in programs on the Milky Way; how stars came to be; Chinese folklore; comparative folklore; star-crossed lovers and princesses.

Main subjects: China; stars; comparative folklore

Eva BOHOLM-OLSSON
Translated by Diane Jonasson

Tuan
Illustrated by Pham van Don.
Farrar, Straus & Giroux, 1988.
ISBN: 91–29–58766–2, pp. 23.

Culture: Vietnamese

The story of a young boy who is bitten by a dog. He lives in a village in the Vietnamese countryside and there is concern about whether or not the dog had rabies. Illustrated with watercolors by Pham van Don, a popular Vietnamese artist. Could be used for programs on Vietnam; rabies and families. The story is, however, somewhat disjointed.

Main subjects: Vietnam; families

Peter BONNICI

Festival, The
Illustrated by Lisa Kopper.
Lerner/Carolrhoda, 1985.
ISBN: 0–87614–229–3.

Culture: Asian Indian

Arjuna, a city boy, visits his grandmother in a small village. His experiences at the festival held in the village are recounted. Provides insight into traditional South Indian culture and customs. Could be used in programs dealing with Asian Indians; intergenerational relationships and family relationships.

Special features: South India
Reviewed in: *Booklist; School Library Journal*
Main subjects: Asian Indian

Rains, The
Illustrated by Lisa Kopper.

Culture: Asian Indian

Arjuna awaits the monsoon season with great anticipation. Could be used in programs dealing with Asian Indians; weather and climate; monsoons.

Special features: South India
Main subjects: Asian Indian; monsoon

Julie BRILLHART

Anna's Goodbye Apron
Albert Whitman & Company, 1990.
ISBN: 0-8075-0375-4, pp. 32.

Culture: Multicultural

An inclusive look at children at play. This picture book would be useful in programs where ethnicity is not the issue but the desire is still to present children from different races interacting together.

Reviewed in: *Booklist; School Library Journal*
Main subjects: Multicultural

Ashley BRYAN

Sh-ko and his Eight Wicked Brothers
Illustrated by Fumio Yoshimura.
Macmillan, 1988.
ISBN: 0-689-31446-9.

Culture: Japanese

This is the story of Sh-ko and how he won the hand of a beautiful princess. He was the youngest of nine brothers and even though he was considered ugly, his kindness won him the princess. Could be used in programs on Japan; folklore; Japanese folklore; comparative folklore; kindness; true beauty; ugliness and princesses.

Reviewed in: *Booklist; Horn Book; School Library Journal*
Main subjects: Japan; kindness; beauty and ugliness; princesses

Fred BURSTEIN

Dancer, The
Illustrated by Joan Auclair.
Bradbury Press (Macmillan), 1993.
ISBN: 0-02-715625-7.

Culture: Multicultural

This story of a young girl's walk across town with her father to go to her ballet lesson is told in English, Spanish and Japanese. Watercolor illustrations accompany the story.

Special features: written in English, Spanish and Japanese
Reviewed in: *Publisher's Weekly; School Library Journal*
Main subjects: Dance class

W. A. CAWTHORNE

Who Killed Cockatoo?
Illustrated by Rodney McRae.
Farrar, Straus & Giroux, 1989.
ISBN: 0–374–38395–2.

Culture: Australian

Based on an adaptation by an Australian teacher and artist in 1870 of the traditional English nursery rhyme 'Who Killed Cock Robin?' McRae uses bold colors and stylized images to create a contemporary picture book. Could be used in programs on Australia; nursery rhymes and comparative tales.

Reviewed in: *Our Family, Our Friends, Our World* by Lyn Miller-Lachmann
Main subjects: Australia

Heidi CHANG

Elaine and the Flying Frog
Illustrated by Heidi Chang.
Random House Stepping Stone, 1991.
ISBN: 679–80870–1, pp. 64.

Culture: Chinese

Elaine Chow is new in school and is the only Chinese American. She and a classmate work together to create a frog kite for their class science project. Could be used in programs dealing with being new in school; Chinese Americans and friendship.

Reviewed in: *Horn Book Guide*
Main subjects: Chinese American; school; friendship

Elaine, Mary Lewis and the Frogs
Crown, 1988.
ISBN: 0–517–56752–0

Culture: Chinese

Elaine Chow moves to Iowa from San Francisco. Her first day experiences at her new school make her feel different from when she was in San Francisco. After becoming involved in a classroom science project, her cultural growing pains subside and her pride in being Chinese American increases. Could be used in programs on new schools; moving; Chinese Americans and cultural differences.

Reviewed in: *Booklist; Horn Book; School Library Journal*
Main subjects: Chinese American; moving; new school

Ann Nolan CLARK

In the land of Small Dragon: a Vietnamese Folktale
Illustrated by Tony Chen.
Viking, 1979.
ISBN: 0–670–39697–4.

Culture: Vietnamese

Vietnamese version of the Cinderella story told in blank verse. Could be used in programs on Cinderella; comparative folklore; Vietnamese folklore; as an example of blank verse.

Special features: the story is told in blank verse.
Main subjects: Vietnam; Cinderella; blank verse; Vietnamese folklore

Shirley CLIMO

Korean Cinderella, The
Illustrated by Ruth Heller.
HarperCollins, 1993.
ISBN: 0–06–020433–8.

Culture: Korean

Korean version of the popular fairy tale recounts the story of Pear Blossom, a stepchild, and a magistrate. The setting is ancient Korea and the magistrate selects Pear Blossom to be his wife. Could be used in programs on Korea; fairy tales; Cinderella and comparative folklore.

Reviewed in: *Publisher's Weekly; School Library Journal*
Main subjects: Korea; fairy tales; Cinderella

Eleanor COERR

Chang's Paper Pony
Series: I Can Read Books.
Illustrated by Deborah Kogan Ray.
HarperCollins, 1988.
ISBN: 0–06–021329–9, pp. 64.

Culture: Chinese

This historical fiction about the American West provides an easy to read story about Chinese Americans who settled in California during the Gold Rush. Chang, the main character, is the son of Chinese immigrants. He wants a pony of his own and tries to get the money by panning for gold. Suitable for programs dealing with the American West, the Gold Rush, the history of Chinese immigration to the United States and units dealing with historical fiction.

Special features: Illustrations which show the simplicity and orderliness of the Chinese immigrants
Reviewed in: *Booklist; School Library Journal*
Main subjects: Asian Americans, American West, Gold Rush, Chinese Americans

Helen COUTANT

First Snow
Illustrated by Mai Vo-Dinh.
Knopf, 1974.
ISBN: 0-394-92831-8, pp. 36.

Culture: Vietnamese

Lien, a young Vietnamese girl, learns the meaning of death after talking with her grandmother who is dying. Snow is used as an analogy for death and the transformation of the spirit when one dies. Black and white drawings illustrate the simple text. Could be used in programs dealing with death; intergenerational relationships; Vietnamese Americans or snow.

Reviewed in: *Booklist; Children's Literature Association Quarterly*
Main subjects: Vietnamese American; death; snow

Stefan CZERNECKI and Timothy RHODES

Singing Snake
Illustrated by Stefan Czernecki.
Hyperion: distributed by Little, Brown, 1993.
ISBN: 1-56282-399-X, pp. 40.

Culture: Australian

How snake tricked lark into singing while sitting in snake's mouth in an attempt to win a singing contest. Could be used in programs on Australia; Australian folklore; comparative folklore; snakes and larks.

Reviewed in: *Booklist*
Main subjects: Australia; folklore; snakes; larks

Emmett DAVIS

Clues in the Desert
Series: Adventure Diary
Illustrated by Julie Downing.
Raintree, 1983.
ISBN: 0-940742-29-2, pp. 32.

Culture: Pakistani

The story of Asif, a Pakistani boy, and his aunt Leela, an archaeologist. Could be used in programs dealing with Pakistan; archaeology and intergenerational relationships. Note that in places the text is a bit disjointed. The illustrations are, however, inviting.

Special features: Architecture, transportation and clothing are presented
Main subjects: Pakistan; archaeology

Demi

Chinese Zoo: Fables and Proverbs, A
Illustrated by Demi.
Harcourt, 1987.
ISBN: 0-15-217510-5.

Culture: Chinese

A collection of fables and proverbs. Could be used in programs on fables; China and proverbs.

Reviewed in: *Booklist; School Library Journal*
Main subjects: China; fables

Chen Ping and his Magic Axe
Illustrated by Demi.
Dodd, 1987.
ISBN: 0-396-08907-0.

Culture: Chinese

How the honesty of a young boy results in his good fortune. Could be used in programs dealing with magic; China; honesty and greed.

Reviewed in: *Bulletin of the Center for Children's Books; Booklist; School Library Journal*
Main subjects: China; magic; greed; honesty

Chingis Khan
Illustrated by Demi.
Henry Holt, 1991.
ISBN: 0-8050-1708-9, pp. 64.

Culture: Chinese

An interpretation of the life of Chingis Khan, one of the rulers of ancient China. Could be used in programs dealing with ancient China; military leaders; rulers and Chingis Khan.

Reviewed in: starred review in *Booklist*; *Horn Book*; *School Library Journal*
Main subjects: Ancient China; Chingis Khan; rulers; leaders; military leaders

Demi's Dragons and Fantastic Creatures
Illustrated by Demi.
Henry Holt, 1993.
ISBN: 0–8050–2564–2, pp. 50.

Culture: Chinese

A collection of mythological creatures in Chinese lore. Different types of dragons are included as well as other mythical creatures like a unicorn, phoenix and spirits such as the guardians of the Heavens. Could be used in programs on comparative folklore; mythology; dragons; magical creatures; spirits; unicorns; phoenix; spirit beings and Chinese folklore.

Main subjects: dragons; unicorns; phoenix; magical creatures; spirits; mythology

Demi's Reflective Fables
Grosset and Dunlap, 1988.
ISBN: 0–448–09281–6, pp. 32.

Culture: Chinese

Collection of thirteen traditional Chinese fables. A mylar mirror is provided on the book's front jacket flap for use by the reader. Can be used in programs dealing with fables; Chinese fables and comparative folklore.

Reviewed in: *School Library Journal*
Main subjects: Chinese fables; mirrors; reflections

Dragon Kites and Dragonflies
Illustrated by Demi.
Harcourt Brace Jovanovich, 1986.
ISBN: 0–15–224199–X.

Culture: Chinese

A collection of Chinese nursery rhymes. Some were adapted from *Chinese Mother Goose Rhymes* (translated by Isaac Taylor Headland, Fleming H. Revell Company, Westwood, NJ, 1900), some from *Chinese Children's Rhymes* (by Ruth Hsu, The Commercial Press Limited, Shanghai, 1935) and some were given verbally to the author by Tze-Si Huang. Could be used in programs on nursery rhymes; kites; dragons; dragonflies; frogs; bridges; boats; lanterns; silk; acrobats; weddings; laziness; tidiness; moon; swans; fireflies and puppets; programs on comparative poetry; comparative nursery rhymes and on Chinese culture.

Reviewed in: *Booklist*; *Horn Book*; *School Library Journal*
Main subjects: nursery rhymes; children's poetry; Chinese

Liang and the Magic Paintbrush
Henry Holt and Company, 1980.
ISBN: 0-8050-0220-0.

Culture: Chinese

Beautifully illustrated book telling the story of Liang, a young Chinese boy, and his wish to be a painter. In a dream he receives a magic paintbrush which brings to life whatever he paints. A greedy emperor tries to take the magic brush from Liang with disastrous results. Could be used in tandem with fables such as the golden goose to teach the price of greed; also in programs dealing with folktales from different lands; with painting; with art appreciation and with magic.

Special features: Good illustrations complement the text.
Awards received: Notable Children's Trade Books in the Field of Social Studies; Reading Rainbow Book
Reviewed in: *Publisher's Weekly; School Library Journal; Bulletin of the Center for Children's Books; Horn Book*
Main subjects: Chinese folktale; magic; painting; art

Artist and the Architect, The
Illustrated by Demi.
Henry Holt, 1991.
ISBN: 0-800-1580-9, pp. 32.

Culture: Chinese

This story deals with envy, talent and trickery. Suitable for programs dealing with ancient China; envy; trickery; architects and artists.

Reviewed in: *Booklist; Kirkus; School Library Journal*
Main subjects: Ancient China; artist; architect

Empty Pot, The
Illustrated by Demi.
Henry Holt, 1990.
ISBN: 0-8050-1217-6, pp. 32.

Culture: Chinese

The story of Ping, an excellent gardener. The Chinese Emperor devises a test to select his heir. The one who can grow the most beautiful flowers from a seed the Emperor gives him will become the heir. Ping surprisingly is unable to get his seed to sprout. Could be used in programs dealing with ancient China; Chinese tales; seeds; plants and gardening.

Reviewed in: Starred review in *Kirkus; Horn Book; Booklist; Publisher's Weekly; School Library Journal*
Main subjects: Ancient China; plants; seeds; gardening

Hallowed Horse: a Folktale from India, The
Illustrated by Demi.
Dodd, 1987.
ISBN: 0-396-08908-9.

Culture: Asian Indian

The King tries to gain possession of a magic horse, which would enable him to overcome his enemies. Could be used in programs on India; horses; magical horses and comparative folklore.

Reviewed in: *Booklist*
Main subjects: India; horses; magic

Magic Boat, The
Illustrated by Demi.
Henry Holt, 1990.
ISBN: 0–8050–1141–2, pp. 32.

Culture: Chinese

The story of a magic boat, its crew and Chang. This book could be used in programs dealing with boats; magic and Chinese tales.

Reviewed in: *Booklist; Horn Book; Kirkus; School Library Journal*
Main subjects: magic; boats

Norah DOOLEY

Everybody Cooks Rice
Illustrated by Peter Thornton.
Carolrhoda Books, 1991.
ISBN: 0–87614–412–1, pp. 32.

Culture: Multicultural

Picture book providing a fun look at people from different cultures. Carrie, a young girl, is looking for her brother who is late for dinner. As she goes to different houses in the neighborhood, she learns each family makes a rice dish for dinner. Could be used for programs on food; lifestyles; cooking and interracial neighborhoods.

Special features: simple rice recipes from different cultures
Reviewed in: *Instructor; Reading Teacher; New York Times Book Review*
Main subjects: multicultural; rice; food; lifestyles

Doris Portwood EVANS

Breakfast with the Birds
Illustrated by Tony Chen.
Putnam, 1972.
ISBN: out of print

Culture: Chinese

The story of a boy and his pet mynah bird. The boy tells fortunes to earn money and is arrested for not having a license to work. The judge lets him go and a generous man gives the boy enough money to treat his bird to breakfast at a special teahouse. Has some flaws yet can be useful if one is careful. It emphasizes tourists and presents Hong Kong in the way a foreigner might perceive the city and so gives a superficial view of the culture. Could be used in programs on birds; Hong Kong; tourists and travel.

Main subjects: Hong Kong; Chinese

Mem FOX

Possum Magic
Illustrated by Julie Vivas.
Harcourt Brace Jovanovich, 1990.
ISBN: 0-15-200572-2, pp. 32.

Culture: Australian

Grandma Poss makes her granddaughter Hush invisible. After a while Hush wants to be visible again, but Grandma has forgotten how to undo the spell. The two circle Australia in their search for the ingredient missing in the spell. Could be used in programs on Australia; animals around the world; opossums; dingoes, wombats, kangaroos and kookaburras.

Reviewed in: *Our Family, Our Friends, Our World* by Lyn Miller-Lachmann
Main subjects: Australia; animals; dingoes, wombats, kookaburras, kangaroos, opossums

Ina R. FRIEDMAN

How My Parents Learned to Eat
Illustrated by Allen Say.
Houghton Mifflin, 1984.
ISBN: 0-395-35379-3, pp. 32.

Culture: Japanese

A young Japanese American girl tells why she is comfortable eating with chopsticks or with a knife and fork. Her father is American and her mother is Japanese. She tells how her father learned to eat with chopsticks and her mother with a fork. Appropriate for programs on interracial marriages; differing manners and customs; foods of the world; Japanese Americans and parents.

Special features: Good illustrations show how the couple blended their different cultural backgrounds; use of chopsticks for eating
Reviewed in: *Multicultural Review*
Main subjects: Japanese Americans; manners and customs; interracial marriages

Hisakazu FUJIMURA

Ho-Limlim: a Rabbit Tale from Japan
Illustrated by Keizaburo Tejima.
Philomel Books (Putnam), 1988.
ISBN: 0-399-22156-5.

Culture: Japanese

Ho-Limlim, a rabbit, lives a carefree life as a youth. As he grows older he settles for a quieter life and realizes home may be the best place of all. Could be used in programs on Japan; rabbits; growing older.

Main subjects: Japan; rabbits; Ainu oral tradition

Chitra GAJADIN

Amal and the Letter from the King
Caroline House, 1992.
ISBN: 1563971208.

Culture: Asian Indian

Amal, a young Asian Indian boy, watches what happens in his village from his window. Useful in programs dealing with India and lifestyles.

Reviewed in: *Publisher's Weekly*; *School Library Journal*
Main subjects: India; lifestyles

Paul GALDONE

Turtle and the Monkey: a Philippine Tale, The
Illustrated by Paul Galdone.
Houghton, 1983.
ISBN: 0-89919-145-2.

Culture: Filipino

Turtle asks for help from monkey to save a banana tree. Useful in programs on monkeys; turtles; banana trees; cooperation; Philippine folklore and comparative folklore.

Main subjects: Philippines; turtles; monkeys

Sherry GARLAND

Lotus Seed, The
Illustrated by Tatsuro Kiuchi.
Harcourt Brace Jovanovich, 1993.
ISBN: 0-15-249465-0.

Culture: Vietnamese

A Vietnamese girl sees the young Emperor of Vietnam cry the day he lost the golden dragon throne. She takes a seed from a lotus pod in the imperial garden to remind her of when she saw the emperor cry. She keeps the seed and takes it with her when, as an adult, she has to flee Vietnam. In later years, her grandson plants the seed and the lotus blooms. Could be used in programs dealing with Vietnam; lotus flowers; the Vietnam War; oppression; emigrants; intergenerational relationships and Vietnamese Americans.

Special features: author's note at the end of the book gives a good brief overview of Vietnam's history
Reviewed in: *Booklinks; Publisher's Weekly; Parents; Horn Book; School Library Journal*
Main subjects: Vietnam; lotus flowers

Why Ducks Sleep on One Leg
Illustrated by Jean Tseng.
Scholastic, Inc., 1993.
ISBN: 0–590–45697–0.

Culture: Vietnamese

This retelling of a Vietnamese folktale explains why ducks sleep while standing on one leg. Three ducks receive only one leg each when they are created. This causes them problems and they seek a way to get a second leg. They get help from a goose and rooster who draft a petition requesting a second leg for each of them. They go to the local village guardian spirit to ask him to take the petition to the Jade Emperor, the ruler of all gods and spirits. Suitable for programs dealing with ducks; animism; comparative religions; spirit beings; folklore and Vietnam. The illustrations are beautiful and could be used in programs on artistic styles.

Special features: author's notes on Vietnam and village life during feudal Vietnam; animism – worship of the spirits of all things in nature
Reviewed in: *Publisher's Weekly; School Library Journal*
Main subjects: ducks; Vietnamese folktale; spirit beings; animism; comparative religion

Christian GARRISON

Dream Eater, The
Illustrated by Diane Capuozzo Goode.
Macmillan Publishing Company, 1986.
ISBN: 0–689–71058–5.

Culture: Japanese

The story of Yukio, a young Japanese boy in ancient Japan. The people in his village are all having bad dreams and are losing sleep because of their nightmares. Yukio rescues a monster called a baku which turns out to be a boon to the village rather than a menace because it eats nightmares. Yukio takes the baku back to his village where the creature eats all the nightmares and the villagers sleep well again. Could be used in programs dealing with dreams; nightmares; monsters and Japan.

Special features: good illustrations suggesting an unrolling scroll of ancient Japan
Awards received: Reading Rainbow Book
Reviewed in: *Children's Book Review Service*
Main subjects: dreams; nightmares; monsters; sleep; Japanese

Mordicai GERSTEIN

Mountains of Tibet, The
HarperCollins, 1987.
ISBN: 0-06-022149-6, pp. 26.

Culture: Tibetan

Story about a boy in Tibet who loves kites. He lives a long life, dies and is given a choice of becoming one with the universe or returning to earth to live another life. He chooses to return to earth and live again as a girl. He returns to earth as a girl in Tibet and as a girl loves kites, essentially becoming what he was in his previous life. Could be used in programs on kites; Tibet; reincarnation and free will.

Reviewed in: *Booklist; Horn Book; School Library Journal*
Main subjects: Tibet; kites; reincarnation; free will

Mirra GINSBURG

Chinese Mirror, The
Illustrated by Margot Zemach.
Harcourt Brace Jovanovich, 1988.
ISBN: 0-15-200420-3.

Culture: Korean

Retelling of a Korean folktale about a man who travels to China and brings back a mirror. Neither he nor the other people in his village had ever seen a mirror. This is the story of their reactions to what they see in the mirror. Could be used in programs dealing with folktales from different countries; Korean folktales; mirrors; the impact of new things on people and how people often misunderstand what they see.

Reviewed in: *Bulletin of the Center for Children's Books; Booklist; School Library Journal*
Main subjects: Korean folktales; mirrors

Rumer GODDEN

Fu-dog
Illustrated by Valerie Littlewood.
Viking, 1989.
ISBN: 0-670-82300-7, pp. 64.

Culture: Chinese

Li-la is of mixed British and Chinese heritage and lives four hours (by train) from London. She and her brother travel to London to find their great-uncle after he sends Li-la a tiny fu-dog for her birthday. Could be used in programs on Chinese in England; Chinese customs; intergenerational relationships; sibling relationships; birthdays and London.

Main subjects: Chinese; friendship; dogs; London

Valiant Chatti-maker, The
Illustrated by Jeroo Roy.
Viking, 1983.
ISBN: 0-670-74236-8.

Culture: Asian Indian

The story of a potter who unexpectedly becomes a hero. Could be used in programs about India; potters and heroes.

Main subjects: India; heroes; potter

Sheila HAMANAKA

Screen of Frogs: an Old Tale
Orchard, 1993.
ISBN: 0531086143.

Culture: Japanese

How Koji, a rich man, learns to respect nature in time to turn his life around. Useful in programs dealing with lifestyles and Japanese culture.

Reviewed in: *Publisher's Weekly; School Library Journal*
Main subjects: Japanese

Oki S. HAN and Stephanie Haboush PLUNKETT

Sir Whong and the Golden Pig
Dial, 1993.
ISBN: 0-8037-1345-2.

Culture: Korean

Folktale about what happens when a stranger secures a loan by using a fake golden pig as collateral. Could be used in programs dealing with Korea and folktales.

Reviewed in: *Booklinks; Kirkus; Publisher's Weekly; Horn Book; School Library Journal*
Main subjects: Korea; Korean folktales

Akiko HAYASHI

Aki and the Fox
Doubleday, 1991.
ISBN: 0–3854–1948–1.

Culture: Japanese

Story of Aki and her toy fox Kon's adventurous journey to Aki's grandmother's house. Kon's arm is damaged and Aki asks her grandmother to mend it. Could be used in programs on journeys; adventures; intergenerational relationships and foxes.

Main subjects: Japanese; journeys; intergenerational relationships; toys; foxes

Marilee HEYER

Weaving of a Dream: a Chinese Folktale, The
Illustrated by Marilee Heyer.
Viking, 1986.
ISBN: 0–670–80555–6.

Culture: Chinese

Story about an old widow and her three sons. Her treasured brocade disappears and she asks her sons to find it. The youngest son finds it, returns it to his mother and out steps the Red Fairy. The three live happily together. Useful in programs on China; Chinese folklore; comparative folklore and fairies.

Reviewed in: *Booklist; School Library Journal*
Main subjects: China; folklore; fairies

Masako HIDAKA

Girl from the Snow Country
Kane/Miller, 1986.
ISBN: 0–916291–06–5.

Culture: Chinese

A girl named Mi-chan from the snow country, who makes snow bunnies. Could be used in programs about snow and China.

Reviewed in: *Booklist; School Library Journal*
Main subjects: China; snow

Elizabeth HILLMAN

Min- Yo and the Moon Dragon
Illustrated by John Wallner.
Harcourt Brace & Company, 1992.
ISBN: 0–15–254230–2, pp. 32.

Culture: Chinese

An original tale about how the stars first appeared in the night sky. The cobweb staircase between the moon and earth is loose. The wise men say the moon is slowly falling toward earth but only the moon dragon knows what is happening. Could be used in programs on China; how things came to be stories; comparative tales; dragons and stars.

Reviewed in: *American Bookseller; Kirkus; Publisher's Weekly*
Main subjects: China; dragons; stars

Margaret HODGES

Voice of the Great Bell, The
Illustrated by Ed Young.
Little, 1989.
ISBN: 0–316–36791–5.

Culture: Chinese

A great bell is made for the Emperor. Useful in programs on bells; China; emperors.

Reviewed in: *Booklist*
Main subjects: China; emperor; bells

Lily Toy HONG

How the Ox Star Fell from Heaven
Illustrated by Lily Toy Hong.
Albert Whitman, 1991.
ISBN: 0–8075–3428–5, pp. 32.

Culture: Chinese

Retelling of a Chinese folktale explaining how man came to have the ox as a beast of burden. Written and illustrated by a Chinese American author, can be used in programs on Chinese Americans; Chinese folklore; world tales or programs on animals.

Reviewed in: starred review in *School Library Journal*; *Kirkus*; *Instructor*; *New York Times Book Review*
Main subjects: Chinese; folktale

Two of Everything
Illustrated by Lily Toy Hong.
Albert Whitman, 1993.
ISBN: 0–8075–8157–7, pp. 32.

Culture: Chinese

Folktale about a brass pot Mr Haktak finds which has magic properties. He discovers that anything that goes into the pot, comes out doubled. Confusion reigns when first Mrs Haktak falls in and then Mr Haktak falls in the magic pot. The soft colors and roundness of the illustrations are especially enjoyable. Could be used in units dealing with magic; comparative folklore or Japanese folktales.

Reviewed in: starred review in *Booklist*; *Horn Book*; *Publisher's Weekly*; *School Library Journal*
Main subjects: China; Chinese folktale; magic

William HOOKS

Peach Boy
Series: I Can Read It Myself
Illustrated by June Otani.
Bantam Little Rooster, 1992.
ISBN: 0–553–07621–3, pp. 48.

Culture: Japanese

An elderly couple's wish for a son is fulfilled when they find a little boy inside a huge peach. Could be used in programs on comparative folklore; tiny people and Japanese folktales.

Main subjects: Japanese folktales; tiny people

Barbara Savadge HORTON

What Comes In Spring
Illustrated by Ed Young.
Knopf, 1992.
ISBN: 0679902686.

Culture: Asian

A mother uses the changing of the seasons to explain to her daughter how the girl's parents met, married and eventually celebrated the birth of their daughter. Could be used in programs on the seasons; reproduction and family relationships.

Reviewed in: *Booklist; Kirkus*
Main subjects: Seasons; reproduction; mothers and daughters

Monica HUGHES

Little Fingerling: a Japanese Folktale
Ideals, 1992.
ISBN: 0824985532.

Culture: Japanese

Folktale about a boy who is only a finger long. Despite his small size, he is able to defeat two monsters by using his wits and courage. Useful in programs dealing with folktales; Japan and courage.

Reviewed in: *Publisher's Weekly*
Main subjects: Japanese; folktales

Jane Hori IKE and Baruch ZIMMERMAN

Japanese Fairytale, A
Illustrated by Jane Hori Ike.
Warne, 1982.
ISBN: 0-7232-6208-X.

Culture: Japanese

Fairytale about a man who gives up his good looks in order to make his bride beautiful. Could be used in programs on kindness; love; Japanese fairytales; comparative fairytales.

Main subjects: Japan; love; kindness

Daisaku IKEDA

Over the Deep Blue Sea
Illustrated by Brian Wildsmith.
Knopf, 1993.
ISBN: 679-84184-9, pp. 32.

Culture: Japanese

Akiko and Hiroshi's encounter with a friend shortly after World War II. The three maintain their friendship even though their countries had been at war. Suitable for programs dealing with World War II; friendship and Japan.

Reviewed in: *School Library Journal*
Main subjects: Japan; Japanese; World War II; friendship

Cherry Tree, The
Illustrated by Brian Wildsmith.
Knopf, 1992.
ISBN: 679–92669–0, pp. 32.

Culture: Japanese

Two Japanese children care for a cherry tree which had not bloomed since before World War II. Could be used in units dealing with nature; Japan and compassion.

Reviewed in: *Publisher's Weekly; School Library Journal*
Main subjects: Japan; Japanese; cherry trees

Princess and the Moon, The
Illustrated by Brian Wildsmith.
Knopf, 1992.
ISBN: 679–93620–3, pp. 32.

Culture: Japanese

The Great Rabbit teaches Sophie that to be treated like a princess she must look for the best in people, including herself. This book could be used in programs dealing with Japanese tales.

Reviewed in: *Growing Point; Junior Bookshelf*
Main subjects: Japan; Japanese

Snow Country Prince, The
Illustrated by Brian Wildsmith.
Knopf, 1991.
ISBN: 679–91965–1, pp. 32.

Culture: Japanese

Mariko and Kazio care for an injured swan while waiting for their parents to return from a distant city. The Snow Country Prince encourages them not to give up. Could be used in programs dealing with separation from parents; swans and Japan.

Reviewed in: *Wilson Library Bulletin*
Main subjects: Japan; Japanese

Momoko ISHII. Translated by Katherine PATERSON

Tongue-cut Sparrow, The
Illustrated by Suekichi Akaba.
Lodestar, 1987.
ISBN: 0-525-67199-4.

Culture: Japanese

The story of an elderly couple and a sparrow. The old man's kindness is rewarded, while his greedy wife gets what she deserves. Could be used in programs on Japan; folklore; Japanese folklore; comparative folklore; kindness; greed and styles of illustrations.

Special features: includes Japanese onomatopoeic words
Reviewed in: *Booklist; Horn Book; School Library Journal*
Main subjects: Japan; folklore; sparrows; birds; kindness; greed

Ryerson JOHNSON

Kenji and the Magic Geese
Illustrated by Jean Tseng.
Simon & Schuster, 1992.
ISBN: 0-671-75974-4.

Culture: Japanese

Kenji's family must sell their prized painting of five geese after floods destroy the family's rice crop. Before the art dealer comes to collect it, Kenji ties the painting of geese to his kite to let them fly high in the sky with the real geese. When he brings the painting to earth, much to his surprise he discovers one goose is missing, and so begins the magical tale. This story provides the reader with a glimpse of the lives of Kenji and his family. Their struggles to survive without starving and their ability to appreciate the beauty of art even when in need are presented in an unintrusive and natural manner. It would lend itself to programs dealing with magic, miracles and art appreciation.

Reviewed in: *Reading Teacher; School Library Journal*
Main subjects: geese; magic; miracles

Tony JOHNSTON

Badger and the Magic Fan: a Japanese Folk Tale, The
Illustrated by Tomie dePaola.
Putnam, 1990.
ISBN: 0-399-21945-5, pp. 28.

Culture: Japanese

Retelling of a Japanese folktale about the Japanese trickster character, the badger, stealing a magic fan from three Tengu. Tengu are Japanese goblins. The fan can make a person's nose grow longer or shorter. The badger uses the fan to trick a princess in order to win her hand. The Tengu children regain the fan and make the badger's nose grow so long it becomes a bridge pole for heavenly workers. There are some flaws in the book, such as drawings that lean towards being stereotypical and some lack of credibility in the story, but it could still be used in programs on comparative folktales; Japanese folktales; magic; magic fans; fans; monsters and goblins.

Reviewed in: *Horn Book*
Main subjects: Japanese; badgers; fans; magic; folktales

Gloria KAMEN

Ringdoves, The
Illustrated by Gloria Kamen.
Macmillan, 1988.
ISBN: 0-689-31312-8.

Culture: Asian Indian

Adaptations of tales that were first told in India about 300 BC. Could be used in programs dealing with India; comparative folklore or the folklore of India.

Reviewed in: *Booklist; School Library Journal*
Main subjects: India; folklore

Carol KENDALL

Wedding of the Rat Family, The
Illustrated by James Watts.
Macmillan, 1988.
ISBN: 0-689-50450-0.

Culture: Chinese

Tale about a search for a suitor for a family's beautiful daughter. After considering a number of powerful, yet inappropriate prospective bridegroom's, the parents find the perfect husband for their daughter. Could be used in programs on Chinese tales; rats; weddings and marriage.

Reviewed in: *Bulletin of the Center for Children's Books; Booklist; School Library Journal*
Main subjects: China; rats; marriage; weddings

Eric KIMMEL

Greatest of All: a Japanese Folktale, The
Holiday House, 1991.
ISBN: 082340885X.

Culture: Japanese

Story of a mouse father's search for the mightiest husband for his daughter. The Emperor, the sun, a cloud, the wind and a wall are all approached before he finds the best one. Could be used in programs dealing with mice; marriage; Japanese folktales and folktales of the world.

Reviewed in: *Booklinks; Kirkus; Publisher's Weekly*
Main subjects: Japanese; folktales

Suzy KLINE

Horrible Harry's Secret
Illustrated by Frank Remkiewicz.
Viking, 1990.
ISBN: 0–670–82470–4, pp. 52.

Culture: Korean

A second grade Korean girl named Song Lee has Asian features but otherwise could be any child. The story does not really enable the reader to learn more about the Korean culture or Korean Americans. This book falls more into the inclusive category of cultural diversity rather than one that will enable the reader to learn about the culture of Korea.

Reviewed in: *Booklist; Horn Book; School Library Journal*
Main subjects: Korean Americans; second grade experiences

Joanna Halpert KRAUS

Tall Boy's Journey
Illustrated by Karen Ritz.
Carolrhoda Books, 1992.
ISBN: 0–87614–746–5, pp. 48.

Culture: Korean

This fictional account of Kim Moo Young, an orphaned Korean boy, explores adoption from the child's point of view. Kim is eight years old when he is sent to the United States to be adopted. He is surrounded by strangers, unfamiliar customs and faced with the difficulties of communicating when he cannot understand the language. His growing frustration and eventual adjustments are covered. Could be used in units on adoption; immigration; Korea; orphans; Korean Americans; interracial families; parenting and lifestyles.

Reviewed in: *Publisher's Weekly; School Library Journal*
Main subjects: adoption; Korea; Korean Americans

Holly H. KWON

Moles and the Mireuk: a Korean Folktale, The
Illustrated by Woodleigh Hubbarb.
Houghton Mifflin, 1993.
ISBN: 0-395-64347-3.

Culture: Korean

Folktale relating the story of a father mole's search for the best husband for his daughter.

Reviewed in: *Horn Book; Publisher's Weekly; School Library Journal*
Main subjects: folktale; best husband

Margaret LEAF

Eyes of the Dragon
Illustrated by Ed Young.
Lothrop, Lee & Shepard/Morrow, 1987.
ISBN: 0-688-06156-7.

Culture: Chinese

Little Li will settle only for the greatest of all dragon painters to decorate the wall around the village. The consequences of his pride is dramatized by the results of his actions. Could be used in programs on China; pride and dragons.

Reviewed in: *Bulletin of the Center for Children's Books; Booklist; School Library Journal*
Main subjects: Chinese; dragons; pride

Jeanne M. LEE

Ba-nam
Illustrated by Jeanne M. Lee.
Henry Holt, 1987.
ISBN: 0-8050-0169-7, pp. 32.

Culture: Vietnamese

The use of full page color art provides insights into the cultural background of the Vietnamese.

Reviewed in: *Bulletin of the Center for Children's Books; Kirkus; Publisher's Weekly*

Legend of the Li River: an Ancient Chinese Tale
Illustrated by Jeanne M. Lee.
Henry Holt, 1983.
ISBN: 0–03–063523–3, pp. 32.

Culture: Chinese

Retelling of a Chinese legend explaining how the hills along the Li River came to be formed. Could be used in programs on rivers; Chinese folklore; comparative folklore and magic.

Reviewed in: *Booklist; Horn Book; Publisher's Weekly; Kirkus*
Main subjects: rivers; Chinese folklore; folklore

Legend of the Milky Way
Illustrated by Jeanne M. Lee.
Henry Holt, 1982.
ISBN: 0–8050–0217–0, pp. 32.

Culture: Chinese

Story about the Weaver Princess and how the Milky Way was created. She comes to earth to find the source of a beautiful melody she has heard. On earth she finds a young shepherd playing his flute. She falls in love with him, marries him and stays on earth with him. Her mother has her brought back to heaven, but the shepherd follows her. The angry mother turns the couple into two stars, separated by the Silver River (the Milky Way) that she created to keep them apart. This book could be used in programs dealing with comparative folklore; creation stories; how things came to be stories; Chinese folklore and stories about princesses.

Awards received: Reading Rainbow Feature
Reviewed in: *Booklist; Horn Book; Kirkus; Publisher's Weekly; School Library Journal*
Main subjects: Chinese folklore; legends; Milky Way; creation stories

Toad is the Uncle of Heaven
Illustrated by Jeanne M. Lee.
Henry Holt, 1985.
ISBN: 0–8050–1146–3, pp. 32.

Culture: Vietnamese

How a toad uses his wits to prevent the anger of the king of heaven. Could be used in programs on toads; Vietnamese folklore; wits and Vietnamese culture.

Awards received: Parents' Choice Honor Award for Illustration
Reviewed in: *Booklist; Horn Book; School Library Journal; Publisher's Weekly; Kirkus*
Main subjects: toads; Vietnamese folklore

Silent Lotus
Farrar Straus & Giroux, 1991.
ISBN: 0374369119.

Culture: Vietnamese

Lotus cannot speak, yet becomes a Khmer court dancer where she learns to tell the legends of the gods through dance. Could be used in programs dealing with muteness; folktales and dance.

Reviewed in: *Booklinks; Booklist; Kirkus; Publisher's Weekly; Horn Book*

Arthur A. LEVINE

Boy who Drew Cats, The
Illustrated by Frederic Clement.
Dial Books, 1993.
ISBN: 0–8037–1173–5.

Culture: Japanese

Retelling based on an ancient Japanese legend of an artist whose drawings of animals were so real that they could come to life. Kenji loves to draw. His mother takes him to a monastery to live because there is not enough food at home for him to be able to eat well and grow. Eventually Kenji leaves the monastery and comes to a temple where he encounters a terrible Goblin Rat. With his skill at painting cats, Kenji magically destroys the Goblin Rat. This book could be used in programs on Japan; Japanese folklore; comparative folklore; cats; artists and illustrating stories.

Special features: each page of text has a large Japanese character at the top of it; a guide to the pronunciation and meaning of the characters is given
Main subjects: Japan; Japanese folklore; cats; artists

Ellen LEVINE

I Hate English!
Illustrated by Steve Bjorkman.
Scholastic, 1989.
ISBN: 0–590–42305–3, pp. 32.

Culture: Chinese

This book is flawed in that the main character has stereotypical exaggerated almond-shaped eyes. Also the way in which Mei Mei, the young girl in the story, resists learning English is not realistic.

Reviewed in: *Multicultural Review; Reading Teacher*
Main subjects: Chinese Americans; Hong Kong

Riki LEVINSON

Our Home is the Sea
Illustrated by Dennis Luzak.
Dutton, 1988.
ISBN: 0-525-44406-8, pp. 26.

Culture: Hong Kong

A boy walks home from school. He lives in Hong Kong and the illustrations show the various sights one would see walking down the streets. He lives on a boat in the harbor and the illustrations reflect this, too. Could be used in programs on Hong Kong; boats; homes; lifestyles; school and comparing and contrasting major cities of different countries.

Reviewed in: *Bulletin of the Center for Children's Books; Horn Book; Emergency Librarian; School Library Journal*
Main subjects: Hong Kong; school; lifestyles; social culture and customs; homes

Richard LEWIS

In the Night, Still Dark
Illustrated by Ed Young.
Atheneum, 1988.
ISBN: 0-689-31310-1, pp. 32.

Culture: Pacific Islands

The Kumulipo, a Hawaiian creation chant, was once sung to newborns to bond them to all other living creatures. Could be used in programs on Hawaii; creation; chants and traditions.

Main subjects: Hawaii; mythology; creation

Betty Jean LIFTON

Joji and the Dragon
Illustrated by Eiichi Mitsui.
Linnet Books, 1989.
ISBN: 0-208-02245-7, pp. 64.

Culture: Japanese

This story is about a scarecrow who doesn't scare crows. Instead, he and the crows have an agreement. He doesn't scare them and they eat worms instead of the crops. The farmer whose field the scarecrow is supposed to protect advertises for someone else to do the job. He hires a dragon and learns in the end that the scarecrow was a better choice. The illustrations are black ink brush drawings that do not immediately capture one's attention. Could be used in programs on scarecrows; farmers; dragons; crows; friendship and Japan.

Main subjects: Japanese; scarecrows; dragons; farmers; crows

Arnold LOBEL

Ming Lo Moves the Mountain
Illustrated by Arnold Lobel.
Greenwillow, 1982.
ISBN: 0-688-00611-6.

Culture: Chinese

Engaging story about a couple who live too close to a mountain. Rocks from the mountain fall on the house and their vegetables are difficult to grow in the shade of the mountain. The woman decides her husband must move the mountain. More than once he goes to the village wise man for help on how to move the mountain. After a few false tries, he succeeds. This book could be used in programs dealing with humor; wisdom; perception of reality; problem solving; illustration styles; art appreciation and China.

Main subjects: China

Morag LOH

Tucking Mommy In
Illustrated by Donna Rawlins.
Orchard Books, 1987.
ISBN: 0-531-08340-3.

Culture: Asian

Two young sisters take care of their mother when she comes home very tired. They help her to bed, help her change clothes, tuck her in bed and tell her a bedtime story. Later, their father comes home and thanks them for being so helpful to their mother. Could be used in programs on families; mothers; siblings and bedtime.

Reviewed in: *Bulletin of the Center for Children's Books; Booklist; School Library Journal*
Main subjects: family; mothers; sisters

Ai-Ling LOUIE

Yeh-shen: a Cinderella Story from China
Illustrated by Ed Young.
Putnam, 1982.
ISBN: 0–399–20900–X.

Culture: Chinese

A Chinese version of the familiar Cinderella fairytale. Could be used in programs on Cinderella; comparative folklore; China and examples of different styles of illustrations.

Main subjects: China; Cinderella; fairytales; magic

Nancy LUENN

Dragon Kite, The
Illustrated by Michael Hague.
Harcourt, 1982.
ISBN: 0–15–224196–5, pp. 32.

Culture: Japanese

Story of Ishikawa, based on a historical thief who lived in Japan during the late 1600s or early 1700s. He stole from the rich to feed the poor. Could be used in programs on comparative folklore; Japanese folktales; thieves; ancient Japan.

Reviewed in: *Publisher's Weekly*
Main subjects: Japan; Japanese folklore; thieves; ancient Japan

Rafe MARTIN

Foolish Rabbit's Big Mistake
Illustrated by Ed Young.
Putnam, 1985.
ISBN: 0–399–21178–0.

Culture: Asian Indian

A retelling of the story of rabbit and his lack of sense. Rabbit believes the world is breaking up and the end of the world is happening. He tells everyone he meets and causes panic until he is shown his fears are ungrounded. (This is one of the Jataka tales.) Can be used in programs on India; comparative folklore; needless fear; foolishness; the importance of learning the facts of a situation before jumping to conclusions and on programs dealing with rabbits as characters in stories.

Reviewed in: *Bulletin of the Center for Children's Books; Booklist; Horn Book*
Main subjects: India; folklore; foolishness; rabbits

Feroza MATHIESON

Very Special Sari: a story set in India, The
Series: Wide World.
Illustrated by Prodeepta Das.
A & C Black; dist. by Childcraft Education Corp., 1988.
ISBN: 0-7136-3064-7, pp. 25.

Culture: Asian Indian

Six year old Gita, an Asian Indian girl, goes on a shopping trip with her mother to buy material for her mother's new sari. The text is illustrated with color photographs. This book could be used in programs dealing with India; family relationships or clothing around the world.

Special features: photographs of an Asian Indian city; clothing
Main subjects: India; Asian Indians; family relationships

Karen Kawamoto McCOY

Tale of Two Tengu, A
Illustrated by Fossey Koen.
Albert Whitman & Company, 1993.
ISBN: 0-8075-7748-0, pp. 32.

Culture: Japanese

Retelling of a traditional Japanese folktale about two goblins named Kenji and Joji. Kenji has a blue nose and Joji has a red one. They constantly argue over which one has the most wonderful nose. Their experiences when they try to determine which is better, a blue nose or a red nose, are recounted. This book could be used in programs dealing with goblins; Japanese folktales; comparative folktales or magic.

Reviewed in: *Publisher's Weekly*
Main subjects: Japan; Japanese folktales; goblins; magic

Gerald McDERMOTT

Stone Cutter: a Japanese Folktale, The
Illustrated by Gerald McDermott.
Penguin, 1975.
ISBN: 0-14-050289-0.

Culture: Japanese

Story about a stone cutter whose greed leads to trouble. This book could be used in programs on Japan; Japanese folktales; greed and comparative folklore.

Main subjects: Japan; greed

Mary MEDICOTT

Tales for Telling: from Around the World
Illustrated by Sue Williams.
Kingfisher Books, 1992.
ISBN: 1-85697-824-9.

Culture: Multicultural

Fifteen folktales from around the world including China and India.

Main subjects: folktales

Laura Krauss MELMED

First Song Ever Sung
Illustrated by Ed Young.
Lothrop, 1993.
ISBN: 0-688-08230-0.

Culture: Japanese

In this picture book a young boy asks what the first song ever sung was and each member of his family replies. The illustrations are borderless and double paged with inky blue washes in a variety of shadings serving as backgrounds for the fourteen paintings that support the story. Could be used in programs on Japan; songs; music; how different people see the same event (perspective) and as an example of different styles of illustration and artwork.

Reviewed in: *Publisher's Weekly; School Library Journal*
Main subjects: Japan; music; songs

Jean MERRILL

Girl Who Loved Caterpillars: a Twelfth Century Tale from Japan, The
Illustrated by Floyd Cooper.
Philomel, 1992.
ISBN: 0399218718.

Culture: Japanese

Story of Izumi, a young woman of twelfth century Japan. Izumi befriends caterpillars and other socially unacceptable things. Could be used in programs on ancient Japan; tolerance; caterpillars and friendship.

Reviewed in: *Booklist; Kirkus; Publisher's Weekly*
Main subjects: Japan; caterpillars; tolerance

Moira MILLER

Moon Dragon, The
Illustrated by Ian Deuchar.
Dial, 1989.
ISBN: 0-8037-0566-2.

Culture: Chinese

Story about a boastful man and what happened to him because of his boasting. This book could be used in programs on China and boasting.

Reviewed in: *Booklist*
Main subjects: China; boasting

Ken MOCHIZUKI

Baseball Saved Us
Illustrated by Dom Lee.
Lee & Low, 1993.
ISBN: 1-880000-01-6.

Culture: Japanese

How a Japanese American boy and others dealt with being sent to an internment camp during World War II. They used baseball as a diversion from the situation they found themselves in and how he continues to play baseball after being allowed to return home. Could be used in programs on Japanese Americans; World War II; internment camps; racism; prejudice and baseball.

Reviewed in: *School Library Journal*
Main subjects: Japanese Americans; World War II; internment camps; racism; prejudice; baseball

Junko MORIMOTO

Mouse's Marriage
Illustrated by Junko Morimoto.
Viking Kestrel, 1986.
ISBN: 0-607-81071-1.

Culture: Japanese

Retelling of a Japanese folktale about a mouse couple's search for the best husband for their daughter is simple yet effective. The illustrations are engaging, the text readable and together they provide a delightful story. The parents search for the best husband for their daughter, approaching in turn the sun, clouds, wind, a wall and finally a mouse who turns out to be the best. This story could be used in programs dealing with comparative folklore; marriage; mice; Japanese folktales and recognition of what makes one right for a certain role (in this case the right husband).

Special features: arranged marriages
Main subjects: mice; marriage; folklore

Inch Boy, The
Illustrated by Junko Morimoto.
Viking, 1986.
ISBN: 0-14-050677-2.

Culture: Japanese

Japanese version of the story of Tom Thumb. Could be used in programs dealing with comparative folklore; fairytales; tiny people and Japanese folklore.

Reviewed in: *Booklist; School Library Journal*
Main subjects: Japan; folklore; fairytales; Japanese folktales; comparative folklore; tiny people

Jill MORRIS

Monkey and the White Bone Demon
Illustrated by Lin Zheng.
Viking, 1984.
ISBN: 0-670-48574-8.

Culture: Chinese

A sixteenth century tale about the monk Hsuan Tsang's search for the ancient Buddhist scriptures. Could be used in programs on ancient China; Buddhism; monks and quests.

Main subjects: China; monks; Buddhism; ancient China

Winifred MORRIS

Magic Leaf, The
Illustrated by Ju-Hong Chen.
Macmillan, 1987.
ISBN: 0-689-31358-6.

Culture: Chinese

Lee Foo shows how he makes mistakes when he tries to pretend he knows more than he does. Could be used in programs on pride and China.

Reviewed in: *Booklist; Horn Book*
Main subjects: China; pride

Arlene MOSEL

Funny Little Woman, The
Illustrated by Blair Lent.
Dutton, 1972.
ISBN: 0–525–30265–4.

Culture: Japanese

This folktale recounts the story of how a little woman is captured by wicked people. Could be used in programs on Japanese folklore; comparative folklore.

Main subjects: Japan; Japanese folklore

Harutaka NAKAWATARI

Sea And I
Farrar, Straus & Giroux, 1992.
ISBN: 0–374–36428–1, pp. 32.

Culture: Japanese

A boy waves goodbye in the morning as his father goes to sea to fish and welcomes him home in the evening when he returns from the day's work. Could be used in programs dealing with the sea; fishermen; family relationships.

Reviewed in: *Publisher's Weekly*
Main subjects: Sea; fishing; family relationships

Keiko NARAHASHI

I Have a Friend
Margaret K. McElderry Books, 1987.
ISBN: 0–689–50432–2, pp. 32.

Culture: Asian

A young Asian boy describes his closest friend which happens to be his shadow. Could be used in programs on friendship and shadows.

Main subjects: Asian; shadows; friendship

Patricia Montgomery NEWTON

Five Sparrows: a Japanese Folktale, The
Illustrated by Patricia Montgomery Newton.
Macmillan, 1982.
ISBN: 0-689-30936-8.

Culture: Japanese

Story about the kindness of an old woman to a sparrow and how she is rewarded. Could be used in programs dealing with kindness; sparrows; birds in folklore; comparative folklore and Japanese folklore.

Main subjects: Japan; sparrows; birds; kindness; folklore; Japanese folklore

Takaaki NOMURA

Grandfather's Town
Kane/Miller, 1991.
ISBN: 09-1629136-7.

Culture: Japanese

Worried that his grandfather is lonely, a young Japanese boy goes with him to the public bath. Could be used in programs on Japanese culture; grandfathers; loneliness; baths and intergenerational relationships.

Main subjects: Japanese; baths; intergenerational relationships; grandfathers; loneliness

Lilith NORMAN

Paddock: a Story in Praise of the Earth, The
Illustrated by Robert Roennfeldt.
Knopf, 1993.
ISBN: 679-83887-2, pp. 32.

Culture: Australian

In Australia, a piece of land is called a paddock. This book portrays the life cycle of a paddock beginning with its origin in rock and lava. The life cycle includes the destruction of the land by man, the crumbling of towns and the land's renewal. Could be used in units dealing with the environment; preservation of the earth and Australia.

Reviewed in: *Publisher's Weekly*
Main subjects: Australia; Pacific Islander; environment

Anna Sibley O'BRIEN

Princess and the Beggar: a Korean Folktale
Scholastic, 1993.
ISBN: 0590460927.

Culture: Korean

A sad princess finds happiness after marrying a beggar. Could be used in programs dealing with Korea; folktales; marriage and the meaning of happiness.

Reviewed in: *Publisher's Weekly; School Library Journal*
Main subjects: Korea; folktales

Yuzo OTSUKA

Suho and the White Horse: a Legend of Mongolia
Illustrated by Suekichi Akaba.
Viking, 1981.
ISBN: 0-670-68149-0.

Culture: Mongolian

Folktale about a young herdsman and his white horse. Could be used in programs on horses; comparative folklore and Mongolia.

Main subjects: Mongolia; folklore; horses

Min PAEK

Aekyung's Dream
Illustrated by Min Paek.
Children's Book Press, 1988.
ISBN: 0-89239-042-5, pp. 22.

Culture: Korean

Aekyung's struggle to adjust to living in the United States. Aekyung is Korean and is faced with the problems of difficulty with English as well as the teasing of her classmates. This picture book was originally published in 1978. It would be useful in programs about immigrants; adapting to new situations; dealing with school; English as a second language and Korean Americans.

Special features: based on first hand experience
Korean and English
Reviewed in: *Multicultural Review*
Main subjects: Korean Americans; immigrants; school

Libuse PALECEK

Magic Grove, The
Illustrated by Josef Palecek.
Picture Book Studio USA, 1985.
ISBN: 0–907234–72–0.

Culture: Asian

Retelling of a Persian folktale recounting the friendship of two old men; the marriage of their children and the kindness of the young couple. Could be used in programs on ancient Persia; comparative folktales; kindness; friendship and marriage.

Reviewed in: *Booklist; School Library Journal*
Main subjects: friendship; marriage; kindness; Persia; folklore

Katherine PATERSON

Tale of the Mandarin Ducks, The
Illustrated by Diane Dillon.
Lodestar Books, 1990.

Culture: Japanese

Retelling of a popular Japanese folktale. A mandarin drake is captured by a selfish lord. As the days go by, the imprisoned duck becomes despondent and its feathers lose their beauty. A compassionate kitchen maid, Yasuko, releases the drake. When the lord learns of the drake's disappearance, he wrongly accuses Shozo, a former samurai. Shozo and Yasuko eventually fall in love. The lord is displeased and attempts to punish them but help for the two comes from an unexpected source. This beautifully illustrated story could be used in programs dealing with comparative folklore; love; compassion; true beauty; caring for others and Japanese art.

Reviewed in: *Horn Book; New York Times Book Review*
Main subjects: ducks; folktale

Darcy PATTISON

River Dragon
Illustrated by Jean Tseng.
Lothrop, Lee & Shepard, 1991.
ISBN: 0–688–10426–6, pp. 32.

Culture: Chinese

Ying Shao must cross the bridge of the river dragon to reach his bride-to-be. His future father-in-law feeds him swallows, a favorite food of the river dragon. Ying Shao must outwit the dragon to safely cross the bridge. Could be used in programs dealing with Chinese tales; dragons and cleverness.

Main subjects: Chinese; dragons; cleverness

Manus PINKWATER

Wingman, The
Bantam Skylark, 1992.
ISBN: 0-553-15958-5, pp. 80.

Culture: Chinese

Story of Donald Chen, the only Chinese student at Public School 132. He deals with loneliness by drawing, reading comic books and going on imaginary adventures with Wingman, a Chinese super hero. Could be used in programs on fantasy; prejudice; loneliness and Chinese Americans.

Reviewed in: *Kirkus, School Library Journal*
Main subjects: Chinese Americans; prejudice

Helena Clare PITTMAN

Gift of the Willows, The
Illustrated by Helena Clare Pittman.
Carolrhoda Books, 1988.
ISBN: 0-87614-354-0, pp. 32.

Culture: Japanese

Story of a potter who saved two willow trees. The trees eventually saved his life, too.

Awards received: IRA-CBC Children's Choice for 1989
Reviewed in: *Teaching PreK-8*
Main subjects: Japan; willows; trees

Grain of Rice, A
Illustrated by Helena Clare Pittman.
Hastings, 1986.
ISBN: 0-8038-9289-6, pp. 80.

Culture: Chinese

Pong Lo, a hardworking servant of the king, outwits the king and wins the Princess for his bride. Could be used in programs dealing with comparative folklore; Chinese tales about marriage and cleverness.

Reviewed in: *Booklist; Kirkus; School Library Journal*
Main subjects: Chinese tales; cleverness

Govinder, RAM

Rama and Sita: an Indian Folk Tale
Bedrick, 1988.
ISBN: 0-87226-171-9.

Culture: Asian Indian

Prince Rama and how he reclaims his place at the royal court. Could be used for programs on India; comparative folklore; folklore of India and royalty.

Reviewed in: *Booklist; School Library Journal*
Main subjects: India; folklore; royalty

Doreen RAPPAPORT

Journey of Meng: a Chinese Legend
Illustrated by Yang Ming-Yi.
Dial, 1991.
ISBN: 0803708963.

Culture: Chinese

A woman searches for her husband, a man forced into slavery to a cruel king. Could be used in programs dealing with slavery and China.

Reviewed in: *Booklist; Book Links; Kirkus; Publisher's Weekly*
Main subjects: China; slavery

Valerie REDDIX

Dragon Kite of the Autumn Moon
Illustrated by Jean Tseng.
Lothrop, Lee & Shepard, 1991.
ISBN: 0-688-11030-4, pp. 30.

Culture: Taiwanese

Tad Tin and his grandfather always make a kite together to release on Kite Day when, according to tradition, it will carry away all one's misfortunes. Could be used in programs on kites; Taiwanese traditions; Kite Day and intergenerational relationships.

Main subjects: Taiwanese traditions; kites; intergenerational relationships

Bjarne REUTER

Princess, and the Sun, Moon, and Stars, The
Illustrated by Otto S. Svend.
Michael Joseph/Viking, 1987.
ISBN: 0-7207-1654-3.

Culture: Chinese

Recreates in brilliant watercolors the ancient world of the Emperors of China. Could be used in programs on ancient China.

Main subjects: ancient China

Nami RHEE

Magic Spring: a Korean Folktale
Putnam, 1993.
ISBN: 0-399-22420-3.

Culture: Korean

The effect a fountain of youth has on three people, an old man and his wife and their greedy neighbor. This book could be used in programs dealing with Korea; folktales; magic; greed and the fountain of youth.

Reviewed in: *Booklinks; Publisher's Weekly; School Library Journal*
Main subjects: Korea; folktales; magic; greed; fountain of youth

Kristina RODANAS

Story of Wali Dad, The
Illustrated by Kristina Rodanas.
Lothrop, 1988.
ISBN: 0-088-07263-1.

Culture: Asian Indian

Story about a poor grass cutter and a princess. The grass cutter buys the princess a beautiful gold bracelet. This book could be used in programs dealing with India; love; sacrifice; princesses; folklore of India and comparative folklore.

Reviewed in: *Booklist; Horn Book; School Library Journal*
Main subjects: India; love; princesses

Dick ROUGHSEY

Giant Devil-dingo, The
Macmillan, 1973.
ISBN: out of print.

Culture: Australian

How dingoes became useful friends of the Aboriginal people. Could be used in programs on Australia; the Dreamtime; Aborigines; dingoes; comparative folklore and legends.

Awards received: Children's Book Council of Australia Picture Book of the Year Award
Reviewed in: *Our Family, Our Friends, Our World* by Lyn Miller-Lachmann
Main subjects: Australia; Aborigines; the Dreamtime; legends; mythology; folklore

Ronald ROY

Thousand Pails of Water, A
Illustrated by Mai Vo-Dinh.
Knopf, 1978.
ISBN: 0-394-93752-X, pp. 26.

Culture: Japanese

A young Japanese boy lives in a fishing village where the main way of making a living is by killing whales. The boy comes upon a beached whale one day and instead of telling the villagers, he tries to save it. He knows the whale will die if it is not kept wet so he vows to pour a thousand pails of water on the whale in an effort to save it. Eventually the villagers discover the boy and the whale and help him save it. This story would lend itself to programs on animal protection; animal rights; the whaling industry; environmental issues; Japan; kindness and compassion.

Main subjects: Japan; fishing; whale hunting; whales; kindness; compassion

Kimiko SAKAI

Sachiko Means Happiness
Illustrated by Tomie Arai.
Children's Book Press, 1990.
ISBN: 0-89239-065-4, pp. 32.

Culture: Japanese

Sachiko and her grandmother share the same name and the young girl is a favorite of her grandmother. However, Sachiko must learn to cope with the changes in her grandmother once the older woman begins experiencing problems due to Alzheimer's. Could be used in programs dealing with compassion; Alzheimer's; Japanese Americans; ageing and intergenerational relationships.

Reviewed in: *School Library Journal*
Main subjects: Japanese Americans; intergenerational relationships; ageing; Alzheimer's disease

Robert D. SAN SOUCI

Enchanted Tapestry, The
Illustrated by Laszlo Gal.
Dial Books for Young Readers, 1987.

Culture: Chinese

Based on several versions of a Chinese folktale. It is the story of three sons and their mother. Their mother weaves beautiful tapestries to earn money for all of them. Eventually she weaves a special tapestry which is lost. Each of her three sons sets out to find the tapestry. The two oldest are swayed from their task by gold; the youngest son perseveres until he finds the tapestry and returns it to his dying mother. Would lend itself to programs on filial piety; mothers and sons; tapestries; love and loyalty; comparative folklore and Chinese folklore.

Reviewed in: *Booklist; School Library Journal*
Main subjects: Chinese folklore; mothers; sons; loyalty; love; tapestries

Samurai's Daughter: a Japanese Legend
Dial, 1992.
ISBN: 0803711352.

Culture: Japanese

Story of a brave girl's journey to be reunited with her father, a samurai warrior. Could be used in programs dealing with samurai; warriors; daughters and fathers, and bravery.

Reviewed in: *Booklist; Kirkus; Publisher's Weekly*
Main subjects: Japan; samurai; father/daughter relationships

Snow Wife
Illustrated by Stephen T. Johnson.
Dial, 1993.
ISBN: 0-8037-1410-6, pp. 32.

Culture: Japanese

A beautiful young woman with thick spreading black hair saves Minokichi, a young woodcutter. He is instructed never to mention her. Later he marries and makes the mistake of telling his wife of the woman who saved him. His wife and the woman are the same and because he did not do as instructed, she disappears. He must convince the gods to return her to him. Could be used in programs on Japanese folktales; comparative folklore; heroes and love.

Reviewed in: *Booklist*
Main subjects: Japan; Japanese folklore; heroes

Isao SASAKI

Snow
The Viking Press, 1982.
ISBN: 0-670-65364-0.

This wordless picture book shows trains coming and going at a train station on a snowy day. Could be used in programs dealing with illustrations; train stations; railroads and snow. No particular culture is apparent. The illustrator, however, is Japanese.

Main subjects: snow; trains; railroads

Satoru SATO

I Wish I Had a Big, Big Tree
Illustrated by Tsutomu Murakami.
Lothrop, Lee & Shepard/Morrow, 1989.
ISBN: 0-688-07304-2, pp. 40.

Culture: Japanese

Karow wants to make pancakes in his treehouse kitchen but first he must find a big tree. Could be used in programs on trees and treehouses.

Main subjects: Trees; treehouses

Allen SAY

Bicycle Man, The
Illustrated by Allen Say.
Houghton Mifflin Company, 1982.
ISBN: 0-395-32254-5.

Culture: Japanese

This sensitive story set less than a year after the end of World War II, tells of sportsday at a Japanese school. Decorating the playground, running races, prizes and a picnic lunch are all part of the day. A surprising event also occurs when two American soldiers unexpectedly appear. The two men, one African American and one Anglo American, put on a show with a bicycle. The gentle illustrations portray the fear, curiosity and ultimately delight the adults and children feel when they are confronted with the two foreigners. This book would lend itself to programs dealing with Japanese; schools; sports; picnics; foods and eating customs; World War II; fear of foreigners; fear of the unknown; foot races and bicycles.

Special features: foods; customs
Reviewed in: *Social Studies; Five Owls*
Main subjects: Japan; World War II; bicycles; festivals; sports

Lost Lake
Houghton Mifflin, 1989.
ISBN: 0-395-50933-5, pp. 32.

Culture: Asian American

Story of a young boy and his father's camping trip in the mountains. The boy lives with his father each summer and usually passes the time by watching television and reading. The week-long camping trip provides an opportunity for the two to become closer. Could be used in programs on camping; fathers and sons, and family relationships.

Main subjects: Asian Americans; family relationships; fathers and sons; camping

River Dream, A
Houghton Mifflin, 1988.
ISBN: 0-395-48294-1, pp. 32.

Culture: Asian

A young boy who is sick in bed goes on a fantastical fishing trip after opening a box from his uncle. Could be used in programs on illness; imagination; fantasies; rivers and fishing.

Main subjects: Fishing; rivers; imagination; uncles

Tree of Cranes
Illustrated by Allen Say.
Houghton Mifflin Company, 1991.
ISBN: 0-395-52024-X, pp. 32.

Culture: Japanese

Engaging story of a young boy's first Christmas. His mother grew up in California and remembered how Christmas was celebrated in the United States. She decorated a pine tree with paper cranes and candles to show her son what a Christmas tree was like and in the morning he found a special present under the tree. This beautifully illustrated book could be used in programs dealing with Christmas; Japanese culture; art appreciation; comparative artistic styles; origami; mothers and sons; intercultural celebrations.

Reviewed in: *Horn Book; School Library Journal; Reading Teacher; New York Times Book Review; Teaching PreK-8*
Main subjects: Christmas; mothers; sons; origami; Japanese culture

Ellen SCHECTER

Sim Chung and the River Dragon: a Folktale from Korea
Illustrated by June Otzui.
Bantam Books, 1993.
ISBN: 0-553-09117-4.

Culture: Korean

The story of Sim Chung, a Korean girl, who tries to help her father regain his eyesight.

Main subjects: folktale

Kathleen SEROS

Sun and Moon: Fairy Tales from Korea
Illustrated by Norman Sibley and Robert Krause.
Hollym LB, 1983.
ISBN: 0-930878-25-6.

Culture: Korean

A collection of seven Korean fairytales. Could be used in programs on comparative fairytales; Korean fairytales and Korean literature.

Main subjects: Korea; Korean fairytales; comparative fairytales

Rashmi SHARMA

Blue Jackal, The
Illustrated by Rashmi Sharma.
Vidya Books, 1993.
ISBN: 1-878099-50-7, pp. 32.

Culture: Asian Indian

Humorous story that illustrates self-esteem for people in a multiracial society is not based on skin color. Could be used in programs on India; tolerance; self-esteem and multiracial societies.

Main subjects: Asian Indians; multiethnic; self-esteem

Aaron SHEPARD

Savitri: a Tale of Ancient India
Illustrated by Vera Rosenberry.
Albert Whitman & Company, 1992.
ISBN: 0-8075-7251-9, pp. 40.

Culture: Asian Indian

Hindu myth telling the story of Princess Savitri and her husband Satyavan. After only a year of marriage, Satyavan is claimed by the god of death, Yama. Princess Savitri wins him back from Yama by using her wit, virtue and strength. Could be used in units or programs dealing with comparative mythology; Asian Indian myths; love and devotion.

Reviewed in: *American Libraries; Kirkus; Publisher's Weekly; School Library Journal*
Main subjects: India; Asian Indian; folktales; Hindu

Marlene SHIGEKAWA

Blue Jay in the Desert
Illustrated by Isao Kikuch.
Polychrome Publishing, 1993.
ISBN: 1–879965–04–6, pp. 36.

Culture: Japanese

A Japanese American boy and his family are placed in an internment camp during World War II. Could be used in programs dealing with Japanese Americans; 1940s; World War II and internment camps.

Main subjects: Japanese Americans; World War II; internment camps

Linda SHUTE

Momotaro: the Peach Boy
Illustrated by Linda Shute.
Lothrop, 1986.
ISBN: 0–688–05864–7.

Culture: Japanese

Retelling of a Japanese folktale about a tiny boy. He is given to a childless couple to be their son. Could be used in programs on comparative folklore; Japanese folktales; fairytales; tiny people and childless couples in folktales.

Reviewed in: *Booklist; Horn Book; School Library Journal*
Main subjects: Japan; tiny people; fairytales; folklore; comparative folklore

Jacquelin SINGH

Fat Gopal
Illustrated by Demi.
Harcourt, 1984.
ISBN: 0–15–227372–7.

Culture: Asian Indian

Fat Gopal, the court clown, accomplishes a number of tasks that seem impossible at first. This could be used in programs dealing with India; folklore of India; comparative folklore; impossible deeds and clowns.

Main subjects: India; clowns; folklore

Peter SIS

Komodo!
Greenwillow Books (Morrow), 1993.
ISBN: 0–688–11584–5.

Culture: Indonesian

This picture book uses elements of fact and fantasy to explore the world of the Komodo Dragons of Indonesia.

Reviewed in: *Horn Book; Publisher's Weekly; School Library Journal*
Main subjects: Komodo Dragons of Indonesia

Dianne SNYDER

Boy of the Three-year Nap, The
Illustrated by Allen Say.
Houghton Mifflin Company, 1988.
ISBN: 0–395–44090–4, pp. 32.

Culture: Japanese

A poor widow's efforts to change her lazy son's habits. She is a seamstress who sews kimonos for rich women and her son, Taro, is lazy. He schemes to marry the daughter of their rich neighbor with unexpected results. Unknown to him, his mother adds a twist of her own to the plan and not only does Taro marry the rich merchant's daughter, he also gets a job. Could be used in programs dealing with laziness; tricksters; mothers and sons; Japanese culture; comparative folklore and Japanese folklore.

Reviewed in: *Publisher's Weekly*
Main subjects: laziness; mothers; sons; Japanese folklore; tricksters

Kiyoshi SOYA

House of Leaves, A
Illustrated by Akiko Hayashi.
Philomel, 1987.
ISBN: 0–399–21422–4, pp. 24.

Culture: Asian

Sarah climbs into leafy shrubbery to stay dry when it unexpectedly rains. The illustrations show the insects (such as a beetle, cabbage butterfly and praying mantis) that she sees as she waits for the rain to stop. Could be used in programs on rain and insects.

Main subjects: Asian; insects; rain

Cathy SPAGNOLI

Judge Rabbit and the Tree Spirit: a Folktale from Cambodia
Children's Book Press, 1991.
ISBN: 0892390719.

Culture: Cambodian

How Judge Rabbit solves the problem of a tree spirit who has assumed human form. Written in English and Khmer. Could be used in programs dealing with rabbits in folklore; Cambodian folktales; tricksters and comparative folktales.

Reviewed in: *Book Links; Kirkus; Publisher's Weekly*
Main subjects: Cambodian folktales; rabbits; tricksters

Claus STAMM

Three Strong Women: a Tall Tale from Japan
Illustrated by Jean Tseng.
Puffin Books, 1990.
ISBN: 0–14–054530–1.

Culture: Japanese

Forever-Mountain, a champion wrestler, believes he is the strongest, most powerful man in the world until he meets Maru-me. Maru-me, her mother and grandmother teach Forever-Mountain what strength really is and help him become strong enough to overcome the other wrestlers in Japan. Could be used in comparative folklore programs; programs on Japanese folklore; programs dealing with the concepts of strength, boasting and humor.

Reviewed in: starred review in *School Library Journal*; *Booklist*
Main subjects: folklore; Japan; power; strength

Catherine STOCK

Emma's Dragon Hunt
Illustrated by Catherine Stock.
Lothrop, Lee & Shepard, 1984.
ISBN: 0–688–02698–2, pp. 32.

Culture: Chinese

Emma's grandfather arrives from China and teaches her about the role of dragons in Chinese mythology. Could be used in programs dealing with dragons; mythology; intergenerational programs; Chinese culture; Chinese Americans and grandparents.

Special features: intergenerational and intercultural; depicts aspects of Chinese culture, art and customs as well as American style of living, eating and clothing
Main subjects: Chinese Americans; manners and customs; folklore; dragons

Michele Maria SURAT

Angel Child, Dragon Child
Illustrated by Vo-dinh Mai.
Raintree, 1983.
ISBN: 0-940742-12-8, pp. 35.

Culture: Vietnamese

The story of Ut (oot), a young Vietnamese girl, and her difficulties adjusting to school in the United States and of how she misses her mother who remained in Vietnam when the rest of the family immigrated. This book could be used in programs dealing with adjusting to a new school; on immigration; on Vietnam; on Vietnamese Americans; on friendship and on missing one's parent.

Special features: Vietnamese words and terms are used throughout the story; a brief explanation of the title, *Angel Child, Dragon Child*, is given in the back of the book; information on the structure of family and personal names as well as the use of family nicknames is given; other aspects of Vietnamese culture are also portrayed
Awards received: Reading Rainbow
Reviewed in: *Children's Literature Association Quarterly; Instructor; Multicultural Review*
Main subjects: Vietnamese immigrants; school; friendship; Vietnamese Americans

Otto S. SVEND

Children of the Yangtze River
Illustrated by Otto S. Svend.
Pelham Books, 1982.
ISBN: out of print

Culture: Chinese

This book shows what it is like in one village along the Yangtze River. The story is told from the point of view of two small children. The river floods the rice fields and when river flooding destroys the houses of the villagers, they all work together to rebuild. Could be used in programs on China; village life; rivers of different countries; the Yangtze River; family life; lifestyles and homes of different countries.

Reviewed in: *Multicultural Review*
Main subjects: China; Yangtze River; rivers; lifestyles; families

Rabindranath TAGORE

Paper Boats
Illustrated by Grayce Bochak.
Boyds Mills Press, 1992.
ISBN: 1-878093-12-6, pp. 32.

Culture: Asian Indian

A young Asian Indian boy dreams of what lies beyond his village. Could be used in programs on Asian Indians; boats; and people of other countries.

Main subjects: Asian Indian; boats; poetry

Fuiko TAKESHITA

Park Bench, The
Illustrated by Mamoru Suzuki.
Kane/Miller, 1988.
ISBN: 0-916291-15-4, pp. 33.

Culture: Japanese

A day in the park as seen from the point of view of a park bench. It goes from dawn to twilight and shows people visiting the park as well as a park employee working in the park. Would lend itself to programs on parks; Japan; benches and the illustrations could be used as an example of one way to use pictures to tell a story.

Special features: the text is in Japanese hiragana and English
Reviewed in: *Multicultural Review*
Main subjects: Japan; parks; benches

Ann TOMPERT

Bamboo Hats and a Rice Cake
Illustrated by Demi.
Crown, 1993.
ISBN: 0-517-59273-8.

Culture: Japanese

An elderly couple do not have enough rice to make cakes for the New Year. Celebrating with rice cakes would ensure they have good fortune during the new year. The wife suggests they sell her wedding kimono to buy the rice. The husband engages in a number of trades and eventually is rewarded for his kindness to the various people he trades with. This beautifully illustrated and interestingly written story would be useful in programs on Japanese folklore; Japan; New Year celebrations; kindness; social customs and illustration techniques.

Special features: the Japanese character for certain words are given in the margins of the illustrations and are used in the text; informative comments by the author and illustrator are at the end of the book; New Year celebrations
Reviewed in: *Publisher's Weekly*
Main subjects: Japan; social customs; kindness; Japanese folklore; New Year celebrations

Grandfather Tang's Story
Illustrated by Robert Andrew Parker.
Crown, 1990.
ISBN: 0-517-57272-0, pp. 30.

Culture: Chinese

Two foxes chase each other and change into different animals. Each time one of the foxes changes, the change includes a tangram. Tangrams are used in the traditional way to illustrate the story. Could be used in programs to introduce tangrams; about foxes; on China and on ways to illustrate stories.

Special features: tangrams
Reviewed in: *Books for Your Children; Childhood Education; Instructor; Language Arts; Social Education; Library Talk; New Advocate*
Main subjects: Chinese; tangrams; foxes

L. Betty TORRE

Luminous Pearl
Illustrated by Carol Inouye.
Orchard Books/Franklin Watts, 1990.
ISBN: 0–531–08490–6, pp. 32.

Culture: Chinese

The Dragon King in his undersea kingdom issues a challenge to two brothers who are suitors for his daughter's hand in marriage. The one who finds a luminous pearl that shines in the night will be the one who wins her hand. Could be used in programs on China; pearls; marriage; princesses; comparative folklore and Chinese folklore.

Main subjects: China; folklore; pearls; marriage; princess

Khanh Tuyet TRAN

Little Weaver of Thai-yen Village, The
Series: Fifth World Tales.
Illustrated by Nancy Hom.
Children's Book Press, 1987.
ISBN: 0–89239–03–1, pp. 24.

Culture: Vietnamese

Based on the experiences of Vietnamese children injured during the Vietnam War. Provides insight into the everyday life of the people of Vietnam. Originally published in 1977, revised version in 1987. Written in English and in Vietnamese and tells of the experiences of Hien, a young Vietnamese girl whose mother and grandmother were killed during bombing on their village. Hien was injured and sent to the United States for surgery. Could be used in programs about the Vietnam War; Vietnam; lifestyles; war and the results of war.

Special features: this bilingual book has beautiful illustrations which capture the feeling of the Vietnamese culture; daily life in Vietnam
Reviewed in: *National Geographic World*
Main subjects: Vietnam War; Vietnam

Rod TRINCA and Kerry ARGENT

One Woolly Wombat
Illustrated by Kerry Argent.
Kane/Miller, 1985.
ISBN: 0–916291–00–6, pp. 32.

Culture: Australian

An original counting rhyme that uses Australian animals as characters to teach children numbers and Australian zoology simultaneously. Could be used in programs on Australia; zoology; animals and numbers.

Reviewed in: *Our Family, Our Friends, Our World* by Lyn Miller-Lachmann
Main subjects: Australia; numbers; zoology; animals

Yoriko TSUTSUI

Anna In Charge
Illustrated by Akiko Hayashi.
Viking, 1989.
ISBN: 0–670–81672–8, pp. 32.

Culture: Japanese

Anna is left in charge of her little sister, Katy, when her mother has to leave the house. Katy disappears while Anna is setting up a game. Could be used in programs on siblings and babysitting.

Main subjects: Japanese; siblings; babysitting

Anna's Secret Friend
Illustrated by Akiko Hayashi.
Viking, 1987.
ISBN: 0–670–81670–1, pp. 32.

Culture: Japanese

A young girl's feelings about moving to a new place and finding new friends. Would lend itself to programs on friendship; moving; endings and beginnings.

Reviewed in: *Multicultural Review; Five Owls*
Main subjects: Japanese American; moving; friendship

Anna's Special Present
Illustrated by Akiko Hayashi.
Viking, 1988.
ISBN: 0–670–81671–X, pp. 32.

Culture: Japanese

Anna's little sister is hospitalized and Anna realizes how much she misses her. She thinks of the perfect gift to give her sister to make her smile. Could be used in programs on sibling relationships; sisters; hospitals and illness.

Main subjects: Japanese American; sibling relationships; sisters; hospitals; illness

Before the Picnic
Illustrated by Akiko Hayashi.
Putnam/Philomel, 1987.
ISBN: 0–399–21458–5, pp. 24.

Culture: Japanese

A young girl named Sashi wants to be helpful to her parents but makes a mess of things. They are patient and loving with her mistakes. Would lend itself to programs on helping others; patience; family life; kindness and life in modern Japan.

Reviewed in: *Multicultural Review*
Main subjects: Japanese; families; patience

Ann TURNER

Through Moon and Stars and Night Skies
Illustrated by James Graham Hale.
HarperCollins, 1990.
ISBN: 0–06–026190–0, pp. 32.

Culture: Asian American

The story of the adoption of a foreign born boy. The story is generic in that the boy's nationality is not made clear nor is it stressed in the story. One does not learn of his culture. By looking at the illustrations, it appears he was born in Vietnam. Could be used in programs that deal with adoption or adoption of foreign born children.

Reviewed in: *Multicultural Review; Language Arts; Reading Teacher; Social Education*
Main subjects: Asian American; adoption; parenting

Yoshiko UCHIDA

Birthday Visitor, The
Illustrated by Charles Robinson.
Scribner, 1975.
ISBN: out of print, pp. 32.

Culture: Japanese

The story of a young girl's birthday. Remove this book from your collection and from programming. It promotes stereotypical behavior, has the Japanese women bowing incorrectly and is dated.

Main subjects: Japanese American; birthdays

Bracelet, The
Philomel, 1994.
ISBN: 0–399–22503–X, pp. 32.

Culture: Japanese

Story of seven year old Emi and her friendship with Laurie, her best friend. Laurie gives Emi a bracelet to remember her by when Emi has to leave. Could be used in programs on friendship; Japanese Americans; World War II and the 1940s.

Main subjects: Japanese Americans; World War II; 1940s; friendship

Magic Purse, The
Illustrated by Keiko Narahashi.
Margaret K. McElderry Books, 1993.
ISBN: 0–689–50559–0.

Culture: Japanese

A young farmer promises to deliver a letter for a young woman. To do so he must brave the terrors of the Red Swamp. The girl gives him a magic purse that if he made sure to always leave one coin in it, the next morning he would find it to be full again. The young man delivers the letter to her parents. In return they give him a golden tray filled with gold coins. He returns home and never wants for money again because of the gifts from the girl and her parents. Would lend itself to programs on Japan; Japanese folklore; comparative folklore; magic and kindness.

Reviewed in: *School Library Journal; Publisher's Weekly*
Main subjects: Japan; Japanese folklore; magic; kindness

Rooster who Understood Japanese, The
Illustrated by Charles Robinson.
Scribner, 1976.
ISBN: out of print, pp. 32.

Culture: Japanese

The problems caused by a rooster's early morning crowing and how they are resolved. Deals mainly with the issue of the rooster without providing information specifically on the Japanese culture. Not a first choice to use in programming.

Main subjects: Japanese American; roosters

Two Foolish Cats, The
Illustrated by Margot Zemach.
Macmillan, 1987.
ISBN: 0–689–50397–0.

Culture: Japanese

Story about two cats and a wise monkey. The two cats argue over rice cakes until the monkey ends their argument.

Reviewed in: *Bulletin of the Center for Children's Books; Booklist; Horn Book*
Main subjects: Japan; rice cakes; cats; monkeys; arguments; foolishness; wisdom

Marie VILLANUEVA

Nene and the Horrible Math Monster
Illustrated by Ria Unson.
Polychrome Pub. Corp., 1993.
ISBN: 1-879965-02-X, pp. 36.

Culture: Filipino

Nene, a Filipino American girl, confronts the myth that all Asians excel at mathematics. Could be used in programs on Filipinos; math and stereotypes.

Main subjects: Filipino; math; stereotyping

Sybil WETTASINGHE

Umbrella Thief, The
Illustrated by Cathy Hirano.
Kane/Miller, 1987.
ISBN: 0-916291-12-X.

Culture: Sri Lankan

Kiri Mama, a Sri Lankan man, introduces umbrellas to the village where he lives after he learns of them when he visits a nearby town. The illustrations are well done and the town scenes are especially appealing. Could be used in programs dealing with Asia; Sri Lanka; saris; umbrellas and inventions.

Main subjects: Sri Lanka; umbrellas

Nadia WHEATLEY

My Place
Illustrated by Donna Rawlins.
Australia in Print, 1989.
ISBN: 0-7328-0010-2.

Culture: Australian

Picture book history of Australia that covers 1788 to 1988. Each decade is covered in a two-page description of what life was like in that year told from the point of view of a child of that era. Could be used in programs on Australia; maps; map-making; historical fiction and historical perspective.

Reviewed in: *Our Family, Our Friends, Our World* by Lyn Miller-Lachmann
Main subjects: Australia; historical fiction; maps

Emily WHITTLE

Fisherman's Tale
Illustrated by Jerry Burdick.
Green Tiger Pr/Simon & Schuster, 1988.
ISBN: 0-88138-101-2, pp. 32.

Culture: Asian

A fisherman finds a pearl that makes him wealthy. When his riches are stolen, he realizes his wealth had not made him happy and nothing of real value had been taken from him. Could be used in programs on fishermen; pearls and happiness.

Main subjects: Fishermen; pearls; happiness

Julie Stewart WILLIAMS

And the Birds Appeared
Illustrated by Robin Yoko Burningham.
University of Hawaii Press, 1988.
ISBN: 0-8248-1194-1.

Culture: Pacific Islands

Retelling of the traditional legend of how birds came to Hawaii. Maui, a cultural hero, uses his magical powers to bring birds to Hawaii. Could be used in programs on Hawaii; birds; comparative folklore; mythical heroes and magical powers.

Main subjects: Hawaii; birds; folklore; Maui; heroes

Barbara Ker WILSON

Acacia Terrace
Illustrated by David Fielding.
Scholastic, 1990.
ISBN: 0-590-42885-3, pp. 40.

Culture: Australian

Picture book overview of Australian history from the mid-1800s to the present based on the story of one family living on Acacia Terrace in Sydney. Could be used in programs on Australia; historical fiction; 1800s and the 1900s.

Reviewed in: *Our Family, Our Friends, Our World* by Lyn Miller-Lachmann
Main subjects: Australia; historical fiction; 1800s; 1900s

Elizabeth WINTHROP

Journey to the Bright Kingdom
Illustrated by Charles Mikolaycak.
Holiday House, 1979.
ISBN: 0-8234-0357-2, pp. 40.

Culture: Japanese

Fairytale about an artist who paints the animals of the forests and fields. She eventually goes blind and after having a baby girl, her dream is to be able to see what her little girl looks like. The girl grows and makes friends with the field mice. The mice guide her and her mother to a magical land called Kakure-sato where no one is sick, or unhappy or blind. While there, the mother is not blind and her dream to see her daughter comes true and she takes the memory with her when they return home. This well written story would be useful in programs on comparative fairytales; Japanese fairytales; mothers; daughters; blindness; kindness; friendship; illustration techniques; parental love and patience.

Special features: Appreciation for nature and art; patience; devotion to a group
Main subjects: Japanese; fairytale; culture; families; blindness

David WISNIEWSKI

Warrior and the Wise Man, The
Lothrop, Lee & Shepard/Morrow, 1989.
ISBN: 0-688-07890-7.

Culture: Japanese

The emperor's sons compete for the throne. To become the successor, one must bring back the five magical elements guarded by five demons. Could be used in programs on magic; challenges; trials; princes and quests.

Reviewed in: *Booklist; Horn Book; School Library Journal*
Main subjects: Magic; demons; trials and challenges

Diane WOLKSTEIN

Magic Wings, The
Illustrated by Robert Andrew Parker.
E.P. Dutton, 1983.
ISBN: 0–525–44275–8.

Culture: Chinese

A poor goose girl wishes to grow wings so that she can fly over the hillside to greet the flowers as they bloom in spring. Soon all the women in the town learn what she is attempting and want to grow wings so they can be the one to fly. Could be used in programs dealing with China; folktales; flying and magic. The storyteller notes in the back are useful and provide suggestions for acting out the story.

Special features: notes for storytellers
Awards received: Parent's Choice Award; A School LIbrary Journal Best Book of the Year; A CBC-NCSS Notable Children's Trade Book in the Field of Social Studies
Reviewed in: *Bulletin of the Center for Children's Books*; starred review in *School Library Journal*; *Horn Book*; *Wilson Library Bulletin*
Main subjects: China; Chinese folktales; flying; magic

Robert WYNDHAM

Chinese Mother Goose Rhymes
Illustrated by Ed Young.
Putnam, 1982.
ISBN: 0–399–20866–6.

Culture: Chinese

More than forty rhymes, riddles, lullabies and games that have amused Chinese children over the centuries. The original Chinese script of each rhyme is printed vertically along the outside margin of the page. Could be used in programs on China; nursery rhymes, riddles, lullabies and games.

Main subjects: Chinese; nursery rhymes

Caryn YACOWITZ

Jade Stone: a Chinese Folktale
Holiday House, 1992.
ISBN: 0823409198.

Culture: Chinese

Chan Lo, a stone carver, is commanded by the emperor to carve a dragon from a piece of perfect jade but discovers the stone wants to be carved into something else. Could be used in programs on ancient China; stone carving; jade; comparative folklore and Chinese folktales.

Reviewed in: *Booklist; Booklinks; Kirkus; Publisher's Weekly*
Main subjects: ancient China; jade; stone carving

Sumiko YAGAWA

Crane Wife
Illustrated by Suekicki Akaba.
Mulberry Books/Morrow, 1981.
ISBN: 0-688-07048-5.

Culture: Japanese

A farmer marries a beautiful stranger, not realizing she is the crane he rescued from death. Could be used in programs on cranes; magical beings; Japanese tales; marriage and wives.

Main subjects: cranes; magical beings; wives; marriage; Japanese tales

Dan YASHINSKY

Storyteller at Fault, the
Illustrated by Nancy Cairine Pitt.
Ragweed Press, 1992.
ISBN: 0-921556-29-2.

Culture: Multicultural

A collection of traditional folktales from Asia, Africa, Europe and the Middle East. Could be used in programming in folktales; Asia; Africa; Europe and the Middle East.

Main subjects: Asian; African; Middle East; European

Chun-Chan YE and Allan BRAILLIE

Bawshou Rescues the Sun: a Han Folktale
Scholastic, 1992.
ISBN: 0590454536.

Culture: Chinese

Story of how the hero Bawshou rescues the sun. Could be used in programs on Chinese folklore; how things came to be and comparative folklore.

Reviewed in: *Kirkus; Publisher's Weekly*
Main subjects: China; folklore; beginnings

Paul YEE

Roses Sing on New Snow: a Delicious Tale
MacMillan, 1992.
ISBN: 0027936228.

Culture: Chinese

Story of Maylin and her greedy father and lazy brothers. She is the real cook in their restaurant and eventually receives the recognition she deserves. Could be used in programs dealing with greed and China.

Reviewed in: *Booklist; Kirkus*
Main subjects: China; greed

Laurence YEP

Man Who Tricked a Ghost, The
Illustrated by Isadore Seltzer.
Troll/Bridgewater, 1993.
ISBN: 0–8167–3030–X, pp. 32.

Culture: Chinese

Story of Sung and how he tricks a ghost. Sung isn't afraid of ghosts since he considers everyone a relation, even otherworldly creatures. Illustrated endnote describes the story's origin. Could be used in programs on ghosts; medieval China and Chinese folklore.

Reviewed in: *Booklist* (starred review)
Main subjects: China folklore; medieval China; ghosts

Shell Woman and the King: a Chinese Folktale
Illustrated by Ming-Yi Yang.
Dial, 1993.
ISBN: 0–8037–1395–9.

Culture: Chinese

Uncle Wu marries Shell, who can assume the form of a seashell at will. He brags about her and the greedy and cruel king imprisons her. Could be used in programs dealing with magical beings; seashells; Chinese folktales and comparative folklore.

Reviewed in: *Publisher's Weekly*
Main subjects: China; Chinese folktales; comparative folklore; seashells; magical beings

Tongues Of Jade
HarperCollins, 1991.
ISBN: 0060224711.

Culture: Chinese

Seventeen Chinese American folktales from various Chinese communities in the US. Could be used in programs dealing with comparative folklore; Chinese Americans and Chinese folktales.

Reviewed in: *Booklist; Kirkus; Publisher's Weekly*
Main subjects: Chinese Americans; folklore

Pen Cat YING

Monkey Creates Havoc in Heaven
Illustrated by Xin Kuan Ling.
Viking, 1989.
ISBN: 0–670–81805–4.

Culture: Chinese

Monkey steals the Dragon King's magical staff and no one is able to catch the thief. Could be used in programs on monkeys; China; Chinese folklore; kings; emperors and comparative folklore.

Main subjects: China; monkey; magic; emperors

Jane Hyatt YOLEN

Seeing Stick, The
Illustrated by Remy Charlip.
Harpercrest, 1977.
ISBN: 0–690–00596–2.

Culture: Chinese

This story set in ancient China tells of a blind princess and a blind old man who teaches her to see with her fingers, mind and heart. Could be used in programs dealing with blindness; perception; reality and illusion; kindness and the meaning of sight.

Reviewed in: *Language Arts; English Journal*
Main subjects: China; blindness; kindness

Emperor and the kite, The
Illustrated by Ed Young.
Philomel Books, 1988.
ISBN: 0–399–21499–2.

Culture: Chinese

The story of tiny Djeow Seow (smallest one) who was the fourth daughter of the Emperor. Because of her size, she was overlooked and ignored. When her father is kidnapped by evil men, little Djeow Seow keeps him alive and eventually helps him escape and return to his throne. First published in 1967 and reissued in 1988. It could be used in programs dealing with fathers and daughters; with the importance of a person's worth not being based on external attributes; loyalty and love; kites.

Reviewed in: Language Arts
Main subjects: kites; fathers; daughters; size; love; loyalty

Girl who Loved the Wind, The
Illustrated by Ed Young.
Thomas Y. Cromwell Company, 1972.
ISBN: 0-690-33100-2.

Culture: Asian

This coming of age story tells of a young girl whose father tries to protect her from reality by creating a palace where only happiness and beautiful things are allowed. The girl, however, eventually learns the world is not always a happy place and escapes her father's control by sailing away on the wind. Would lend itself to programs dealing with reality; of parents attempting to shield their children from the world; of the wind; of loneliness and programs on Asian tales.

Main subjects: wind; coming of age

Seventh Mandarin, The
Illustrated by Ed Young.
Seabury Press, 1970.

Culture: Asian

This story tells of a king and his seven advisors. The kingdom is not identified other than 'in the East'. The king is a good king but uninformed of the reality of life outside the palace walls. One night he dreams of the people of the kingdom outside the walls and learns everything is not as he believed. The story line is good; the illustrations indistinct and no specific cultural information is readily evident. Not a first choice to use in a program but, with recognition of its limitations, could be included in programs dealing with reality and illusion and in comparative tales.

Reviewed in: *Language Arts*
Main subjects: kites; kings

Ed YOUNG

Lon Po Po
Philomel, 1989.
ISBN: 0-399-21619-7, pp. 32.

Culture: Chinese

Chinese version of Little Red Riding Hood. Could be used in programs on comparative folklore; wolves in folklore and Chinese folktales.

Awards received: Caldecott Medal Winner
Reviewed in: *Booklist*
Main subjects: China; Chinese folktale; comparative folklore; wolves

Red Thread
Philomel, 1993.
ISBN: 0-399-21969-2.

Culture: Chinese

Wei Gu, a young Chinese man, meets a spirit who tells his future. Could be used on programs dealing with Chinese; spirits; ghosts; the supernatural or fortune telling.

Reviewed in: *Publisher's Weekly; School Library Journal*
Main subjects: Chinese

Nathan ZIMELMAN

I Will Tell You of Peach Stone
Illustrated by Haru Wells.
Lothrop, Lee & Shepard Co., 1976.
ISBN: 0-688-51662-9.

Culture: Chinese

Old Man told the children of the village stories of how the sun was created, how man came to be and other tales of wonder. Old Man's companion was a dog named Peach Stone, so named because he liked to eat peaches. One winter Old Man developed a plan to go on an adventure with Peach Stone. When spring returned, he and Peach Stone set out to spread peaches to the rest of the world. Could be used in programs dealing with folktales on how things came to be; comparative folktales (such as Johnny Appleseed); on journeys; on friendships between man and dogs and on Chinese tales.

Main subjects: peaches; storytelling

FICTION – FOURTH THROUGH SIXTH GRADE

Lloyd ALEXANDER

Remarkable Journey of Prince Jen, The
Dutton, 1991.
ISBN: 0525448268.

Culture: Chinese

Story of Prince Jen and his journey. He has six unusual gifts that prove their worth on his perilous adventure. Could be used in programs on China; princes; quests; journeys.

Reviewed in: *Booklist; Booklinks; Kirkus; Publisher's Weekly*
Main subjects: China; princes; quests

Jean F. ANDREWS

Secret in the Dorm Attic, The
Series: Flying Fingers Club
Gallaudet University Press, 1990.
ISBN: 0–930323–66–1, pp. 100.

Culture: Pakistani

One in the series of the Flying Fingers Club. Saleem is a deaf boy from Pakistan. Information about Pakistan is given. In the illustrations, Saleem's clothing and hairstyle are very American appearing. Could be used in programs dealing with deafness; prejudice; friendship; sign language and Pakistan.

Reviewed in: *Library Talk; School Library Journal; Small Press Book Review*
Main subjects: Pakistani; deaf; sign language; prejudice

Asian Cultural Centre of UNESCO (eds)

Folk Tales from Asia for Children Everywhere: Book Three
Weatherhill, 1975.
ISBN: 0-8348-1034-4.

Culture: Asian

Nine folktales. Could be used in programs on comparative folklore; Asian folktales or Asian literature.

Main subjects: Asia; folklore

Allan BAILLIE

Little Brother
Viking-Penguin, 1992.
ISBN: 0670843814.

Culture: Cambodian

Vithy's attempt to rescue his older brother. The story takes place in Cambodia after the Vietnamese War. Vithy must overcome social upheaval, the jungle and his inability to trust to rescue his brother. Could be used in programs dealing with Cambodia; siblings and rescues.

Reviewed in: *Booklist; Kirkus; Publisher's Weekly*
Main subjects: Cambodia; siblings

Betsy BANG

Demons of Rajpur; Five Tales from Bengal
Illustrated by Molly Garrett Bang.
Greenwillow, 1980.
ISBN: 0-688-80263-X, pp. 81.

Culture: Asian Indian

Five Bengali tales of magic that are faithful to traditional demon tales. Could be used in programs on demons; Asian Indian folklore; comparative folklore and magic.

Main subjects: Asian Indian; magic; demons

Molly BANG

Dawn
Morrow, 1983.
ISBN: 0-688-02404-1.

Culture: Japanese

This Japanese tale is a variation on the story of Orpheus. Could be used in programs dealing with Japanese folklore; Japan and comparative folklore.

Main subjects: Japan; folklore

Milo Cleveland BEACH

Adventures of Rama, The
Smithsonian Institution, 1983.
ISBN: 0–934686–51–3.

Culture: Asian Indian

Stories from the *Ramayana,* a Hindu epic. Could be used in programs on India; Hinduism; comparative literature and folklore.

Main subjects: India; *Ramayana*; Hinduism; epic literature

David BIRCH

King's Chessboard, The
Illustrated by Davis Grebu.
Dial, 1988.
ISBN: 0–3087–0367–8.

Culture: Asian Indian

How a man's wisdom helps him to outsmart a vain king. Could be used in programs on India; vanity and wisdom.

Reviewed in: *Booklist; School Library Journal*
Main subjects: India; wisdom; vanity

Errol BROOME

Dear Mr Sprouts
Knopf, 1993.
ISBN: 679–83714–0, pp. 128.

Culture: Australian

The story of a schoolgirl and a farm boy. The boy finds a packet of seeds and a letter from a schoolgirl. The two correspond and over the years their friendship grows like the trees grow from the seeds. Could be used in programs about Australia and friendship.

Reviewed in: *Magpies*
Main subjects: Australia; Pacific Islander; friendship

Eve BUNTING

Happy Funeral, The
Illustrated by Mai Vo-Dinh.
HarperCollins, 1982.
ISBN: out of print, pp. 40.

Culture: Chinese

How a young girl deals with the death of her grandfather. The funeral and rituals surrounding it are also described. Useful in programs dealing with death; funerals; intergenerational relationships and Chinese Americans.

Special features: funeral customs and the rituals surrounding death in the Chinese American culture
Reviewed in: *Multicultural Review*
Main subjects: Chinese American; death; intergenerational; mourning; funerals

F. R. CARPENTER

Tales of a Chinese Grandmother
Illustrated by Malthe Hasselrus.
Amereon LB, 1973.
ISBN: 0–89190–481–6.

Culture: Chinese

Thirty Chinese stories.

Main subjects: China

Margaret and Raymond CHANG

In the Eye of War
Macmillan/Margaret K. McElderry, 1990.
ISBN: 0–689–50503–5, pp. 197.

Culture: Chinese

Account based on Raymond Chang's boyhood in Shanghai during World War II. It describes the Japanese occupation of Shanghai through the eyes of a child and his family. Could be used in programs on Shanghai; Japanese occupation; World War II.

Reviewed in: *Booklist*
Main subjects: Chinese; Shanghai; World War II

Sook Nyul CHOI

Year of Impossible Goodbyes
Houghton Mifflin, 1991.
ISBN: 0-395-57419-6.

Culture: Korean

A young Korean girl's life in Korea during the 1940s. Her experiences during the occupation of North Korea by the Japanese, and later of life under the rule of the Communists, and her eventual escape to South Korea are recounted. This historical novel could be used in programs dealing with Korea; World War II; Communism and oppression.

Special features: Japanese occupation of Korea
Reviewed in: *Booklinks; Booklist; Kirkus; Publisher's Weekly; Wilson LIbrary Bulletin*
Main subjects: Korea; World War II

Matt CHRISTOPHER

Shortstop from Tokyo
Illustrated by Harvey Kidder.
Little, Brown, 1988.
ISBN: 0-316-13992-1, pp. 121.

Culture: Japanese

A Japanese American boy named Sam Suzuki becomes shortstop on a boy's baseball team. Readers who enjoy baseball will like the play by play ballgame descriptions. Originally published in the 1970s. Does not provide much insight into the Japanese American culture, but could be used in programs dealing with baseball and friendship.

Reviewed in: *Horn Book; New York Times Book Review; School Library Journal*
Main subjects: Japanese American; baseball; friendship

Claude CLEMENT

Painter and the Wild Swans, The
Illustrated by Frederic Clement.
Dutton/Dial, 1986.
ISBN: 0-8037-0268-X, pp. 21.

Culture: Japanese

This story is told in four ways within the book: a poem written in Japanese calligraphy appears alongside each painting; in an English translation; in English text and then written in full at the end. The story is about a painter who falls so in love with the beauty of wild swans in winter that he begins following them. Eventually he comes to identify so completely with the swans that he can't remember if he is a swan or a human. Could be used in programs showing different ways to tell a story; on swans; animals; Japan; illustrating stories and the meaning of beauty.

Main subjects: Japan; swans

Eleanor COERR

Mieko and the Fifth Treasure
Putnam, 1993.
ISBN: 0-399-22434-3.

Culture: Japanese

Ten year old Mieko recounts her feelings in the aftermath of the dropping of the atomic bomb on Nagasaki. Could be used in programs on Japan; World War II; Nagasaki and the atomic bomb.

Reviewed in: *Booklinks; Publisher's Weekly; School Library Journal*
Main subjects: Japan; World War II; atomic bomb; Nagasaki

Linda CREW

Children of the River
Delacorte Press, 1989.
ISBN: 0-440-50122-9, pp. 213.

Culture: Cambodian

Sundara Sovann, a Cambodian refugee living in Oregon, wants to fit in at her high school but faces problems when the traditional ways of her family clash with American culture. Could be used in programs on Cambodian Americans; refugee experiences; cultural clashes and peer pressure.

Awards received: IRA Children's Book Award
Reviewed in: *Booklist; Kirkus; Publisher's Weekly; School Library Journal*
Main subjects: Cambodian; refugee experiences; prejudice

Emily CROFFORD

Born in the Year of Courage
Carolrhoda Books, 1991.
ISBN: 0-87614-679-5, pp. 184.

Culture: Japanese

Historical fiction telling the story of Manjiro, a Japanese teenager in the 1860s. He is shipwrecked on an island and later picked up by an American whaling ship. Manjiro joins the ship's crew and becomes instrumental in developing friendly trade relations between the United States and Japan. Could be used in programs dealing with the history of Japanese/American relations; how one person can make a difference and on the 1860s. Would also lend itself to a booktalk to young people.

Reviewed in: *School Library Journal*
Main subjects: Japan; Japanese American; historical fiction

Sarah ELLIS

Next-door Neighbors
Macmillan, 1990.
ISBN: 0-689-50495-0, pp. 154.

Culture: Chinese

Peggy moves to a new town where she is befriended by Sing, the Chinese gardner of Peggy's rich next-door neighbor. Could be used in programs on moving; intercultural and intergenerational friendship as well as friendship in general.

Awards received: School Library Journal Best Book of 1990
Reviewed in: *School Library Journal*
Main subjects: friendship; new town; moving; intercultural friendships; intergenerational friendships

Betty Vander ELS

Bombers' Moon, The
Farrar, Straus & Giroux, 1985.
ISBN: 0-374-30864, pp. 167.

Culture: Chinese

Fictional tale about a young girl and boy living in China who are sent away from their missionary parents when the Japanese invade China. It covers the two years they spent in schools away from their parents. Thoughts on war, relationships with other students and teachers and with each other are all part of the story. Could be used in programs on China; World War II; separation from parents; growing up in a culture different from one's own; war; friendships; sibling relationships; teachers and students.

Reviewed in: *Bulletin of the Center for Children's Books; Booklist; Horn Book*
Main subjects: China; World War II; separation; teachers; students

Alan FUJIWARA

Baachan! Geechan! Arigato: a Story of Japanese Canadians
Illustrated by Tom McNeely.
Momiji, 1989.
ISBN: out of print, pp. 32.

Culture: Chinese

A recreation of the events after the attack on Pearl Harbor. Japanese Canadians were taken from their West Coast homes and placed in internment camps in the British Columbia interior. This story features Masao and Sumiko who came as young immigrants to Canada. They and their children were placed in an internment camp and chose to remain in Canada after they were released. Could be used in programs on Japanese Canadians; internment camps; World War II and the 1940s.

Reviewed in: *Our Family, Our Friends, Our World* by Lyn Miller-Lachmann
Main subjects: Chinese Canadians; grandparents; Canada; internment camps; World War II; 1940s

Sherry GARLAND

Lotus Seed, The
Illustrated by Tatsuro Kiuchi.
Harcourt Brace Jovanovich, 1993.
ISBN: 0-15-249465-0.

Culture: Vietnamese

A Vietnamese girl sees the young Emperor of Vietnam cry the day he lost the golden dragon throne. She takes a seed from a lotus pod in the imperial garden to remind her when she saw the emperor cry. She keeps the seed and takes it with her when, as an adult, she has to flee Vietnam. In later years, her grandson plants the seed and the lotus blooms. Could be used in programs dealing with Vietnam; lotus flowers; the Vietnam War; oppression; emigrants; intergenerational relationships and Vietnamese Americans.

Special features: author's note at the end of the book gives a good brief overview of Vietnam's history
Reviewed in: *Booklinks; Publisher's Weekly; Parents; Horn Book; School Library Journal*
Main subjects: Vietnam; lotus flowers

Song of the Buffalo Boy
Harcourt Brace & Jovanovich, 1992.
ISBN: 0152771077.

Culture: Vietnamese

Seventeen year old Loi is shunned and mistreated because she is of mixed heritage. She runs away to Ho Chi Minh City to escape an arranged marriage and to try to go to the United States to find her American father. Could be used in programs dealing with prejudice; interracial relationships; Amerasian children and Vietnam.

Reviewed in: *Booklist; Kirkus; Publisher's Weekly*
Main subjects: Vietnam; Amerasian children

Sheila GARRIGUE

Eternal Spring of Mr Ito, The
Bradbury, 1985.
ISBN: 0–02–737300–2, pp. 163.

Culture: Japanese

The suffering of a Japanese Canadian family as they are shipped off to a remote settlement is described by a young British girl living in Vancouver during World War II. Could be used in programs dealing with World War II; Japanese Canadians and relocation camps.

Reviewed in: *Booklist; Horn Book; School Library Journal*
Main subjects: Japanese Canadians; internment camps; World War II

Rumer GODDEN

Valiant Chatti-maker, The
Illustrated by Jeroo Roy.
Viking, 1983.
ISBN: 0–670–74236–8.

Culture: Asian Indian

A potter unexpectedly becomes a hero. Could be used in programs dealing with India; potters and heroes.

Main subjects: India; heroes; potter

Barbara Diamond GOLDIN

Red Means Good Fortune
Illustrated by Wenhai Ma.
Viking, 1994.
ISBN: 0–670–85352–6, pp. 64.

Culture: Chinese

Story of Jin Mun and his family in San Francisco's Chinatown in 1868 and what happens when he befriends Wai Hing, a poor slave girl. Could be used in programs on slavery; Chinese Americans; immigrants; the 1860s; friendship and slavery.

Reviewed in: *School Library Journal*
Main subjects: Chinese Americans; San Francisco's Chinatown; 1860s; friendship; slavery

Nancy Price GRAFF

Where a River Runs: a Portrait of a Refugee Family
Photos by Richard Howard.
Little, Brown, 1993.
ISBN: 0-316-32287-3.

Culture: Cambodian

In depth photo essay about a Cambodian family's flight from civil war in their country to Boston in 1983. Photos show the three generations at school, at home and with friends. Includes a 32 sample question list which immigrants and refugees are required to answer before becoming citizens.

Reviewed in: *Booklist; Publisher's Weekly*
Main subjects: Cambodian Americans; refugees; family life

Erik Christian HAUGAARD

Boy and the Samurai
Houghton Mifflin, 1991.
ISBN: 0395563984.

Culture: Japanese

Saru, an orphan of the streets of sixteenth-century Japan, tries to help a samurai rescue his wife from imprisonment by a warlord. Could be used in programs dealing with ancient Japan; samurais; war; orphans and rescues.

Reviewed in: *Booklist; Booklinks; Kirkus*
Main subjects: ancient Japan; samurai; war; warriors

Marilee HEYER

Weaving of a Dream: a Chinese Folktale, The
Illustrated by Marilee Heyer.
Viking, 1986.
ISBN: 0-670-80555-6.

Culture: Chinese

Story about an old widow and her three sons. Her treasured brocade disappears and she asks her sons to find it. The youngest son finds it, returns it to his mother and out steps the Red Fairy. The three live happily together. Could be used in programs on China; Chinese folklore; comparative folklore and fairies.

Reviewed in: *Booklist; School Library Journal*
Main subjects: China; folklore; fairies

Minfong HO

Clay Marble
Farrar, Straus & Giroux, 1991.
ISBN: 0374313407.

Culture: Cambodian

Twelve year old Dara becomes separated from her family in a refugee camp in war torn Cambodia during the late 1970s. Could be used in programs dealing with Cambodia; refugees; separation from parents and war.

Reviewed in: *Booklist; Kirkus; Publisher's Weekly*
Main subjects: Cambodia; refugee camps

Margaret HODGES

Voice of the Great Bell, The
Illustrated by Ed Young.
Little, 1989.
ISBN: 0-316-36791-5.

Culture: Chinese

A great bell is made for the Emperor. Could be used in programs on bells; China; emperors.

Reviewed in: *Booklist*
Main subjects: China; emperor; bells

Dorothy HOOBLER

Aloha Means Come Back: the Story of a World War II Girl
Series: Her Story
Silver Burdett Press, 1991.
ISBN: 0-382-02148-7, pp. 64.

Culture: Japanese

Two young people, a Hawaiian of Japanese descent, and a military brat, try to maintain their friendship after the bombing of Pearl Harbor. Could be used in programs on friendship; prejudice; World War II and Japanese Americans.

Main subjects: Japanese Americans; World War II; friendship; prejudice

Ellen HOWARD

Her Own Song
Atheneum, 1988.
ISBN: 0-689-31444-2, pp. 160.

Culture: Chinese

Historical novel set on the West Coast around the turn of the century, telling the story of an eleven year old girl's discovery of her origins. The practise of baby-selling and the climate of prejudice towards Chinese during this period are explored. Could be used in programs dealing with prejudice; babyselling; adoption and California.

Special features: babyselling
Reviewed in: *Bulletin of the Center for Children's Books; Booklist; School Library Journal*
Main subjects: Chinese American; babyselling; California; adoption

Momoko ISHII Translated by Katherine Paterson

Tongue-cut Sparrow, The
Illustrated by Suekichi Akaba.
Lodestar, 1987.
ISBN: 0-525-67199-4.

Culture: Japanese

The story of an elderly couple and a sparrow. The old man's kindness is rewarded, while his greedy wife gets what she deserves. Could be used in programs on Japan; folklore; Japanese folklore; comparative folklore; kindness; greed and styles of illustrations.

Special features: includes Japanese onomatopoeic words
Reviewed in: *Booklist; Horn Book; School Library Journal*
Main subjects: Japan; folklore; sparrows; birds; kindness; greed

M. A. JAGENDORF and Virginia WENG

Magic Boat and Other Chinese Folk Stories, The
Illustrated by Lo Koon-Chiu.
Vanguard, 1980.
ISBN: 0-8149-0823-3.

Culture: Chinese

A collection of thirty-three folktales, the majority from the Han people of China. Could be used in programs on China; Chinese folklore and comparative folklore.

Main subjects: China; folklore; Han people of China

Vancy KASPER

Street of Three Directions
Overlea House, 1988.
ISBN: 0–7172–2481–3, pp. 141.

Culture: Chinese

Amanda, who is Chinese, and James, who is black, are rivals academically and both have entered a school photography contest. They learn to overcome their rivalry, to overcome their family's objections to their friendship and to work together to solve a mystery at school. Could be used in programs on interracial friendship; prejudice and Chinese Canadians.

Reviewed in: *Our Family, Our Friends, Our World* by Lyn Miller-Lachmann
Main subjects: Chinese Canadian; friendship; prejudice

Carol KENDALL

Sweet and Sour: Tales from China
Houghton, 1979.
ISBN: 0–395–28958–0.

Culture: Chinese

A collection of Chinese folktales. Could be used in programs on China; folklore; comparative folklore and Chinese folklore.

Main subjects: China; Chinese folklore

Robin KLEIN

Hating Allison Ashley
Viking, 1987.
ISBN: 0–670–80864–4, pp. 182.

Culture: Australian

Sixth grader Erica Yurken has difficulty accepting new comer Allison Ashley. Allison seems to have all the advantages of an upper-middle class home plus she is beautiful and talented. After a period of time the two work through their problems and become friends. Could be used in programs on friendship and acceptance.

Reviewed in: *Our Family, Our Friends, Our World* by Lyn Miller-Lachmann
Main subjects: Australia; friendship; envy

Joy KOGAWA

Naomi's Road
Illustrated by Matt Gould.
Oxford University Press, 1988.
ISBN: 0-19-540547-1, pp. 82.

Culture: Japanese

Naomi Nakane's mother leaves the family to return to Japan to care for her sick mother. Naomi's father and brother are sent to a Japanese internment camp and little Naomi is left in the care of her aunt. Could be used in programs on Japanese Canadians; internment camps; World War II; prejudice; 1940s and interracial friendship.

Reviewed in: *Booklist; School Library Journal*
Main subjects: Japanese Canadians; internment camps; World War II; 1940s; friendship; prejudice

Joanna Halpert KRAUS

Tall Boy's Journey
Illustrated by Karen Ritz.
Carolrhoda Books, 1992.
ISBN: 0-87614-746-5, pp. 48.

Culture: Korean

This fictional account of Kim Moo Young, an orphaned Korean boy, explores adoption from the child's point of view. Kim is eight years old when he is sent to the United States to be adopted. He is surrounded by strangers, unfamiliar customs and faced with the difficulties of communicating when he cannot understand the language. His growing frustration and eventual adjustments are covered. Could be used in units on adoption; immigration; Korea; orphans; Korean Americans; interracial families; parenting and lifestyles.

Reviewed in: *Publisher's Weekly; School Library Journal*
Main subjects: adoption; Korea; Korean Americans

Stephen KRENSKY

Iron Dragon Never Sleeps
Illustrated by John Fulwieler.
Delacorte, 1994.
ISBN: 0385311710, pp. 80.

Culture: Chinese

Story of ten year old Winnie Tucker during the summer of 1867. Her father is a mining engineer for the Central Pacific railroad in Cisco, California. The railroad weathers a labor strike by Chinese immigrant workers and Winnie's perspective of the world is changed by her interaction with Lee Cheng, a young Chinese tea carrier. Could be used in programs dealing with the 1860s; the transcontinental railroad and Chinese immigrant workers.

Reviewed in: *Publisher's Weekly*
Main subjects: Chinese Americans; transcontinental railroad; 1860s; immigrants

Eleanor Frances LATTIMORE

Little Pear and His Friends
Harcourt Brace & Company, 1991.
ISBN: 0–15–246863–1.

Culture: Chinese

Six year old Little Pear gets into trouble with his friend Big Head. This is a sequel to Little Pear. Could be used in programs on China; lifestyles; early 1900s and friendship.

Main subjects: China; friendship; 1900s

Marie LEE

Finding My Voice
Houghton Mifflin, 1992.
ISBN: 0395621348.

Culture: Korean

Ellen Sung's senior year and her struggles to deal with prejudice and parental pressure. Could be used in programs dealing with peer pressure; prejudice; parental pressure; senior year and Korean Americans.

Reviewed in: *Booklist; Kirkus; Publisher's Weekly*
Main subjects: Korean Americans; prejudice; family relationships

Sonia LEVITIN

Golem and the Dragon Girl
Dial, 1993.
ISBN: 0-8037-1280-4, pp. 192.

Culture: Chinese

Story of the friendship between Laurel whose grandparents are from China and Jonathan who has a Jewish background and how the two work together to solve a mystery. Laurel's parents sell their house and buy a larger one in anticipation of her grandparents' arrival from China. Jonathan's mother and new stepfather buy Laurel's old house. Laurel and Jonathan become convinced the house is haunted and investigate the odd happenings. Could be used in programs dealing with racism; ethnic pride; family loyalty; intergenerational relationships; cross cultural friendships; mysteries; teamwork and ghosts.

Reviewed in: *Publisher's Weekly*
Main subjects: China; Chinese Americans; intergenerational relationships; cross cultural friendship; ghosts

Elizabeth Foreman LEWIS

Young Fu of the Upper Yangtze
Illustrated by Ed Young.
Dell Yearling, 1973.
ISBN: 0-440-49043-X, pp. 288.

Culture: Chinese

Story of Young Fu, apprentice coppersmith, and his life in Chungking during the 1920s. Could be used in programs dealing with China; courage and good fortune and the 1920s.

Awards received: Newbery Medal Book
Reviewed in: *New York Times Book Review*
Main subjects: China; courage; good fortune; 1920s

He LIYI. Edited by Philip Niel

Spring of Butterflies and other Folktales of China's Minority Peoples, The
Lothrop, 1986.
ISBN: 0-688-06192-3.

Culture: Chinese

A collection of tales from China's minority people.

Reviewed in: *Bulletin of the Center for Children's Books; School Library Journal*
Main subjects: China; minority people of China

Bettey Bao LORD

In the Year of the Boar and Jackie Robinson
Illustrated by Marc Simont.
Harper, 1984.
ISBN: 0–06–024004–0, pp. 176.

Culture: Chinese

In 1947 Shirley Temple Wong moves to Brooklyn from China. She finds it difficult to make friends until she discovers baseball. Could be used in programs on Chinese Americans; immigrant experiences; post-World War II; Brooklyn and baseball.

Awards received: ALA Notable Childrens Book (1984)
Main subjects: Chinese American; immigrant experiences; baseball; Brooklyn

Dianne MACMILLAN and Dorothy FREEMAN

My Best Friend Duc Tran: Meeting a Vietnamese American Family
Series: My Best Friend
Illustrated by Mary Jane Begin.
Julian Messner, 1987.
ISBN: out of print, pp. 38.

Culture: Vietnamese

Duc Tran introduces his American friend Eddie Johnson to the Vietnamese way of life. The illustrations portray the family behaving just as other Americans do while at the same time showing how they have incorporated their heritage into their lives. Provides insight into the Vietnamese American way of life, and would be useful in programs dealing with Vietnamese Americans; friendship; traditions and customs.

Special features: includes a bibliography; family unity, Vietnamese customs, family celebrations and Vietnamese foods and holidays are portrayed
Reviewed in: *Booklist; School Library Journal*
Main subjects: Vietnamese American; friendship

My Best Friend Mee-yung Kim
Series: My Best Friend
Julian Messner, 1989.

Shows how Mee-yung Kim and her family maintain their heritage while at the same time adapt to the American way of life. An informative and educational book that could be used in programs dealing with friendship.

Special features: bibliography and glossary of terms
Reviewed in: *Children's Literature Association Quarterly*
Main subjects: Friendship

Margaret MAHY

Good Fortunes Gang
Illustrated by Marion Young.
Delacorte, 1993.
ISBN: 0–385–31015–3, pp. 80.

Culture: Australian

Pete Fortune and his family move from Australia to New Zealand where he meets numerous relatives. Pete wants to join 'the Good Fortunes Gang' controlled by his tough cousin Tracey and he must spend a night in a graveyard to be admitted to the club. Could be used in programs on Australia; New Zealand; moving; peer pressure and family relationships.

Reviewed in: *Publisher's Weekly*
Main subjects: Australia; New Zealand; peer pressure; moving; family relationships

Janice MARRIOTT

Letters to Lesley
Knopf, 1991.
ISBN: 679–81595–3, pp. 144.

Culture: Australian

Amusing story telling of Henry's efforts to play matchmaker. He tries to marry his mother off to his pen pal's wealthy father. Could be used in programs dealing with family relationships and with Australia.

Reviewed in: starred review in *Booklist*
Main subjects: Australia; Pacific Islander

Ann M. MARTIN

Yours Truly, Shirley
Holiday House, 1988.
ISBN: 0–8234–0719–5, pp. 133.

Culture: Vietnamese

This story dealing with sibling rivalry could be any nationality. The fact that Jackie, the main character, is an adopted Vietnamese girl does not mean the reader will learn much of Vietnam or its culture. Jackie's American sister is dyslexic and her older American brother is gifted. Concentrates on the issue of sibling rivalry rather than Jackie's nationality. Although it does not provide information about Vietnam or Vietnamese customs, could be used in programs dealing with adoption; Vietnamese Americans; sibling rivalry and dyslexia. Be aware that there are sentences which perpetrate stereotypes.

Main subjects: Vietnamese American; adoption; dyslexia; sibling rivalry

Toshi MARUKI

Hiroshima No Pika
Lothrop, Lee & Shepard, 1982.
ISBN: 0-688-01297-3, pp. 48.

Culture: Japanese

Fictionalized account of a seven-year-old Hiroshima child and her mother's experiences when the United States dropped an atomic bomb on Hiroshima during World War II. Could be used in programs on Japan; World War II; atomic bombs; nuclear weapons; war; 1940s and Hiroshima.

Main subjects: Japan; World War II; Hiroshima; nuclear war; atomic bombs; war; 1940s

Christobel MATTINGLEY

Miracle Tree, The
Illustrated by Marianne Yamaguchi.
Harcourt Brace Jovanovich, 1985.
ISBN: 0-15-200530-7, pp. 32.

Culture: Japanese

The story of Hanako, her husband and her mother. Hanako, against her mother's wishes, marries a man of whom her mother disapproves. The atomic blast at Nagasaki injures her badly, destroying her beauty. For twenty years she hides herself away. Later, near death, she writes a poem, folds it into a paper crane and throws it out of her window to the gardener she has watched for years tending a tree. She knows he is her husband and she wants to see him and her mother once more. Her wish is granted. Could be used in programs on World War II; Japan; Nagasaki; atomic bomb; origami; family relationships and forgiveness.

Main subjects: Japan; atomic bomb; Nagasaki; families; origami; World War II

Joyce McDONALD

Mail-order Kid
Putnam, 1988.
ISBN: 0-399-21513-1, pp. 125.

Culture: Korean

This story tells of the difficulties Flip Doty has in accepting his adopted younger brother Todd. Flip orders a fox through the mail to keep as a pet, but the parents find out what he has done and tell him he can't keep the fox. Flip insists, using the fact that his younger brother was selected for adoption by mail order as the reason he should be allowed to keep the animal. Could be used in programs dealing with adoption; Korean Americans; mail order and wild animals as pets. Although the book avoids dealing with the realities of the legal problems of keeping a wild animal as a pet, it could be used to introduce the issue.

Reviewed in: *Bulletin of the Center for Children's Books*; *Booklist*; *School Library Journal*
Main subjects: Korean American; adoption

Kyoko MORI

Shizuko's Daughter
Henry Holt, 1993.
ISBN: 0–8050–2557–X, pp. 256.

Story of an Asian girl whose mother commits suicide. Could be used in programs dealing with suicide; grief; mourning; mothers and daughters.

Special features: notes on the setting and glossary
Reviewed in: starred reviews in *Publisher's Weekly* and *Kirkus*; *Booklist*
Main subjects: suicide; mothers; daughters; grief; mourning

Lensey NAMIOKA

Coming of the Bear
HarperCollins, 1992.
ISBN: 0060202890.

Culture: Japanese

Story of two unemployed samurai and the Ainus, a primitive people on a northern Japanese island. The two are saved from drowning by the Ainus. Later, their loyalties are tested when the possibility of war between the Ainus and a band of Japanese settlers arises. Could be used in programs on ancient Japan; Ainus; samurai; friendship and war.

Reviewed in: *Booklist*; *Kirkus*
Main subjects: Japan; Ainus; war; friendship; samurai

Yang the Youngest and His Terrible Ear
Joy Street, 1992.
ISBN: 0316597015.

Culture: Chinese

Story of Yingtao, a musically untalented boy who must give a violin performance to attract new students for his father, a music teacher. Could be used in programs dealing with Chinese Americans; immigrants; music lessons and family relationships.

Reviewed in: *Booklist*; *Kirkus*; *Publisher's Weekly*
Main subjects: Chinese Americans; family relationships; music lessons

Ruth PARK

Playing Beatie Bow
Penguin/Puffin, 1984.
ISBN: 0-14-031460-1, pp. 196.

Culture: Australian

Abigail Kirk lives in contemporary Sydney. One day she follows an odd young girl into an apartment building and finds herself transported one hundred years back in time. There she learns about life in Sydney during the last century and after adventures and difficulties, returns to her own time. Could be used in programs dealing with Australia; Sydney; time travel and historical fiction.

Awards received: 1981 Best Australian Children's Book Award.
Reviewed in: *Our Family, Our Friends, Our World* by Lyn Miller-Lachmann
Main subjects: Australia; time travel; Sydney

Gregory PATENT

Shanghai Passage
Illustrated by Ted Lewin.
Clarion, 1990.
ISBN: 0-89919-743-4, pp. 115.

Culture: Chinese

Story of a boy born in Britain, living in Shanghai with his extended family during the 1940s. His father is Russian and his mother is Iraqi. Black and white ink drawings illustrate the story. Could be used in programs dealing with China in the 1940s; World War II; the 1940s in general; Shanghai; extended families and bicultural families.

Reviewed in: *Horn Book*; *New York Times Book Review*
Main subjects: China; lifestyles; Shanghai; families; World War II; 1940s

Katherine PATERSON

Park's Quest
Dutton/Lodestar, 1988.
ISBN: 0-525-67258-3, pp. 148.

Culture: Vietnamese

This is the story of eleven year old half Vietnamese, half American Park's quest to find out about his American father. Park is a devotee of chivalry and King Arthur and expects his father's family to live up to his images of them as knights and ladies or gentlemen and ladies. They do not. In addition, he discovers he has a Vietnamese half-sister who lives with his father's family. An insightful look at a difficult time in the United State's recent history. Could be used in programs dealing with the Vietnam War; Amerasian children; chivalry; family relationships.

Special features: children of American soldiers and Vietnamese women
Reviewed in: *Bulletin of the Center for Children's Books*; *Horn Book*; *School Library Journal*
Main subjects: Vietnamese Americans

Mitali PERKINS

Sunita Experiment, The
Joy Street Books/Little, Brown, 1993.
ISBN: 0-316-69943-8.

Culture: Asian Indian

A young girl's attempt to balance her traditional Asian Indian culture with life in the United States.

Reviewed in: *New York Times Book Review*; *Publisher's Weekly*; *School Library Journal*

Joan PHIPSON

Tide Flowing, The
Atheneum, 1981.
ISBN: out of print, pp. 156.

Culture: Australian

Mark is a boy growing up in a Sydney suburb in a middle-class family. While he and his mother are sailing to Sydney from Tasmania, his mother falls overboard during a storm and dies. Mark goes to stay with his father's parents in Sydney but has difficulty dealing with his mother's death and feels abandoned by his father. Could be used in programs dealing with Australia; death; friendship and alienation.

Reviewed in: *Our Family, Our Friends, Our World* by Lyn Miller-Lachmann
Main subjects: Australia; Sydney; death; alienation; friendship

Helena Clare PITTMAN

Gift of the Willows, The
Illustrated by Helena Clare Pittman.
Carolrhoda Books, 1988.
ISBN: 0–87614–354–0, pp. 32.

Culture: Japanese

The story of a potter who saves two willow trees. The trees eventually save his life, too.

Awards received: IRA-CBC Children's Choice for 1989
Reviewed in: *Teaching PreK-8*; *Booklist*; *Publisher's Weekly*; *School Library Journal*
Main subjects: Japan; willows; trees

Govinder RAM

Rama and Sita: an Indian Folk Tale
Bedrick, 1988.
ISBN: 0–87226–171–9.

Culture: Asian Indian

Prince Rama and how he reclaims his place at the royal court. Could be used for programs on India; comparative folklore; folklore of India and royalty.

Reviewed in: *Booklist*; *School Library Journal*
Main subjects: India; folklore; royalty

Catherine Edwards SADLER

Heaven's Reward: Fairy Tales from China
Illustrated by Cheng Mung Yun.
Macmillan, 1985.
ISBN: 0–689–31127–3.

Culture: Chinese

A collection of six stories, each set in a different period of China's history. Could be used in programs on China and comparative folklore.

Reviewed in: *Booklist*; *School Library Journal*
Main subjects: China; folklore

Marcia SAVIN

Moon Bridge
Scholastic, 1992.
ISBN: 0590458736.

Culture: Japanese

Story of the friendship between Mitzi Fujimoto and Ruthie Fox. The two girls live in San Francisco during the 1940s. The girls' friendship is changed when Mitzi's family is forced into an internment camp during World War II. Could be used in programs on World War II; Japanese Americans during the 1940s; internment camps and friendship.

Reviewed in: *Booklist*; *Book Links*; *Publisher's Weekly*
Main subjects: Japanese Americans; internment camps; World War II; friendship

Allen SAY

Feast of Lanterns, The
HarperCollins, 1976.
ISBN: out of print, pp. 57.

Culture: Japanese

Two young boys leave their safe island fishing village to go to the mainland. There they have a delightful adventure exploring the small town they find themselves in. Line drawings illustrate the story. Could be used in programs on Japan; customs and culture; Feast of Lanterns; adventures and lifestyles.

Main subjects: Japan; adventures; customs and culture; Feast of Lanterns

Miriam SCHLEIN

Year of the Panda, The
Illustrated by Kam Mak.
HarperCollins, 1990.
ISBN: 0–690–04866–1, pp. 83.

Culture: Chinese

A young boy named Lu Yi finds a baby panda and keeps it to raise. The needs of pandas, their struggle to survive and the efforts of the Chinese government Panda Rescue Center are all part of the story. Could be used in programs on pandas; China; animals; endangered species and environmental issues.

Reviewed in: *Multicultural Review*
Main subjects: China; pandas; endangered species; animals; environmental issues

Aaron SHEPARD

Savitri: a Tale of Ancient India
Illustrated by Vera Rosenberry.
Albert Whitman & Company, 1992.
ISBN: 0–8075–7251–9, pp. 40.

Culture: Asian Indian

Hindu myth telling the story of Princess Savitri and her husband Satyavan. After only a year of marriage, Satyavan is claimed by the god of death, Yama. Princess Savitri wins him back from Yama by using her wit, virtue and strength. Could be used in units or programs dealing with comparative mythology; Asian Indian myths; love and devotion.

Reviewed in: *American Libraries*; *Kirkus*; *Publisher's Weekly*; *School Library Journal*
Main subjects: India; Asian Indian; folktales; Hindu

Gary SOTO

Pacific Crossing
Harcourt Brace & Company, 1992.
ISBN: 0-15-259187-7, pp. 144.

Culture: Japanese

Lincoln and Tony (Mexican Americans) practise the martial art of kempo and are selected as exchange students to Japan. They fly from San Francisco to Tokyo where Lincoln learns his Japanese family, and people everywhere, are not unlike his family back home in California. Could be used in programs on martial arts; exchange students; Japan; lifestyles and families; intercultural friendships.

Reviewed in: *American Bookseller*; *Horn Book*; *Kirkus*; *Publisher's Weekly*
Main subjects: Japan; exchange students; lifestyles; martial arts; kempo; Mexican American; barrio

Cathy SPAGNOLI

Judge Rabbit and the Tree Spirit: a Folktale from Cambodia
Children's Book Press, 1991.
ISBN: 0892390719.

Culture: Cambodian

How Judge Rabbit solves the problem of a tree spirit who has assumed human form. Written in English and Khmer. Could be used in programs dealing with rabbits in folklore; Cambodian folktales; tricksters and comparative folktales.

Reviewed in: *Booklinks*; *Kirkus*; *Publisher's Weekly*
Main subjects: Cambodian folktales; rabbits; tricksters

Eleanor SPENCE

Devil's Hole, The
Lothrop, Lee & Shepard, 1977.
ISBN: out of print, pp. 215.

Culture: Australian

Douglas and his family live in a small coastal Australian town. After the birth of his younger brother Carl, the family moves to Sydney where Carl can attend a special school. Eventually Carl is diagnosed as being autistic. Could be used in programs on autism; Australia; family relationships and disabilities.

Reviewed in: *Our Family, Our Friends, Our World* by Lyn Miller-Lachmann
Main subjects: Australia; autism; disabilities; sibling relationships

Colin THIELE

Fire in the Stone
HarperCollins, 1974.
ISBN: out of print, pp. 305.

Culture: Australian

Ernie Ryan lives in a remote mining town in South Australia. He works an old mine claim of his father's and finds some opals. These are stolen and Ernie, with the help of two friends, search for the thief. Could be used in programs on Australia; mining; opals; friendship and racism.

Awards received: Edgar Allan Poe Special Award Winner
Reviewed in: *Our Family, Our Friends, Our World* by Lyn Miller-Lachmann
Main subjects: Australia; Aborigines; racism; friendship; mystery; opals; mining

Shadow Shark
HarperCollins, 1988.
ISBN: 0–06–026179–X, pp. 214.

Culture: Australian

Joe and Meg are cousins who share the same birthday. After his father's death, Meg's parents take Joe into their family and the two cousins begin to get to know each other better. Joe's move from Melbourne, a large city to Cockle Bay, a small coastal town in South Australia is woven into the story. Could be used in programs dealing with Australia; loyalty; friendship; family relationships and moving.

Reviewed in: *Our Family, Our Friends, Our World* by Lyn Miller-Lachmann
Main subjects: Australia; loyalty; survival; family relationships

Brian THOMPSON

Story of Prince Rama, The
Illustrated by Jeroo Roy.
Viking, 1985.
ISBN: 0–670–80117–8.

Culture: Asian Indian

An introduction to the Hindu epic, the *Ramayana*. Could be used in programs on India; Hinduism; the *Ramayana*; epics; folklore and comparative folklore.

Reviewed in: *Bulletin of the Center for Children's Books*; *Booklist*; *School Library Journal*
Main subjects: India; folklore; *Ramayana*; Hinduism

S. T. TUNG

One Small Dog
Illustrated by Ted Lewin.
Dodd, Mead, 1975.
ISBN: out of print, pp. 160.

Culture: Chinese

The story of Sung, a young boy, and his dog Luck. In China during the 1950s the government ordered all dogs be killed. Sung attempts to save his pet by taking it to Hong Kong where he will be safe. Along the way the dog is stolen and winds up in a one man traveling circus. Sung decides to leave his dog with the circus. Could be used in programs on dogs; China; communism; the 1950s and pets.

Main subjects: China; 1950s; communism; pets

Yoshiko UCHIDA

Best Bad Thing, The
Atheneum, 1983.
ISBN: 0-689-50290-7, pp. 120.

Culture: Japanese

Sequel to *A Jar of Dreams* continuing the story of Rinko, a Japanese American girl living in California during the Depression. Could be used in programs on Japanese Americans; the Great Depression; friendship and California. It provides many insights into Japanese culture and customs.

Awards received: Junior Literary Guild Selection Outstanding Book; Commonwealth Club of California Silver Medal for Excellence, 1981
Main subjects: Japanese Americans; California; friendship; Great Depression

Happiest Ending, The
Atheneum, 1985.
ISBN: 0-689-50326-1

Culture: Japanese

This story tells of the arranged marriage of a Japanese girl.

Reviewed in: *School Library Journal*

Journey Home, The
Illustrated by Charles Robinson.
Atheneum, 1978.
ISBN: 0-689-50126-9, pp. 131.

Culture: Japanese

The story of Yuki, a Japanese American girl, and her family's attempts to adjust after being released from a Japanese American internment camp. Sequel to *Journey to Topaz*, the concentration camp in Utah they were sent to during World War II. Could be used in programs dealing with Japanese Americans; Japanese who served in the US armed forces during World War II; Japanese internment camps; postwar anti-Japanese attitudes and adjustment to life after war.

Special features: Japanese internment camps
Awards received: Junior Literary Guild Outstanding Book
Reviewed in: *Los Angeles Times Book Review*; *Five Owls*
Main subjects: Japanese American; World War II; Japanese Internment camp

Journey to Topaz
Illustrated by Donald Carrick.
Scribner, 1971.
ISBN: out of print, pp. 149.

Culture: Japanese

Story of eleven year old Yuki Sakane and what happens to her and her family after the Japanese bomb Pearl Harbor. She was born in America, but her parents are prohibited by law from becoming citizens of the United States. Yuki and her family are sent to a Japanese internment camp in Utah, and this book tells of their experiences. This historical fiction would be useful in programs dealing with Japanese American history; Japanese internment camps; prejudice; World War II and family relationships.

Special features: Japanese internment camp
Reviewed in: *School Library Journal*; *Booklist*
Main subjects: Japanese American; Japanese internment camps; World War II; California

Magic Listening Cap: More Folk Tales from Japan
Illustrated by Yoshiko Uchida.
Harcourt, 1983.
ISBN: 0-88739-016-1.

Culture: Japanese

Collection of Japanese folktales which could be used in programs on Japanese folklore and comparative folklore.

Main subjects: Japan; Japanese folktales; comparative folklore

Lynette Dyer VUONG

Brocaded Slipper and Other Vietnamese Tales, The
Illustrated by Vo-Dinh Mai.
Harper, 1982.
ISBN: 0-317-56669-5.

Culture: Vietnamese

Five Vietnamese fairytales. Could be used in programs on Vietnamese folklore and fairytales; comparative folklore or fairytales.

Main subjects: Vietnam; Vietnamese folklore; comparative folklore

Yoko Kawashima WATKINS

Tales from the Bamboo Grove
Bradbury, 1992.
ISBN: 0027925250.

Culture: Japanese

A collection of Japanese folktales recalled from the author's childhood. Could be used in programs on Japanese folktales; childhood experiences.

Reviewed in: *Kirkus*; *Publisher's Weekly*
Main subjects: Japanese folklore; childhood

Diane WOLKSTEIN

White Wave: a Chinese Tale
Illustrated by Ed Young.
Harper, 1979.
ISBN: 0-690-03894-1.

Culture: Chinese

Story of a young boy and the goddess who promised to help him. Could be used in programs on China; Chinese folklore; magic and comparative folklore.

Main subjects: China; magic

Patricia WRIGHTSON

Ice Is Coming
Atheneum, 1977.
ISBN: out of print, pp. 223.

Culture: Australian

In this battle between good and evil, Wirrun, an Aborigine, becomes part of an effort to stop ice from covering the continent. He must find a primordial fire spirit called the Eldest Nargun and convince the spirit to help stop the spread of the ice. Could be used in programs on Australia; Aborigines; fire and ice; good and evil.

Reviewed in: *Our Family, Our Friends, Our World* by Lyn Miller-Lachmann
Main subjects: Australia; Aborigines; folklore; ice; fire; good; evil

Paul YEE

Tales from Gold Mountain: Stories of the Chinese in the New World
Illustrated by Simon Ng.
Macmillan, 1989.
ISBN: 0-02-793621-X, pp. 64.

Culture: Chinese

Stories of Chinese immigrants' hopes and dreams when they came to the New World and the disappointments they faced in a strange land. Could be used in programs on Chinese immigrants; cultural differences; moving and Chinese Americans.

Reviewed in: *Booklist*
Main subjects: Chinese Americans; immigrant experiences

Laurence YEP

Sea Glass
HarperCollins, 1979.
ISBN: out of print, pp. 213.

Culture: Chinese

Thirteen year old Craig Chin, a Chinese American boy, must adjust to living in a new town after moving from San Francisco's Chinatown. Could be used in programs dealing with Chinese Americans; intergenerational relationships; friendship and family relationships.

Main subjects: Chinese American; intergenerational relationships; friendship

Star Fisher
William Morrow, 1991.
ISBN: 0688093655.

Culture: Chinese

Story of fifteen year old Joan Lee and the adjustments she and her family must make when they move from Ohio to West Virginia in the 1920s. Could be used in programs dealing with the 1920s; Chinese Americans and moving.

Reviewed in: *Booklist*; *Publisher's Weekly*
Main subjects: Chinese Americans; the 1920s; moving

Tongues of Jade
HarperCollins, 1991.
ISBN: 0060224711.

Culture: Chinese

Seventeen Chinese American folktales from various Chinese communities in the US. Could be used in programs dealing with comparative folklore; Chinese Americans and Chinese folktales.

Reviewed in: *Booklist*; *Kirkus*; *Publisher's Weekly*
Main subjects: Chinese Americans; folklore

NONFICTION – PRESCHOOL THROUGH THIRD GRADE

Donna BAILEY

Australia
Series: Where We Live
Steck-Vaughn, 1990.
ISBN: 0-8114-2547-9, pp. 32.

Culture: Australian

Overview of the people, places, animals and climate of Australia. Includes an index and is illustrated with color photographs. Could be used in programs on Australia and lifestyles.

Reviewed in: series reviewed by *School Library Journal*
Main subjects: Australia; geography; culture; animals; Aborigines

Hong Kong
Series: Where We Live
Steck-Vaughn, 1990.
ISBN: 0-8114-2552-5, pp. 32.

Culture: Hong Kong

Overview of the people, places and sites of Hong Kong. Includes an index and is illustrated with color photographs. Could be used in programs on Hong Kong; cultures and lifestyles.

Reviewed in: series reviewed in *School LIbrary Journal*
Main subjects: Hong Kong; culture; lifestyles

India
Series: Where We Live
Steck-Vaughn, 1990.
ISBN: 0-8114-2548-7, pp. 32.

Culture: Asian Indian

Shows the lifestyle of an Indian farming family. They raise livestock and grow crops which they sell at the capital city marketplace. Includes an index and is illustrated with color photographs. Could be used in programs on India; lifestyles and cultures.

Reviewed in: series reviewed in *School Library Journal*
Main subjects: India; lifestyles; culture

Japan
Series: Where We Live
Steck-Vaughn, 1990.
ISBN: 0–8114–2554–1, pp. 32.

Culture: Japanese

Shows a family in Tokyo – what they eat, where they play, their school and how they celebrate holidays. Includes an index and is illustrated with color photographs. Could be used in programs on Japan; lifestyles and cultures.

Reviewed in: series reviewed in *School Library Journal*
Main subjects: Japan; culture; lifestyles

Philippines
Series: Where We Live
Steck-Vaughn, 1990.
ISBN: 0–8114–2564–9, pp. 32.

Culture: Filipino

Introduction to the people, places, crops and climate of the Philippines. Includes an index and is illustrated with color photographs. Could be used in programs on the Philippines; lifestyles and cultures.

Reviewed in: series reviewed in *School Library Journal*
Main subjects: Philippines; lifestyles; cultures

Thailand
Series: Where We Live
Steck-Vaughn, 1990.
ISBN: 0–8114–2570–3, pp. 32.

Culture: Thai

Introduces Thailand and the capital city Bangkok. Includes an index and is illustrated with color photographs. Could be used in programs on Thailand; lifestyles and cultures.

Reviewed in: series reviewed in *School Library Journal*
Main subjects: Thailand; lifestyles; cultures

Barbara BEIRNE

Pianist's Debut: Preparing for the Concert Stage, A
Photos by Barbara Beirne.
Carolrhoda Books, 1990.
ISBN: 0–87614–432–6, pp. 56.

Culture: Korean

Photo-biography of Leah Yoon, an aspiring pianist who is a Korean American and studies piano on a full scholarship at Julliard. She also attends the Professional Children's School. Good photographs in this upbeat portrait. Would lend itself to discussions on careers; pianists; musicians; biographies; achievements of young people and programs dealing with Korean Americans.

Reviewed in: *Kirkus*
Main subjects: Korean American; Korean; pianist; musician

Xiong BLIA. Adapted by Cathy Spagnoli

Nine-in-one Grr! Grr! A Folktale from the Hmong People of Laos
Illustrated by Nancy Hom.
Children's Book Press, 1989.
ISBN: 0–89239–048–4, pp. 32.

Culture: Laotian

A folktale about tigers. The tigers are blessed by a god with having nine cubs each year if Tiger remembers to say 'nine-in-one, Grr! Grr!'. The land is being overrun with tigers until a smart little bird gets Tiger to say 'one-in-nine, Grr! Grr!' instead of 'nine-in-one, Grr! Grr!'. Could be used in programs on Laos; Hmong; tigers; folktales; illustration styles and comparative folklore.

Special features: illustrations based on traditional Hmong embroidery styles and motifs
Reviewed in: *Language Arts; Reading Teacher; Emergency Librarian; Five Owls; Instructor*
Main subjects: Laos; Hmong; folktales; tigers

Geoff BURNS

Take a Trip to New Zealand
Series: Take a Trip
Franklin Watts, 1983.
ISBN: 0–531–03761–4, pp. 32.

Culture: New Zealander

An overview of New Zealand with simple sentences and color photos. Provides bits of information on various topics and includes an index. Could be used as an introduction to New Zealand; in programs on New Zealand and its geography.

Reviewed in: *Our Family, Our Friends, Our World* by Lyn Miller-Lachmann
Main subjects: New Zealand; geography

Thelma CATTERWELL

Sebastian Lives in a Hat
Illustrated by Kerry Argent.
Kane/Miller, 1990.
ISBN: 0-9162-9130-8, pp. 32.

Culture: Australian

Sebastian, an orphaned wombat, finds a new home in a brown wool hat in the author's house. Could be used in programs on orphaned animals; zoology; Australia and wombats.

Awards received: 1985 Whitley Award for Best Children's Book (given by the Royal Zoological Society of New South Wales)
Reviewed in: *Our Family, Our Friends, Our World* by Lyn Miller-Lachmann
Main subjects: Australia; wombats; hats; animals; zoology

Judith Hoffman CORWIN

Asian Crafts
Franklin Watts, 1993.
ISBN: 0531110133.

Culture: Japanese

Step by step instructions on how to make ancient and modern crafts, toys and foods from various countries in Asia. Could be used in programs dealing with Asia; Japan; food; toys; crafts and Asian culture.

Special features: step by step instructions
Reviewed in: *Booklinks*
Main subjects: Asian crafts; Asian foods; Japanese crafts; Japanese foods

Pamela DELL

I.M. Pei
Series: Picture Story Biographies
Children's Press, 1993.
ISBN: 0-516-04186-X, pp. 32.

Culture: Chinese

Biography of Chinese American architect I.M. Pei. Could be used in programs on Chinese Americans and on biographies.

Reviewed in: *Booklist*
Main subjects: Chinese Americans; architects; biographies

Michael Chang: Tennis Champion
Children's Press, 1992.
ISBN: 0516041851.

Culture: Chinese

Biography of Michael Chang, the youngest man to win the prestigious French Open tennis tournament, in 1989. This book would be useful in programs dealing with sports; tennis and Chinese Americans.

Main subjects: Chinese American; tennis; sports; biography

Judy DONNELLY

Wall of Names: the Story of the Vietnam Veterans Memorial, A
Series: Step Into Reading Step 4
Random House, 1991.
ISBN: 679-80169-3, pp. 48.

Culture: Vietnamese

History of the Vietnam War and the Vietnam Veterans Memorial, with photos to illustrate the text. The response of those who visit the Memorial is included. Could be used in programs dealing with veterans; war; the Vietnam War and the Vietnam Veterans Memorial.

Reviewed in: *Booklist; Newsweek*
Main subjects: Vietnam; Vietnam War; veterans

Stephanie FEENEY

A is for Aloha
Illustrated by Hella Hammid.
University of Hawaii Press, 1980.
ISBN: 0-8248-0722-7.

Culture: Pacific Islands

Alphabet book that uses large print letters, words and black and white photographs to teach children the letters of the alphabet and to identify people, places and activities of Hawaiian children. Could be used in programs on learning the alphabet; example of different alphabet books; how to use art to transmit information and programs dealing with how artists can interpret the same information in a variety of ways.

Main subjects: Hawaii; Pacific Islands; alphabet

Hawaii is a Rainbow
Illustrated by Jeff Reese.
University of Hawaii Press, 1985.
ISBN: 0–8248–1007–4.

Culture: Pacific Islands

Picture book that uses the colors of the rainbow and photos of people, places, plants and animals of Hawaii to teach children the colors of the rainbow and at the same time, to introduce them to Hawaii. Could be used in programs on Hawaii; colors; rainbows and how to teach through the use of art.

Reviewed in: *Booklist; School LIbrary Journal*
Main subjects: Pacific Islands; Hawaii; rainbows; colors

Leonard Everett FISHER

Great Wall of China, The
Illustrated by Leonard Everett Fisher.
Macmillan, 1986.
ISBN: 0–02–735220–X, pp. 32.

Culture: Chinese

The building of the Great Wall of China. The illustrations are black, white and shades of grey. They effectively support the text. Emperor Chin Shih Huang Ti was responsible for connecting the many walls which had been built before his time into one Great Wall. He united China into one empire, rather than a number of small states. Although he did many positive things for China, he was also known for his ruthlessness, inhumanity and arrogance. Could be used in programs on China's early history; the Great Wall of China; comparing and contrasting walls such as the Great Wall of China and the Berlin Wall; emperors of different countries; emperors of China; Emperor Chin Shih Huang Ti; great leaders of different countries and time periods.

Main subjects: Chinese; Great Wall; Emperor Chin Shih Huang Ti; culture and customs

Mary Ann FRASER

On Top of the World
Illustrated by Mary Ann Fraser.
Henry Holt, 1991.
ISBN: 0–8050–1587–7, pp. 40.

Culture: Tibetian

Story of Edmund Hillary and Tenzing Norgay's successful climb of Mount Everest. Could be used in programs dealing with mountains; mountain climbing; adventurers; sports; Tibet; Edmund Hillary and Tenzing Norgay.

Reviewed in: *Booklist; School Library Journal; Kirkus*
Main subjects: Mount Everest; adventurers; mountains; mountain climbing; sports

Ten Mile Day
Illustrated by Mary Ann Fraser.
Henry Holt, 1993.
ISBN: 0–8050–1902–2, pp. 40.

Culture: multicultural

This story of how the Transcontinental Railroad was built is informative and multicultural. Could be used in programs on transportation; railroads; nineteenth century American history and immigrants.

Special features: illustrated glossary
Reviewed in: *School Library Journal*
Main subjects: railroads; America; transportation; Transcontinental Railroad

Nance Lui FYSON and Richard GREEN

Family in China, A
Series: Families the World Over
Lerner, 1985.
ISBN: 0–8225–1653–5, pp. 32.

Culture: Chinese

Provides information on lifestyles of rural and city life in China. Could be used in programs on China and lifestyles.

Reviewed in: *Booklist; School Library Journal*
Main subjects: China; lifestyles

Linda Walvoord GIRARD

We Adopted You, Benjamin Koo
Illustrated by Linda Shute.
Albert Whitman, 1989.
ISBN: 0–8075–8694–3, pp. 32.

Culture: Korean

Nine year old Benjamin tells how he was born in Korea and brought to the United States for adoption by an American family. Well done and useful for programs dealing with adoption, Korean Americans and parenting.

Special features: a true story told in the first person; Benjamin is a nonstereotypical Asian American.
Reviewed in: *The Bulletin of the Center for Children's Books*
Main subjects: Korean American; adoption

Reijo HARKONEN

Children of China, The
Series: The World's Children
Photos by Matti A. Pitkanen.
Carolrhoda Books, 1990.
ISBN: 0–87614–394–X.

Culture: Chinese

The lives of children in China, with beautiful color photographs. Could be used to introduce China; children in other countries; lifestyles and comparative lifestyles; Asia and Chinese.

Special features: pronunciation guide and index
Reviewed in: *School Library Journal*
Main subjects: China; Chinese; Asian

Children of Nepal, The
Series: The World's Children
Photos by Matti A. Pitkanen.
Carolrhoda Books 1990.
ISBN: 0–87614–395–8, pp. 48.

Culture: Nepalese

This import from Finland has lost some of its usefulness due to an awkward text and its failure to focus on children. Good color photos give the reader a feeling of traveling in Nepal. Could be used to introduce Nepal and Asia and in programs dealing with differing lifestyles.

Special features: pronunciation guide, index and map
Reviewed in: *School Library Journal*
Main subjects: Nepal; Asia

Jim HASKINS

Count Your Way Through China
Series: Count Your Way
Carolrhoda, 1987.
ISBN: 0–87614–302–8, pp. 21.

Culture: Chinese

Introduces concepts about China through the use of the numbers one through ten. Could be used in programs on learning numbers; counting and China.

Awards received: Notable Children's Trade Book in the Field of Social Studies
Reviewed in: *Booklist; School Library Journal*
Main subjects: China; numbers; counting

Count Your Way Through India
Series: Count Your Way
Illustrated by Liz B. Dobson.
Lerner/Carolrhoda, 1990.
ISBN: 0–87614–414–8, pp. 24.

Culture: Asian Indian

Hindi is the national language of India and in this counting book children can learn to count to ten in Hindi. Can be used in programs dealing with counting; language of other countries and India.

Special features: Hindi language
Reviewed in: *Library Talk; Language Arts; Horn Book*
Main subjects: India; Asian Indian; counting; Hindi language

Count Your Way Through Japan
Series: Count Your Way
Illustrated by Martin Skoro.
Lerner/Carolrhoda, 1987.
ISBN: 0–87614–301–X, pp. 20.

Culture: Japanese

Follows the format of introductory notes on the language followed by the first ten numerals. The drawings are colorful showing an item from the culture to represent the number on that page. The facing page has a paragraph telling what the item is and the number as it is written in Japanese and as an Arabic numeral. Could be used in programs to teach counting; on Japanese culture and on languages.

Reviewed in: *Booklist; School Library Journal*
Main subjects: Japan; counting

Count Your Way Through Korea
Series: Count Your Way
Carolrhoda, 1989.
ISBN: 0–87614–348–6, pp. 24.

Culture: Korean

Introduces concepts about Korea through the use of the numbers one through ten. Could be used in programs on counting, numbers and Korea.

Main subjects: Korea; counting; numbers

Susan KUKLIN

When I See my Doctor
Bradbury Press, 1988.
ISBN: 0–02–751232–0.

Culture: Asian

What happens when a child goes to the doctor for a checkup. The young boy in the story is Thomas Gilliland and his appearance is Asian. The author follows Thomas as he visits the doctor and photographs the boy during his annual checkup. Good color photographs. Could be used in programs dealing with visiting the doctor; medical care and medical examinations.

Special features: instruments used in the examination are explained
Reviewed in: *Booklist; School Library Journal*
Main subjects: medical examination; medical care; doctors

Keith LYE

Take a Trip to Indonesia
Series: Take a Trip
Franklin Watts, 1985.
ISBN: 0-531-04940-X, pp. 32.

Culture: Indonesian

Brief information about Indonesia, including topics such as geography, ethnic mix, schools, markets and transportation. Color photos with brief text to present the information. Could be used in programs to introduce Indonesia; life in other countries and comparative lifestyles.

Reviewed in: *Booklist; School Library Journal*
Main subjects: Indonesia; lifestyles

Take a Trip to Nepal
Series: Take a Trip
Franklin Watts, 1988.
ISBN: 0-531-10557-1, pp. 32.

Culture: Nepalese

Color photographs and a simple text introduce young children to the country of Nepal, but this book may not excite children about Nepal since the photographs do not portray child-oriented activities. Could be used to introduce programs on Asia and Nepal.

Reviewed in: *Booklist; School Library Journal*
Main subjects: Nepal; Asia; lifestyles

Barbara MARGOLIES

Kanu of Kathmandu: a Journey in Nepal
Four Winds Press, 1992.
ISBN: 0027622827.

Culture: Nepalese

Kanu, a young Nepalese boy, visits several villages of Nepal during which many traditional activities and customs are observed. Useful in programs dealing with other countries and cultures; lifestyles; family relationships and Nepal.

Reviewed in: *Booklinks; Booklist; Publisher's Weekly*
Main subjects: Nepal; Nepalese; lifestyles; family relationships

Sally MASON

Take a Trip to China
Series: Take a Trip
Photos by Sally Mason.
Franklin Watts, 1981.
ISBN: 0-531-04317-7, pp. 32.

Culture: Chinese

An introduction to China for young children, containing large text, large color photos and brief information about aspects such as the people, type of occupations; art; food; agriculture and shopping. Could be used as an introduction for young children to China; comparative lifestyles and other countries.

Special features: index
Reviewed in: *Language Arts*
Main subjects: China; lifestyles; culture and customs

Junko MORIMOTO

My Hiroshima
Illustrated by Junko Morimoto.
Viking, 1987.
ISBN: 0-670-83181-6, pp. 30.

Culture: Japanese

Simple and effective account of what it was like in Hiroshima before and after the atomic bomb. The way children were taught in school to be ready for war and their immersion in militarism are presented. Pen and ink drawings with a color wash, black and white photos and color photos are all used to add to the text. The author makes an effective case for peace and the sanctity of life rather than war and death. Could be used in programs dealing with war; propaganda; Japan; World War II; the atomic bomb; Hiroshima; peace; compassion and survivors of war.

Reviewed in: *Booklist; School Library Journal; Publisher's Weekly; Horn Book; Bulletin of the Center for Children's Books; Journal of Youth Services in Libraries*
Main subjects: Japan; Hiroshima; World War II; atomic bomb; 1940s; war; peace

Dokuohtei NAKANO

Easy Origami
Illustrated by Eric Kenneway.
Viking, 1986.
ISBN: 0-670-80382-0, pp. 64.

Culture: Japanese

Easy to follow step by step instructions and diagrams to make boats, snakes and other creatures. Could be used in programs on paper folding; origami; activities.

Awards received: Reading Rainbow Book
Reviewed in: *Booklist; School Library Journal*
Main subjects: Japan; origami; paper folding

Ta Huay PENG

Fun with Chinese Festivals
Illustrated by Leong Kum Chuen.
Heian International, 1991.
ISBN: 0-89346-358-2, pp. 96.

Culture: Chinese

Contains information on over seventy-five Chinese festivals. Could be used in programs on Chinese holidays; comparative holidays and festivals.

Main subjects: Chinese festivals; holidays

Jan REYNOLDS

Himalaya
Series: Vanishing Cultures
Illustrated by Jan Reynolds.
Harcourt Brace & Company, 1991.
ISBN: 0-15-234465-9, pp. 32.

Culture: Tibetan

Photographer Jan Reynolds lived with a family in the Himalayas and documented the daily life of the salt traders who travel by yak from Tibet to Nepal. Could be used in programs on Tibet; Himalayas; lifestyles and salt traders.

Awards received: NCSSS-CBC Notable Children's Trade Book in the Field of Social Studies
Reviewed in: *American Bookseller; Publisher's Weekly; School Library Journal*
Main subjects: Tibet; Nepal; Himalayas; mountains; lifestyles

Allen SAY

El Chino
Houghton, 1990.
ISBN: 0-395-52023-1, pp. 32.

Culture: Chinese

A picture book biography of Bong Way Wong, a Chinese American civil engineer. He is the fourth child of Chinese immigrants and while on a visit to Spain, watches a bullfight and falls in love with the sport. Could be used in programs on Chinese Americans; matadors; biographies and bullfights.

Reviewed in: *Booklist*
Main subjects: Chinese Americans; matadors; bullfighting

Grandfather's Journey
Houghton Mifflin, 1993.
ISBN: 0-395-57035-2, pp. 32.

Culture: Japanese

Say tells the story of his grandfather's journey from Japan to the United States where he lived for many years before taking his family back to Japan. Could be used in programs dealing with Japan; Japanese Americans; immigrant experiences.

Reviewed in: *Publisher's Weekly*
Main subjects: Japanese Americans; immigrant experiences; Japan

Phyllis SHALANT

Look What We've Brought You from Vietnam
Illustrated by Joanna Roy.
Julian Messner, 1988.
ISBN: 0-671-65978-2, pp. 48.

Culture: Vietnamese

Contains crafts, games, folktales, recipes, songs and other cultural activities from Vietnam. Could be used in programs on Vietnamese Americans; cultural activities; comparative folklore; games; foods and crafts.

Reviewed in: *Booklist*
Main subjects: Vietnam; folktales; games; songs; foods; crafts

Charnan SIMON

Seiji Ozawa: Symphony Conductor
Children's Press, 1992.
ISBN: 0516041827.

Culture: Japanese

Biography on the career of Seiji Ozawa, a Japanese symphony conductor famous for directing major western orchestras throughout the world. Could be used in programs dealing with biographies; famous Japanese; symphonies and conductors.

Reviewed in: *School Library Journal*
Main subjects: Japanese; symphony; biography; conductor

Harriet Langsam SOBOL

We Don't Look Like our Mom and Dad
Illustrated by Patricia Agree.
Coward, McCann, 1984.
ISBN: 0-698-20608-8, pp. 32.

Culture: Korean

Black and white photo essay about the life of the Levin family. The parents are American and their two adopted sons are Korean. Would be useful in programs dealing with adoption; immigration; interracial families and Asian American immigrants.

Special features: excellent photographs of real people experiencing varying emotions; other Asian American children with Asian parents are part of the boys' world
Reviewed in: *Multicultural Review*
Main subjects: Korean Americans; adoption

Ruth THOMSON

Family in Thailand, A
Series: Families the World Over
Lerner, 1988.
ISBN: 0-8225-1684-5, pp. 32.

Culture: Thai

Introduces the culture of Thailand by focusing on Thai children. Color photographs illustrate the text. Could be used in programs on Thailand; lifestyles; families and cultures.

Reviewed in: *Booklist*
Main subjects: Thailand; families; lifestyles; cultures

Percy TRESIZE

Peopling of Australia, The
Illustrated by Percy Tresize.
Gareth Stevens, 1988.
ISBN: 1–55532–950–0, pp. 32.

Culture: Australian

Provides information on Australia's history from its beginnings as part of the supercontinent Gondwanaland up until 1788. Could be used in programs dealing with Australia and its history.

Reviewed in: *Booklist; School Library Journal*
Main subjects: Australia; history

Yukio TSUCHIYA

Faithful Elephants: a True Story of Animals, People and War
Illustrated by Ted Lewin.
Houghton Mifflin, 1988.
ISBN: 0–395–46555–9, pp. 32.

Culture: Japanese

Translated from Japanese and originally written in the 1950s. Deals with the decision to kill zoo animals during World War II to prevent them from escaping (because of possible damage to the zoo from bombing) and running loose in the city. Conveys the feelings of the 1950s and dwells on the process of death of the animals such as the starvation of the elephants. This book is flawed and one needs to be aware of its limitations, the spirit of the times in which it was written and have a clear understanding of why and how to use it in programs. With proper preparation, it could be used in programs on war; World War II; difficult decisions; animal issues; zoos in times of war.

Reviewed in: *Horn Book*
Main subjects: Japan; war; elephants; zoos; zoo animals; death

Kate WATERS and Madeline SLOVENZ-LOW

Lion Dancer: Ernie Wan's Chinese New Year
Scholastic, 1990.
ISBN: 0–590–43046–7, pp. 32.

Culture: Chinese

Beautiful photographs of a Chinese family's celebration of the New Year expose children to the culture of Chinese Americans. Ernie Wan lives in Chinatown in New York City and this book accurately pictures the lifestyle of this Chinese American family in the 1980s. Also includes an example of the Chinese horoscope.

Special features: photographs of a Chinese American family which reveal the importance their ancient customs still hold for them even though they live and participate in the modern world; Buddhist rituals; Chinese festival; celebration of the Chinese New Year in Chinatown in New York City
Reviewed in: *Multicultural Review*
Main subjects: Chinese Americans; Chinese New Year; dance; Chinese horoscope

Joanne Stewart WETZEL

Christmas Box, The
Illustrated by Barry Root.
Knopf, 1992.
ISBN: 679-91789-1, pp. 32.

Culture: Japanese

One Christmas when the author was young, her father couldn't be home for the holiday. He was a soldier stationed in Japan and sent her a box filled with photos and presents. This is the story of her Christmas box. Could be used in programs on Christmas; Japan and families.

Reviewed in: *Horn Book; Publisher's Weekly; Booklist*
Main subjects: Japan; Japanese; Christmas

Clara YEN

Why Rat Comes First: a Story of the Chinese Zodiac
Children's Book Press, 1991.
ISBN: 0892390727.

Culture: Chinese

The Chinese calendar cycle is twelve years and this book explains why Rat comes first in the cycle. Could be used in programs dealing with calendars; China and the zodiac.

Reviewed in: *Booklist; Kirkus; Publisher's Weekly*
Main subjects: Calendars; zodiac

Ling YU

Family in Taiwan, A
Series: Families the World Over
Lerner, 1990.
ISBN: 0-8225-1685-3, pp. 32.

Culture: Taiwanese

Introduces the lifestyle and culture of Taiwan through focusing on one family. Illustrated with color photographs. Could be used in programs on Taiwan; lifestyles and cultures.

Reviewed in: *School Library Journal*
Main subjects: Taiwan; lifestyles; cultures

Zheng ZHENSUN

Young Painter: the Life and Paintings of Wang Yani, A
Scholastic, 1991.
ISBN: 0590449060.

Culture: Chinese

Wang Yani, a young Chinese girl, began painting at the age of three and became the youngest artist to have a one person exhibition at the Smithsonian Institute. Could be used in programs dealing with art; artists; famous women; women; famous Chinese and Chinese.

Reviewed in: *Booklinks; Booklist; Kirkus; New York Times Book Review*
Main subjects: Chinese; artist; art; women; famous Chinese

NONFICTION – FOURTH THROUGH SIXTH GRADE

Buddhist Festivals

Series: Holidays and Festivals
Rourke Publications, 1989.
ISBN: 0–86592–984–X, pp. 48.

Culture: Asian Indian

Buddhism – its history, traditions, beliefs, festivals and celebrations. Could be used in programs dealing with India; Asian Indians; religions of the world; festivals and celebrations.

Main subjects: India; Asian Indian; Buddhism; festivals; holidays; religions of the world

Hindu Festivals

Series: Holidays and Festivals
Rourke Publications, 1989.
ISBN: 0–86592–986–6.

Culture: Asian Indian

The history, traditions, beliefs, celebrations and festivals of the Hindus. Color photographs illustrate the text. Could be used in programs dealing with India; Asian Indians; Hinduism; religions of the world; celebrations and festivals.

Main subjects: India; Asian Indians; Hindu; religions of the world; holidays; festivals

Muslim Festivals

Series: Holidays and Festivals
Rourke Publications, 1987.
ISBN: 0–86592–979–3.

Culture: Asian Indian

The history, beliefs, traditions, festivals and celebrations of Muslims. Could be used in programs dealing with India; Asian Indians; Muslims; religions of the world; festivals and holidays.

Main subjects: India; Asian Indians; Muslims; religions of the world; festivals; holidays

Ronda ARMITAGE

New Zealand
Series: Countries of the World
Illustrated by Chris Fairclough and Stefan Chabluk.
Franklin Watts, 1988.
ISBN: 0–531–18158–8, pp. 48.

Culture: New Zealand

Covers history, family life, culture and art of New Zealand in an introductory manner. Includes an index, glossary and brief bibliography. Could be used in programs on New Zealand; Pacific Islanders and the Maoris.

Reviewed in: *Booklist; School Library Journal*
Main subjects: New Zealand; Pacific Islanders; Maori

Caroline ARNOLD

Australia Today
Series: First Books
Franklin Watts, 1987.
ISBN: 0–531–10377–3, pp. 96.

Culture: Australian

Overview of the history, geography, people and resources of Australia, with information on the Aborigines, English settlers and other immigrants. A chronology and index are included. Could be used in programs on Australia; geography; history and Aborigines.

Reviewed in: *Booklist; School Library Journal*
Main subjects: Australia; Aborigines; history; geography

Walk on the Great Barrier Reef, A
Carolrhoda, 1988.
ISBN: 0–87614–285–4, pp. 48.

Culture: Australian

Describes the plants and animals of Australia's Great Barrier Reef, with full color photographs. Could be used in programs on the Great Barrier Reef; reef plants and animals; reefs of the world and Australia.

Awards received: Outstanding Science Trade Book for Children, NSTA-CBC 1988; Best Children's Science Book Selection, Science Books & Films 1988.
Reviewed in: *Booklist; School LIbrary Journal*
Main subjects: Australia; Great Barrier Reef; reefs; coral

Brent ASHABRANNER

Land of Yesterday, Land of Tomorrow: Discovering Chinese Central Asia
Cobblehill, 1992.
ISBN: 0525650865.

Culture: Chinese

Xinjiang province in China. The photographs and text enable the reader to catch a glimpse of a part of China that was closed to foreigners by the communist government. Could be used in programs dealing with China; Xinjiang; communism or life in other countries.

Reviewed in: *Booklinks; Kirkus; School Library Journal; Horn Book*
Main subjects: China; Xinjiang; communism

Gwynneth ASHBY

Family in South Korea, A
Series: Families the World Over
Lerner, 1987.
ISBN: 0-8225-1675-6, pp. 32.

Culture: Korean

Introduction to the lifestyle of a South Korean family, illustrated with color photographs. Could be used in programs on South Korea; lifestyles and cultures.

Reviewed in: *Booklist; School Library Journal*
Main subjects: Korea; South Korea; lifestyles; cultures

Patricia BAHREE

Hindu World, The
Series: Religions of the World
Trafalgar Sq./David & Charles, 1989.
ISBN: out of print, pp. 45.

Culture: Asian Indian

Information packed details about Hindu festivals, philosophy and rituals. Could be used to introduce Hindu way of life; religions of the world; rituals and festivals.

Special features: Hindu religion; religion and philosophy; rituals and festivals
Main subjects: India; Asian Indian; religion

Barbara BEIRNE

Pianist's Debut: Preparing for the Concert Stage, A
Photos by Barbara Beirne.
Carolrhoda Books, 1990.
ISBN: 0-87614-432-6, pp. 56.

Culture: Korean

Photobiography of Leah Yoon, an aspiring pianist. She is a Korean American who studied piano on a full scholarship at Julliard. She also attended the Professional Children's School. Upbeat portrait with good photographs. Would lend itself to discussions on careers; pianists; musicians; biographies; achievements of young people and programs dealing with Korean Americans.

Reviewed in: *Kirkus*
Main subjects: Korean American; Korean; pianist; musician

Gay BENNETT

Family in Sri Lanka, A
Series: Families the World Over
Illustrated by Christopher Cormack.
Lerner, 1985.
ISBN: 0-8225-1661-6, pp. 32.

Culture: Sri Lankan

Shows through photographs and text the everyday routines of twelve year old Niman and his family. They live in a small farming community in the heart of the world's most important cinnamon growing area. Could be used in programs dealing with Sri Lanka; family life; farming and cinnamon.

Reviewed in: *Booklist*
Main subjects: Sri Lanka; family life; cinnamon

Robert and Corinne BORJA

Making Chinese Papercuts
Albert Whitman & Company, 1980.
ISBN: 0-8075-4948-7, pp. 40.

Culture: Chinese

This informative book provides instructions for designing, cutting and coloring papercuts, and also tells the historical significance of this ancient Chinese craft. Would be useful for activities; craft projects; exploring ancient Chinese crafts; comparative craft projects and papercutting programs.

Special features: Chinese papercutting craft
Reviewed in: *Booklist; School Library Journal*
Main subjects: Chinese papercutting; crafts

Tricia BROWN

Chinese New Year
Photos by Fran Ortiz.
Henry Holt, 1987.
ISBN: 0-8050-0497-1, pp. 48.

Culture: Chinese

Preparations for the Chinese New Year in San Francisco's Chinatown. The text is informative; the photographs are black and white. Could be used for programs dealing with the Chinese New Year; San Francisco or Chinese Americans.

Special features: photographs of the preparations for the Chinese New Year in San Francisco; Chinese New Year
Reviewed in: *Publisher's Weekly; Booklist; Bulletin of the Center for Children's Books; Notable Children's Trade Book in the Field of Social Studies*
Main subjects: Chinese American; Chinese New Year; San Francisco

Lee Ann: the Story of a Vietnamese American Girl
Photos by Ted Thai.
Putnam, 1991.
ISBN: 0-399-21842-4, pp. 48.

Culture: Vietnamese

The story of Lee Ann, a Vietnamese American girl and her family. Her school activities, family relationships and weekend activities are portrayed, as well as their celebration of TET, the Vietnamese New Year. Could be used in programs dealing with Vietnamese Americans; Asians; holidays; New Year's Day celebrations; lifestyles; family relationships and TET.

Reviewed in: *Booklinks; Publisher's Weekly*
Main subjects: Vietnamese American; lifestyles; TET

Rollo BROWNE

Aboriginal Family, An
Series: Families the World Over
Illustrated by Chris Fairclough.
Lerner, 1985.
ISBN: 0-8225-1655-1, pp. 32.

Culture: Australian

Focuses on Lynette Joshua and her family. She is eleven and provides the reader with a sense of the traditional life of the Aborigines. Gives information on religious ceremonies; family relationships; hunting and gathering activities and current issues facing the Aborigines. Can be used in programs on lifestyles; Australia and Aborigines.

Awards received: Notable Children's Trade Book in the Field of Social Studies
Reviewed in: *Booklist; School Library Journal*
Main subjects: Australia; Aborigines; lifestyles

Family in Australia, A
Series: Families the World Over
Illustrated by Chris Fairclough.
Lerner, 1987.
ISBN: 0–8225–1671–3, pp. 32.

Culture: Australian

Twelve year old David Baker lives on the northern coast of Australia near Cape Arnhem. Looks at his life and various activities such as attending school, boating, surfing, swimming and playing rugby. Could be used in programs on Australia; lifestyles and Aborigines.

Reviewed in: *Booklist; School Library Journal*
Main subjects: Australia; lifestyles

Muriel Paskin CARRISON

Cambodian Folk Stories from the Gatiloke
Charles E. Tuttle, 1987.
ISBN: 0–8048–1518–6, pp. 139.

Culture: Cambodian

Folktales translated from the Gatiloke, the original collection of Cambodian oral folktales. The introduction provides background on Cambodian folktales and information on Buddha and Buddhism is included. At the end of each tale, historical and cultural information is given. Could be used in programs on Cambodia; comparative folklore; Cambodian folklore; Buddhism and comparative religion.

Special features: glossary and appendix with historical, geographical and cultural information
Main subjects: Cambodia; folktales; comparative folklore; Buddhism

Sylvia CASSEDY

Red Dragonfly on my Shoulder
HarperCollins, 1992.
ISBN: 0–0602–2625–0.

Culture: Japanese

Thirteen haiku about animals, translated from the Japanese. Could be used in programs on Japanese poetry; haiku; styles of poetry and animals.

Main subjects: Japanese; haiku; poetry; animals

Anthony CHAN

Hmong Textile Designs
Illustrated by Anthony Chan.
Stemmer House, 1990.
ISBN: 0–88045–113–0, pp. 43.

Culture: Laotian

Examples of Hmong textile designs. The introduction provides information on Hmong beliefs and history. The textile designs are black and white. Could be used in programs on textiles; Hmong; art styles; culture and art; art appreciation and embroidery.

Main subjects: Laos; Hmong; textiles; embroidery

Howard CHUA-EOAN

Aquino
Series: World Leaders, Past and Present
Chelsea House, 1988.

Culture: Filipino

Corazon Aquino as a person and the political situation in the Philippines relevant to her election as president. Illustrated with news photos. Would lend itself to programs on the Philippines; Corazon Aquino; famous women and political leaders.

Special features: a time line, index and bibliography.
Main subjects: Philippines; Corazon Aquino; famous women

Vicki COBB

This Place is Crowded: Japan
Series: Imagine Living Here
Walker, 1992.
ISBN: 0-8027-8154-4.

Culture: Japanese

Information on the lives and customs of people in Japan. Could be used in programs on Japan; lifestyles and cities.

Reviewed in: *Booklist*
Main subjects: Japan; lifestyles; cities

Elanor COERR

Sadako and the Thousand Paper Cranes
Illustrated by Ronald Himler.
Dell Yearling, 1977.
ISBN: 0-440-47465-5, pp. 64.

Culture: Japanese

Biography of Sadako Sasaki, a Japanese girl who died of leukemia ten years after being exposed to radiation at the bombing of Hiroshima. Could be used in programs dealing with World War II; Hiroshima; death; atomic bomb and Japan.

Reviewed in: *Booklist; Horn Book; Kirkus; Children's Book Review*
Main subjects: Japanese; World War II; atomic bomb; Hiroshima; death

David CUMMING

India
Series: Countries of the World
Illustrated by Jimmy Holmes.
Franklin Watts, 1989.
ISBN: 0-531-18271-1, pp. 48.

Culture: Asian Indian

Information on the history, wildlife and education in India, with examples of city versus village life including what the people eat and drink and recreational activities. The chapters are short and the text readable; illustrated with color photographs. Would be useful in programs dealing with India; Asian Indians; city life; village life; foods of the world and life in other countries.

Special features: index, glossary and bibliography; India
Reviewed in: *School Library Journal*
Main subjects: India; Asian Indian

Prodeepta DAS

Inside India
Series: Inside
Illustrated by Prodeepta Das.
Franklin Watts, 1990.
ISBN: 0-531-14045-8, pp. 32.

Culture: Asian Indian

The history and family life of Asian Indians in India, including comparisons of city and villages. The text is brief and the photographs are in color. Good graphics give facts about the size and population of India. Would be useful in introducing programs dealing with India; Asian Indians; aspects of life in India and the history of India.

Special features: map and graphics
Reviewed in: *Horn Book*; *School Library Journal*
Main subjects: India; Asian Indians

Judy DONNELLY

Wall of Names: the Story of the Vietnam Veterans Memorial, A
Series: Step Into Reading Step 4
Random House, 1991.
ISBN: 679-80169-3, pp. 48.

Culture: Vietnamese

A history of the Vietnam War and the Vietnam Veterans Memorial, with photos to illustrate the text. The response of those who visit the Memorial is included. Could be used in programs dealing with veterans; war; the Vietnam War and the Vietnam Veterans Memorial.

Reviewed in: *Booklist*; *Newsweek*
Main subjects: Vietnam; Vietnam War; veterans

Judith ELKIN

Family in Japan, A
Series: Families the World Over
Illustrated by Stuart Atkin.
Lerner, 1987.
ISBN: 0-8225-1672-1, pp. 32.

Culture: Japanese

Introduction to life in modern Japan focusing on the daily routines of a young Japanese boy. Large color photos and large print text, but in depth information is not provided. Could be used as an introduction to aspects of life in modern Japan, however, does not provide much detail and does not cover problems of life in Japan. If one is aware of the limitations of the book, then it could be used in programs on families; lifestyles and children of other countries.

Special features: glossary
Reviewed in: *Booklist*
Main subjects: Japan; families; lifestyle

Leila FOSTER

Nien Cheng: Courage in China
Children's Press, Inc., 1992.
ISBN: 0516032798.

Culture: Chinese

The story of Nien Cheng, a Chinese woman in Shanghai who was imprisoned during the Cultural Revolution. Could be used in programs dealing with women; Shanghai; the Cultural Revolution or China.

Reviewed in: *School Library Journal*
Main subjects: Chinese; women; Cultural Revolution; Shanghai

Mary Ann FRASER

On Top of the World
Illustrated by Mary Ann Fraser.
Henry Holt, 1991.
ISBN: 0-8050-1587-7, pp. 40.

Culture: Tibetan

The story of Edmund Hillary and Tenzing Norgay's successful climb of Mount Everest. Could be used in programs dealing with mountains; mountain climbing; adventurers; sports; Tibet; Edmund Hillary and Tenzing Norgay.

Reviewed in: *Booklist; School Library Journal; Kirkus*
Main subjects: Mount Everest; adventurers; mountains; mountain climbing; sports

Ten Mile Day
Illustrated by Mary Ann Fraser.
Henry Holt, 1993.
ISBN: 0-8050-1902-2, pp. 40.

Culture: Multicultural

How the Transcontinental Railroad was built – informative and multicultural. Could be used in programs on transportation; railroads; nineteenth century American history and immigrants.

Special features: an illustrated glossary
Reviewed in: *School Library Journal*
Main subjects: railroads; America; transportation; Transcontinental Railroad

Jean FRITZ

Homesick: My Own Story
Illustrated by Margot Tomer.
Putnam, 1982.
ISBN: 0–399–20933–6, pp. 176.

Culture: Chinese

Autobiography of writer Jean Fritz tells of her growing up in China in the 1920s during the struggle for power between the communists and nationalists. She learned to speak Chinese as well as English and attended a British school. When she was twelve she moved to the United States and discovered she felt as much a foreigner there as she did in China. Would lend itself to programs on cultural diversity; friendship; moving; change; growing up in two cultures; the 1920s and China.

Reviewed in: *English Journal*
Main subjects: China; 1920s; biography; cultural diversity

Dan GARRETT and Warrill GRINROD

Australia
Series: World in View
Steck-Vaughn, 1990.
ISBN: 0–8114–2429–4, pp. 96.

Culture: Australian

Basic information on the history and geography of Australia. Could be used in programs on Australia; Aborigines; history and geography of Australia.

Reviewed in: *Our Family, Our Friends, Our World* by Lyn Miller-Lachmann
Main subjects: Australia; Aborigines; lifestyles; history and geography

D. V. GEORGES

Asia
Series: New True Books
Children's Press, 1986.
ISBN: 0–516–01288–6, pp. 48.

Culture: Asian

A brief overview of Asia, with large print text and color photographs; maps for each country covered. Could be used in programs on an introduction to Asia or one dealing with maps.

Special features: glossary and index
Main subjects: Asia

Australia
Series: New True Books
Children's Press, 1986.
ISBN: 0-516-41290-6, pp. 48.

Culture: Australian

Covers a variety of topics related to science and geography with little cultural and social information. Includes an index and glossary. Could be used in introductory programs dealing with geography and Australia.

Reviewed in: *Our Family, Our Friends, Our World* by Lyn Miller-Lachmann
Main subjects: Australia; geography

Patricia Reilly GIFF

Mother Teresa: Sister to the Poor
Series: Women of Our Time
Illustrated by Ted Lewin.
Viking, 1986.
ISBN: 0-670-81096-7, pp. 58.

Culture: Asian Indian

Well written biography of Mother Teresa tells the story of her life and work in India among the poor simply and effectively, with good illustrations. Could be used for programs dealing with women; religion; the poor; biographies and famous people.

Reviewed in: *Bulletin of the Center for Children's Books; Booklist; School Library Journal*
Main subjects: Mother Teresa; India

Alice GILBREATH

Great Barrier Reef: a Treasure in the Sea, The
Dillon, 1986.
ISBN: 0-87518-300-X.

Culture: Australian

Overview of the Great Barrier Reef of Australia. Could be used in programs on the Great Barrier Reef; Australia; corals and reefs of the world.

Reviewed in: *Booklist; School Library Journal*
Main subjects: Australia; Great Barrier Reef; reefs; corals

Denise GOFF

Early China
Gloucester, 1986.
ISBN: 0–531–17025–X.

Culture: Chinese

Overview of history of China with emphasis on the Han dynasty. Could be used in programs on history, China and the Han dynasty.

Reviewed in: *Booklist*
Main subjects: China; history; Han dynasty

Mace GOLDFARB

Fighters, Refugees, Immigrants: a Story of the Hmong
Carolrhoda Books, 1982.
ISBN: 0–87614–197–1.

Culture: Laotian

Full color photographs are used to present the difficult life of the Hmong and their reasons for fleeing their country. Could be used in programs on immigrants; refugees; war; Asians; Hmong and Asian Americans.

Main subjects: Laotian; Laos; Hmong; immigrants; refugees

Bridget GOOM

Family in Singapore, A
Series: Families the World Over
Illustrated by Jenny Mathews.
Lerner, 1986.
ISBN: 0–8225–1663–2, pp. 32.

Culture: Singaporean

Chor Ling, a twelve year old girl, lives on the island nation of Singapore. Shows what life is like for her and her family; photos illustrate the text. Could be used in programs on lifestyles; Singapore; other cultures and families.

Reviewed in: *Booklist; School Library Journal*
Main subjects: Singapore; families; lifestyles

Susan GORDON

Asian Indians
Series: Recent American Immigrants
Franklin Watts, 1990.

Culture: Asian Indian

Asian Indians, their old way of life and their life as Americans; why they emigrated to the United States; with contributions by Asian Indians. This excellent resource can be used by children as a research tool or by teachers and librarians to introduce programs on Asian Indians or emigrants.

Special features: bibliography and index; Asian Indians
Reviewed in: *Bulletin of the Center for Children's Books; Horn Book; Library Talk*
Main subjects: Asian Indians

Carol GREENE

Indira Nehru Gandhi: Ruler of India
Series: Picture-story Biographies
Children's Press, 1985.
ISBN: 0-516-03478-2, pp. 32.

Culture: Asian Indian

Introduction to the life of Indira Nehru Gandhi, with black and white photos. A simple chronology is included. Could be used in programs dealing with famous women; biographies; women leaders; India and Asian Indians.

Main subjects: India; Asian Indians; Indira Nehru Gandhi; women; biography

Japan
Series: Enchantment of the World
Children's Press, 1983.
ISBN: 0-516-02769-7.

Culture: Japanese

An introductory description to the history, culture and geography of Japan, with numerous color photographs, maps and a mini-facts section. Could be used in programs on Japan's history, geography and culture.

Main subjects: Japan; geography; history; culture

K. J. GREGORY

Yellow River, The
Silver, 1980.
ISBN: 0-382-06371-6.

Culture: Chinese

Life and sites along China's Yellow River. Could be used in programs on rivers of the world; rivers of China; geography and China.

Main subjects: China; rivers; Yellow River

Emily GUNNER and Shirley McCONKY

Family in Australia, A
Series: Families Around the World
Franklin Watts, 1985.
ISBN: 0-531-03824-6, pp. 32.

Culture: Australian

Focuses on the King family and their farm. Could be used in programs on Australia and lifestyles.

Reviewed in: *Booklist; School Library Journal*
Main subjects: Australia; lifestyles

Sheila HAMANAKA

Journey: Japanese Americans, Racism, and Renewal
Orchard Books/Franklin Watts, 1990.
ISBN: 0-531-08449-3.

Culture: Japanese

Photo essay inspired by a twenty five foot mural that documented the experiences of Japanese Americans imprisoned in the United States during World War II. The painting is a documentary and memorial to the painter's family and the 120,000 Japanese Americans that were interned in the camps. Could be used in programs on Japanese American experiences during World War II; war; internment camps; concentration camps and racism.

Awards received: School Library Journal Best Books of 1990
Reviewed in: *Kirkus; School Library Journal*
Main subjects: Japanese Americans; World War II; internment camps; war; racism

Reijo HARKONEN

Children of China, The
Series: The World's Children
Photos by Matti A. Pitkanen.
Carolrhoda Books, 1990.
ISBN: 0-87614-394-X.

Culture: Chinese

Introduces children to the lives of children in China, with beautiful color photographs. Could be used to introduce China; children in other countries; lifestyles and comparative lifestyles; Asia and Chinese.

Special features: pronunciation guide and index
Reviewed in: *School Library Journal*
Main subjects: China; Chinese; Asian

Children of Nepal, The
Series: The World's Children
Photos by Matti A. Pitkanen.
Carolrhoda Books, 1990.
ISBN: 0–87614–395–8, pp. 48.

Culture: Nepalese

This import from Finland has lost some of its usefulness due to awkward text and its failure to focus on children. Good color photos give the reader a feeling of traveling in Nepal. Could be used to introduce Nepal and Asia and in programs dealing with differing lifestyles.

Special features: pronunciation guide, index and map
Reviewed in: *School Library Journal*
Main subjects: Nepal; Asia

Tomike HIGA

Girl with the White Flag
Dell Yearling, 1992.
ISBN: 0–440–40720–6, pp. 128.

Culture: Japanese

Autobiographical recounting of the author's survival as a seven year old on Okinawa. Could be used in programs dealing with war; World War II; Japan; survival and the 1940s.

Reviewed in: *School Library Journal; Voice of Youth Advocates*
Main subjects: World War II; 1940s

Charles HIGHAM

Maoris, The
Lerner, 1983.
ISBN: 0–8225–1229–7, pp. 48.

Culture: New Zealand

History of the Maoris of New Zealand, with index and glossary. Could be used in programs on New Zealand and the Maoris.

Reviewed in: *Our Family, Our Friends, Our World* by Lyn Miller-Lachmann
Main subjects: New Zealand; Maoris; history

Dorothy and Thomas HOOBLER

Vietnam: Why We Fought
Knopf, 1990.
ISBN: 394–81943–8, pp. 208.

Culture: Vietnamese

Well written book providing photographs and maps to help explain the United States' involvement in Vietnam. Why they lost the Vietnam War and what can be learned from the experience are also covered. Can be used in units dealing with Vietnam; war; diplomacy; foreign affairs; the 1960s and the Vietnam War.

Special features: photographs and maps
Awards received: National Council for Social Studies Notable Children's Trade Book
Reviewed in: starred review in *School Library Journal*; *New York Times Book Review*
Main subjects: Vietnam; Vietnamese War

Diane HOYT-GOLDSMITH

Hoang Anh: a Vietnamese American Boy
Holiday House, 1992.
ISBN: 0823409481.

Culture: Vietnamese

Hoang Anh describes his life and the traditional culture and customs that shape his family life. Could be used in programs on lifestyles; Vietnamese Americans and family relationships.

Reviewed in: *Booklinks; Booklist; Kirkus; Publisher's Weekly*
Main subjects: Vietnamese; Vietnamese American; lifestyles; family relationships

Nigel HUNTER

Gandhi
Series: Great Lives
Franklin Watts, 1986.
ISBN: 0–531–18093–X, pp. 32.

Culture: Asian Indian

Biography covering the highlights of Gandhi's life, with color illustrations and historical photos. Could be used in programs dealing with Gandhi; Asian Indians; India; civil rights and passive resistance.

Special features: index, chronology, glossary and bibliography
Main subjects: Gandhi; India

Quang Nhoung HUYNH

Land I Lost: Adventures of a Boy in Vietnam, The
Harper, 1982.
ISBN: 0–06–024593–X, pp. 115.

Culture: Vietnamese

A Vietnamese American's memories of his youth in Vietnam before war disrupted his life. Could be used in programs on Vietnam; war; displacement and Vietnamese Americans.

Reviewed in: *Booklist*
Main subjects: Vietnam; war; Vietnamese Americans; displacement

Peter JACOBSEN and Preben KRISTENSEN

Family in India, A
Series: Families Around the World
Franklin Watts, 1984.
ISBN: 0–531–03788–6, pp. 32.

Culture: Asian Indian

This look at a family that lives in a village near New Delhi in India provides insight into the changes taking place in that country. Illustrated with photographs. Could be used in programs dealing with India; Asian Indians; family relationships and lifestyles.

Special features: index, fact page and glossary
Main subjects: India; Asian Indian; family relationships

Madhur JAFFREY

Seasons of Splendor: Tales, Myths and Legends of India
Illustrated by Michael Foreman.
Atheneum, 1985.
ISBN: 0–689–31141–9, pp. 128.

Culture: Asian Indian

A collection of folktales told throughout the year in conjunction with various festivals and holidays. Some of the stories are from the great Indian epics, others are made up by the author's family and others are from traditional folklore. The illustrations include full page paintings as well as smaller paintings and drawings. Could be used in programs dealing with India; Asian Indians; folklore; myths; legends; holidays; festivals and customs; also as a source of folktales to learn for storytelling programs.

Special features: pronunciation guide and glossary
Reviewed in: *Bulletin of the Center for Children's Books; Booklist*
Main subjects: India; Asian Indian; folktales; myths

Ian JAMES

Australia
Series: Inside
Franklin Watts, 1989.
ISBN: 0-531-10759-0, pp. 32.

Culture: Australian

Highpoints of Australian geography, family life, arts and industry. Could be used in introductory programs on Australia and lifestyles around the world.

Reviewed in: *Our Family, Our Friends, Our World* by Lyn Miller-Lachmann
Main subjects: Australia

Neil JOHNSON

Step Into China
Series: Step Into
Illustrated by Neil Johnson.
Julian Messner, 1988.
ISBN: 0-671-64338-X, pp. 32.

Culture: Chinese

A good overview of China and life in China, with color photographs which would appeal to young children. The photos are large and surround a paragraph or two of text. Covers topics such as school, games, language and work. Would be useful in programs giving an introduction to China; Asian countries; lifestyles around the world; how other people live and the culture of China.

Main subjects: China; lifestyles; cultures and customs

Rebecca L. JOHNSON

Great Barrier Reef: a Living Laboratory, The
Carolrhoda, 1991.
ISBN: 0-8225-1596-2, pp. 64.

Culture: Australian

First hand account of marine research on Australia's Great Barrier Reef. Could be used in programs on marine biology; marine research; Great Barrier Reef; corals; reefs of the world and Australia.

Main subjects: Australia; Great Barrier Reef; marine research; corals

Sukhbir Singh KAPOOR

Sikh Festivals
Series: Holidays and Festivals
Rourke Publications, 1989.
ISBN: 0-86592-984-X, pp. 48.

Culture: Asian Indian

Provides insight into the history and culture of the Sikh in India. Sikhs in North America are mentioned. Comparisons between Sikhism and Christianity are made. Color and black and white photos illustrate the text. Would be useful in programs dealing with India; Asian Indians; Sikhism; religions of the world; holidays and festivals.

Main subjects: India; Asian Indians; holidays; festivals; religions of the world; Sikh history and customs

Marylee KNOWLTON and Mark SACHNER

Burma
Series: Children of the World
Illustrated by Takashi Morieda.
Gareth Stevens, 1987.
ISBN: 1-55532-159-3, pp. 64.

Culture: Burmese

The daily life of a young Burmese boy and his family. Color photos present aspects such as his house, school and neighborhood. Information is provided at the end of the book on research project ideas and activities. Could be used to introduce children to Burma; other cultures; family life around the world; children in other countries and lifestyles.

Special features: map and index; background information on Burma
Main subjects: Burma; families; lifestyles

Marylee KNOWLTON and David K. WRIGHT

India
Series: Children of the World
Illustrated by Uchiyama Sumio.
Gareth Stevens, 1988.
ISBN: 1–55532–208–5, pp. 64.

Culture: Asian Indian

The life of Vikram Singh, an Indian boy. The first part of the book uses photos to portray his environment and lifestyle. The second part gives factual information about India. However, Vikram's family lifestyle is not typical. His family is part of India's small upper class. The color photographs are appealing. Would be useful in programs dealing with India; Asian Indians; family relationships and lifestyles. Additional sources will need to be added to provide information on the caste system and on the partition of India and Pakistan.

Special features: activities, resources and index
Reviewed in: *Booklist*
Main subjects: India; Asian Indian; family relationships; lifestyles

Kathleen KRULL

City Within a City: How Kids Live in New York's Chinatown
Lodestar, 1994.
ISBN: 0525674381, pp. 48.

Culture: Chinese

Stories of Sze Ki Chau and Chao Liu, recent immigrants to the United States. The two observe traditional Chinese holidays and talk about the problems of dealing with two cultures. Could be used in programs on immigrants; cultural adjustments and Chinese Americans.

Reviewed in: *Booklist*
Main subjects: Chinese Americans; lifestyles; immigrants

Emilie U. LEPTHIEN

Corazon Aquino: President of the Philippines
Series: Picture-story Biographies
Children's Press, 1987.
ISBN: 0–516–04170–3, pp. 32.

Culture: Filipino

Biography of Corazon Aquino which focuses on her as a person and ends with her election as president of the Philippines. Includes family photos and news photos. Would lend itself to programs on famous women; the Philippines; biographies; Corazon Aquino and political figures.

Special features: a timeline
Main subjects: Philippines; Corazon Aquino; biographies; famous women

Paul LIGHTFOOT

Mekong, The
Series: Rivers of the World
Silver Burdett, 1981.
ISBN: 0–382–06520–4, pp. 67.

Culture: Asian

Photos along the course of the Mekong River from its beginnings in Tibet through Thailand to the sea, with informative and provocative text. Could be used in programs dealing with rivers of the world; Tibet; Thailand; Asia and comparative lifestyles.

Special features: glossary, index, bibliography, map and factual information page
Main subjects: rivers; Mekong River; Asian rivers

Sing LIM

West Coast Chinese Boy
Tundra, 1979.
ISBN: 0–88776–121–6, pp. 64.

Culture: Chinese

Artist Sing Lim's account of growing up in Vancouver, which had the second largest Chinese community in North America, during the 1920s. Could be used in programs on Chinese immigrants; Chinese Canadians; Vancouver and the 1920s.

Main subjects: Chinese Canadians; Vancouver; 1920s.

Trudie MacDOUGALL

Beyond Dreamtime: the Life and Lore of the Aboriginal Australian
Illustrated by Pat Cummings.
Coward, McCann, 1978.
ISBN: out of print, pp. 64.

Culture: Australian

Describes Aboriginal life in different regions of Australia and includes several legends of the Dreamtime. Could be used in programs on Australia; Aborigines; Dreamtime; legends; comparative folklore and lifestyles.

Reviewed in: *Our Family, Our Friends, Our World* by Lyn Miller-Lachmann
Main subjects: Australia; Aborigines; legends

Jodine MAYBERRY

Chinese
Series: Recent American Immigrants
Franklin Watts, 1990.

Culture: Chinese

Excellent information about Chinese American emigrants. A good reference tool for children or can be used by teachers and librarians to introduce programs on Chinese Americans or emigrants to the United States.

Reviewed in: *Booklist; Horn Book; Library Talk*
Main subjects: Chinese Americans; immigration

Filipinos
Series: Recent American Immigrants
Franklin Watts, 1990.
ISBN: 0-531-10978-X, pp. 64.

Culture: Filipino

A valuable resource with clear charts, easy to read maps and photos (both black and white and color). Demographics, a clear outline of the book and a well designed layout make the book easy to read and to use. Concise biographies on Asian Americans are given in sidebars. The way the immigrants came to the United States, their old way of life and new lifestyle are explored. An excellent research tool for children to learn more about Philippine Americans. Teachers and librarians could use this book to introduce programs on the Philippines, Philippine Americans or emigrants.

Special features: bibliography and index, charts and maps; Philippine American
Reviewed in: *Horn Book; Library Talk*
Main subjects: Philippine Americans; Filipinos; immigration

Robert McCLUNG

Lili: a Giant Panda of Sichuan
Illustrated by Irene Brady.
Morrow, 1988.
ISBN: 0-688-06943-6.

Culture: Chinese

Story of Lili, one of less than a thousand pandas living in the wild, illustrates efforts to prevent pandas from becoming an extinct species. Could be used in programs on China; pandas; endangered species and animal preservation.

Reviewed in: *Bulletin of the Center for Children's Books; Booklist; School LIbrary Journal*
Main subjects: China; pandas; endangered species

Kay McDEARMON

Giant Pandas
Dodd, Mead, 1986.
ISBN: out of print, pp. 62.

Culture: Chinese

A pair of giant pandas are given to a US zoo by the government of China. Black and white illustrations and photographs. Information about giant pandas as well as the threat to their survival as a species. Could be used in programs on giant pandas; China; animals around the world; endangered species; animals in zoos and environmental issues.

Reviewed in: *Booklist*
Main subjects: China; animals; pandas; endangered species; zoos

William McGUIRE

Southeast Asians
Series: Recent American Immigrants
Franklin Watts, 1991.
ISBN: 0-531-11108-3.

Culture: Asians

Factual account of how over a million refugees from Southeast Asia (Vietnam, Laos and Cambodia) have struggled to adapt to American culture while retaining their own heritage. Could be used in programs on refugees; Southeast Asian refugee experiences; Vietnamese, Laotian and Cambodian refugee experiences.

Main subjects: Vietnam; Laos; Cambodia; refugees; war; Indochina

Nancy Durrell McKENNA

Family in Hong Kong, A
Series: Families the World Over
Lerner, 1987.
ISBN: 0-8225-1676-4, pp. 32.

Culture: Hong Kong

One family's lifestyle in Hong Kong, illustrated with color photographs. Could be used in programs on Hong Kong; lifestyles and cultures.

Reviewed in: *School Library Journal*
Main subjects: Hong Kong; families; lifestyles; cultures

Sylvia McNAIR

Indonesia
Series: Enchantment of the World
Children's Press, 1993.
ISBN: 0–516–02618–6, pp. 128.

Culture: Indonesian

Information on the life, geography and history of Indonesia, with index. Could be used in programs on geography; history, lifestyles and Indonesia.

Reviewed in: *Booklist*
Main subjects: Indonesia; geography; history

Janet Nomura MOREY and Wendy DUNN

Famous Asian Americans
Cobblehill, 1992.
ISBN: 0525650806.

Culture: Chinese

Fourteen short biographies of Chinese Americans including chapters on Ellison Onizuka, An Wang, Michael Chang and Jose Aruego. Could be used in programs on biographies; Chinese Americans or famous Americans.

Reviewed in: *Booklinks; Kirkus*
Main subjects: Chinese Americans

Huynh Quang NHUONG

Land I Lost, The
Illustrated by Vo-Dinh Mai.
Harper & Row, 1982.
ISBN: 0–06–024593–X. pp. 115.

Culture: Vietnamese

A collection of personal reminiscences of growing up in Vietnam; An interesting and informative biography. Could be used in programs on Vietnam; social life and customs; water buffalos and animals.

Main subjects: Vietnam; social life and customs

Ta Huay PENG

Fun with Chinese Festivals
Illustrated by Leong Kum Chuen.
Heian International, 1991.
ISBN: 0–89346–358–2, p. 96.

Culture: Chinese

Information on over seventy-five Chinese festivals. Could be used in programs on Chinese holidays; comparative holidays and festivals.

Main subjects: Chinese festivals; holidays

Susan PEPPER

Australia
Series: Passport to ...
Franklin Watts, 1987.
ISBN: 0–531–10270–X, pp. 48.

Culture: Australian

Information on Australia's history and geography, with graphs and charts. Could be used in programs on Australia; geography and history.

Reviewed in: *Booklist; School Library Journal*
Main subjects: Australia; geography; history

Margaret RAU

Red Earth, Blue Sky: the Australian Outback
HarperCollins, 1981.
ISBN: 0–690–04081–4, pp. 118.

Culture: Australian

Contemporary life in isolated regions of the Australian outback (sheep stations, deserts, mines and remote towns). Gives a brief history of the land, people and European settlers. Could be used in programs on lifestyles; Australia and the outback.

Reviewed in: *Our Family, Our Friends, Our World* by Lyn Miller-Lachmann
Main subjects: Australia; outback; lifestyles; Aborigines

Jan REYNOLDS

Down Under
Series: Vanishing Cultures
Illustrated by Jan Reynolds.
Harcourt Brace & Company, 1992.
ISBN: 0–15–224182–5, pp. 32.

Culture: Australian

Photographer Jan Reynolds documented one Tiwi family on a walkabout. The Tiwi believe that by going on walkabout they can enter the time when the land was created and that the land where they live, Bathurst Island just off the northern coast of Australia, is sacred. Could be used in programs on Australia; Aborigines; Tiwi; walkabout and world views.

Reviewed in: *American Bookseller; Kirkus; School Library Journal*
Main subjects: Australia; Aborigines; Tiwi

Mike ROSEN

Conquest of Everest, The
Series: Great Journeys
Illustrated by Doug Post.
Franklin Watts, 1990.
ISBN: 0–531–18319–X, pp. 32.

Culture: Nepalese

The story of various expeditions to climb Mount Everest, the tallest mountain in the world, in the Himalayan mountain range which lies between India and the Tibet region of China. Could be used in programs dealing with mountains; Nepal; the Himalayas; Asia; mountain climbing; sports; women and mountain climbing.

Special features: two pages on women on Everest
Main subjects: Nepal; Mount Everest; Asia; mountain climbing; sports

Catherine Edwards SADLER

Two Chinese Families
Illustrated by Alan Sadler.
Atheneum, 1981.
ISBN: 0–689–30865–5, pp. 70.

Culture: Chinese

Life in Guilin, a small town in southern China. On one page a couple of paragraphs of text tells about the inhabitants' lives; on the facing page, a photograph illustrates the text. Could be used in programs on China; families around the world and lifestyles.

Main subjects: China; family life; lifestyles

Margaret SCARIANO

Picture Life of Corazon Aquino, The
Franklin Watts, 1987.
ISBN: 0–531–10296–3.

Culture: Filipino

Simplistic biography which is not balanced in its presentation of Corazon Aquino and the political situation in the Philippines during the period relevant to her election as president. Example of a flawed biography. Use it with caution, if at all.

Reviewed in: *Booklist*
Main subjects: Philippines; famous women; political leaders; Corazon Aquino

Alisa and Alan SCARSBROOK

Family in Pakistan, A
Series: Families the World Over
Lerner, 1985.
ISBN: 0–8225–1662–4, pp. 32.

Culture: Pakistani

The life of fourteen year old Assim Mahmood and his family provide the reader with an overview of rural and urban lifestyles in Pakistan; illustrated with photographs. Could be used in programs on Pakistan; lifestyles and Asia.

Reviewed in: *Booklist*
Main subjects: Pakistan; lifestyles; Asia

Amy SHUI and Stuart THOMPSON

Chinese Food and Drink
Series: Food and Drink
Franklin Watts, 1987.
ISBN: 0–531–18129–4, pp. 44.

Culture: Chinese

Introduction to Chinese cuisine with some recipes, information on food in history, cultivation, meals, markets and etiquette. The role of food in Chinese medicine, and customs dealing with tea, soup and special foods for festivals are also covered. Could be used in programs dealing with China; Chinese cuisine; customs; food and cooking.

Special features: glossary, bibliography and index
Main subjects: China; food; recipes; customs and cultures

Fay STANLEY

Last Princess: the Story of Princess Ka'iulani of Hawaii, The
Illustrated by Diane Stanley.
Four Winds Press, 1991.
ISBN: 0–02–786785–4, pp. 40.

Culture: Pacific Islands

Picture biography of Ka'iulani, the last princess of Hawaii, including notes on the Hawaiian language and an extensive bibliography. Could be used in programs on Hawaii; biographies and real life princesses.

Reviewed in: *Booklist*
Main subjects: Hawaii; princess; biography

Shizuye TAKASHIMA

Child in Prison Camp, A
Illustrated by Shizuye Takashima.
Tundra, 1971.
ISBN: 0–88776–241–7, pp. 100.

Culture: Japanese

Slightly fictionalized account of Takashima's stay in a Canadian internment camp when she was a small child. After the war ended, her family chose to stay in Canada and relocated to Toronto where Takashima established herself as a talented artist. Could be used in programs on Japanese Canadians; internment camps; prejudice and World War II.

Reviewed in: *Our Family, Our Friends, Our World* by Lyn Miller-Lachmann
Main subjects: Japanese Canadians; internment camps; World War II; 1940s

Sally TALAN and Rhoda SHERWOOD

China
Series: Children of the World
Illustrated by Yasuhiko Miyazima.
Gareth Stevens, 1988.
ISBN: 1-55532-207-7, pp. 64.

Culture: Chinese

Shows what life is like for an eleven year old Chinese girl and her family, describing religion, school, work, festivals and daily life, with color photos. Information on China, research project ideas and activities are provided at the end of the book. Could be used to introduce children to China; lifestyles in other countries; children in other countries; school; customs and culture.

Special features: map and index
Main subjects: China; lifestyles; families

Alice TERADA

Under the Starfruit Tree: Folktales from Vietnam
Illustrated by Janet Larsen.
University of Hawaii Press, 1989.
ISBN: 0-8248-1252-2, pp. 136.

Culture: Vietnamese

Vietnamese tales translated into English by native speakers and grouped into four categories: foibles of man and quirks of animals; tales of the lowlands and highlands; the spirit world; food, love and laughter. Could be used in programs on Vietnam; comparative folklore and Vietnamese folklore.

Main subjects: Vietnam; folklore; supernatural beings

Vivian L. THOMPSON

Hawaiian Myths of Earth, Sea, and Sky
Illustrated by Marilyn Kahalewai.
University of Hawaii Press, 1988.
ISBN: 0-8248-1171-2, pp. 88.

Culture: Pacific Islands

Twelve myths of how the gods created earth and life. Could be used in programs on Hawaii; mythology; legends; comparative folklore and Hawaiian folklore.

Main subjects: Hawaii; myths; legends; creation; folklore

Hawaiian Tales of Heroes and Champions
Illustrated by Herbert Kawainui Kane.
University of Hawaii Press, 1971.
ISBN: 0-8234-0192-8.

Culture: Pacific Islands

Tales of shape-shifters, magic powers and rare weapons; heroes and champions. Could be used in programs on Hawaii; comparative folklore; heroes; champions; mythology; legends and Hawaiian folklore.

Main subjects: Hawaii; heroes; champions; myths; legends; folklore

Peggy THOMSON

City Kids in China
Illustrated by Paul Conklin.
HarperCollins, 1991.
ISBN: 0-06-021654-9.

Culture: Chinese

Photo essay on children in China who live in cities. Could be used in programs on lifestyles; China and city life.

Reviewed in: *Booklist*
Main subjects: China; cities; lifestyles

Gioia TIMPANELLI

Tales from the Roof of the World: Folktales of Tibet
Illustrated by Elizabeth Kelly Lockwood.
Viking, 1984.
ISBN: 0-670-71249-3, pp. 53.

Culture: Tibetan

Four Tibetan folktales. Buddhist symbols are used in the borders of each page and notes at the end of the book explain their significance. The tales deal with karma, magic, love and forgiveness. Could be used in programs on comparative folktales; Tibet; Buddhism; comparative religion and Tibetan folklore.

Main subjects: Tibet; folktales; comparative folklore; Buddhism

Suelyn Ching TUNE

How Maui Slowed the Sun
Illustrated by Robin Yoko Burningham.
University of Hawaii Press, 1988.
ISBN: 0-8248-1083-X, pp. 32.

Culture: Pacific Islands

Maui lassoed the sun and forced it to slow down so men would have more time in the day to fish and work the fields; women would have more time to dry clothes and children more time to play. Could be used in programs on Hawaii; mythology; legends; heroes; comparative folklore and Hawaiian folklore.

Main subjects: Hawaii; Hawaiian folklore; legends; mythology

Yoshiko UCHIDA

Invisible Thread: an Autobiography, The
Julian Messner, 1991.
ISBN: 0-671-74163-2, pp. 152.

Culture: Japanese

Story of the author's childhood in Berkeley, California. She was a Nisei, second generation Japanese American. She and her family were confined to a concentration camp during World War II. Could be used in programs dealing with Japanese Americans; Nisei; concentration camps and World War II.

Awards received: ALA Best Books for Young Adults 1993
Reviewed in: *Booklist; Book Links*
Main subjects: Japanese Americans; Nisei; World War II; Japanese internment camps

David K. WRIGHT

Hong Kong
Series: Children of the World
Photos by David K. Wright.
Gareth Stevens Children's Books, 1990.
ISBN: 0-8368-0382-5, pp. 64.

Culture: Hong Kong

Introduces children to daily life in Hong Kong. It tells about ten year old Elisa and her family through photographs and text. Also provides information on Hong Kong's geography, demographics, language, currency, educational system, culture, industry and natural resources. Could be used to introduce children to Hong Kong; in programs on lifestyles; on China and foreign countries.

Special features: bibliography, research topics, activity projects and discussion of various aspects of life in Hong Kong
Main subjects: Hong Kong

Dana Ying-Hui WU and Jeffery Dao-Sheng TUNG

Chinese-American Experience
Series: Coming to America
Millbrook, 1993.
ISBN: 1-56294-271-9, pp. 64.

Culture: Chinese

Candid and unsentimental look at why Chinese immigrants came to the United States, what they left behind, the journey, what they found when they got here and how they are doing now. Includes some detailed history of the country they left. Black and white as well as color photos are used and box inserts provide additional information. Includes a good map and brief bibliography. Could be used in programs on Chinese Americans; immigrant experiences; history of immigration in the United States and changes in immigration laws.

Reviewed in: *Booklist*
Main subjects: Chinese Americans; immigrant experience; US history

Akinobu YANAGI

Australia
Series: Children of the World
Gareth Stevens, 1988.
ISBN: 1-55532-222-0, pp. 64.

Culture: Australian

Pictorial essay about a ten year old Australian boy named Scott Lowe. His parents work at a zoo which provides additional interest. The book includes a reference section, a short reading list, a glossary, an index and ideas for research projects and activities. Could be used in programs on Australia; zoos; lifestyles and family relationships.

Reviewed in: *Our Family, Our Friends, Our World* by Lyn Miller-Lachmann
Main subjects: Australia; lifestyles; zoos

Clara YEN

Why Rat Comes First: a Story of the Chinese Zodiac
Children's Book Press, 1991.
ISBN: 0892390727.

Culture: Chinese

The Chinese calendar cycle is twelve years and this book explains why Rat comes first in the cycle. Could be used in programs dealing with calendars; China and the zodiac.

Reviewed in: *Booklist; Kirkus; Publisher's Weekly*
Main subjects: Calendars; zodiac

Laurence YEP

Lost Garden, The
Julian Messner, 1991.
ISBN: 0671741608.

Culture: Chinese

The author tells of growing up in San Francisco, of being a Chinese American and how he learned to celebrate his ethnic heritage through his writing. Could be used in programs dealing with authors; autobiographies; Chinese Americans and San Francisco.

Reviewed in: *Booklinks; Kirkus; Publisher's Weekly; School Library Journal*
Main subjects: Chinese Americans; San Francisco; writers

Rainbow People, The
Illustrated by David Wiesner.
HarperCollins, 1989.
ISBN: 0-06-026761-5, pp. 190.

Culture: Chinese

Twenty folktales originally told by Chinese American immigrants. The stories are arranged by theme. Could be used in programs on folktales; Chinese Americans; Chinese folklore and comparative folklore.

Reviewed in: *Booklist; Kirkus*
Main subjects: Chinese Americans; folktales

Zheng ZHENSUN

Young Painter: the Life and Paintings of Wang Yani, A
Scholastic, 1991.
ISBN: 0590449060.

Culture: Chinese

Wang Yani, a young Chinese girl, began painting at the age of three and became the youngest artist to have a one person exhibition at the Smithsonian Institute. Could be used in programs dealing with art; artists; famous women; women; famous Chinese and Chinese.

Reviewed in: *Booklinks; Booklist; Kirkus; New York Times Book Review*
Main subjects: Chinese; artists; art; women; famous Chinese

APPENDICES

Alphabetical listing by author

                                                                       Culture

Buddhist Festivals	Asian Indian
Children's Sports In China	Asian
Hindu Festivals	Asian Indian
Muslim Festivals	Asian Indian
Andrews, Secret in the Dorm Attic, The	Pakistani
Alexander, Remarkable Journey of Prince Jen, The	Chinese
Allen, Panda	Chinese
Armitage, New Zealand	New Zealand
Armstrong, Chin Yu Min and the Ginger Cat	Chinese
Arnold, Australia Today	Australian
Walk on the Great Barrier Reef, A	Australian
Aruego, Crocodile's Tale: a Philippine Folk Story, A	Filipino
Ashabranner, Land of Yesterday, Land of Tomorrow: Discovering Chinese Central Asia	Chinese
Ashby, Family in South Korea, A	Korean
Ashley, Cleversticks	Chinese
Asian Cultural Centre, Folk Tales from Asia for Children Everywhere: Book Three	Asian
Bahree, Hindu World, The	Asian Indian
Bailey, Australia	Australian
Hong Kong	Hong Kong
India	Asian Indian
Japan	Japanese
Philippines	Filipino
Thailand	Thai
Baillie, Little Brother	Cambodian
Baker, Magic Fan, The	Japanese
Where the Forest Meets the Sea	Australian
Bang, Dawn	Japanese
Demons of Rajpur; Five Tales from Bengal	Asian Indian
Paper Crane, The	Japanese
Tye May and the Magic Brush	Chinese
Beach, Adventures of Rama, The	Asian Indian
Beirne, Pianist's Debut: Preparing for the Concert Stage, A	Korean

Culture

Bennett, Family in Sri Lanka, A	Sri Lankan
Birch, King's Chessboard, The	Asian Indian
Birdseye, Song of Stars, A	Chinese
Blia, Nine-in-one Grr! Grr! a Folktale from the Hmong People of Laos	Laotian
Boholm-Olsson, Tuan	Vietnamese
Bonnici, Festival, The	Asian Indian
Rains, The	Asian Indian
Borja, Making Chinese Papercuts	Chinese
Brillhart, Anna's Goodbye Apron	Multicultural
Broome, Dear Mr Sprouts	Australian
Brown, Chinese New Year	Chinese
Lee Ann: the story of a Vietnamese American Girl	Vietnamese
Browne, Aboriginal Family, An	Australian
Family in Australia, A	Australian
Bryan, Sh-ko and his Eight Wicked Brothers	Japanese
Bunting, Happy Funeral, The	Chinese
Burns, Take a Trip to New Zealand	New Zealand
Burstein, Dancer, The	Multicultural
Carpenter, Tales of a Chinese Grandmother	Chinese
Carrison, Cambodian Folk Stories from the Gatiloke	Cambodian
Cassedy, Red Dragonfly on My Shoulder	Japanese
Catterwell, Sebastian Lives in a Hat	Australian
Cawthorne, Who Killed Cockatoo?	Australian
Chan, Hmong Textile Designs	Laotian
Chang, Elaine and the Flying Frog	Chinese
Elaine, Mary Lewis and the Frogs	Chinese
In the Eye of War	Chinese
Choi, Year of Impossible Goodbyes	Korean
Christopher, Shortstop from Tokyo	Japanese
Chua-Eoan, Aquino	Filipino
Clark, In the Land of Small Dragon: a Vietnamese Folktale	Vietnamese
Clement, Painter and the Wild Swans, The	Japanese
Climo, Korean Cinderella, The	Korean
Cobb, This Place is Crowded: Japan	Japanese
Coerr, Chang's Paper Pony	Chinese
Mieko and the Fifth Treasure	Japanese
Sadako and the Thousand Paper Cranes	Japanese
Corwin, Asian Crafts	Japanese
Coutant, First Snow	Vietnamese
Crew, Children of the River	Cambodian
Crofford, Born in the Year of Courage	Japanese
Cumming, India	Asian Indian
Czernecki, Singing Snake	Australian
Das, Inside India	Asian Indian

Culture

Davis, Clues in the Desert	Pakistani
Dell, I. M. Pei	Chinese
Michael Chang: Tennis Champion	Chinese
Demi, Artist and the Architect, The	Chinese
Chen Ping and his Magic Axe	Chinese
Chinese Zoo: Fables and Proverbs, A	Chinese
Chingis Khan	Chinese
Demi's Dragons and Fantastic Creatures	Chinese
Dragon Kites and Dragonflies	Chinese
Empty Pot, The	Chinese
Hallowed Horse: a Folktale from India, The	Asian Indian
In the Eyes of the Cat: Japanese Poetry for all Seasons	Japanese
Liang and the Magic Paintbrush	Chinese
Magic Boat, The	Chinese
Donnelly, Wall of Names: the story of the Vietnam Veterans Memorial, A	Vietnamese
Dooley, Everybody Cooks Rice	Multicultural
Elkin, Family in Japan, A	Japanese
Ellis, Next-door Neighbors	Chinese
Els, Bombers' Moon, The	Chinese
Evans, Breakfast with the Birds	Chinese
Feeney, A is for Aloha	Pacific Islands
Hawaii is a Rainbow	Pacific Islands
Fisher, Great Wall of China, The	Chinese
Foster, Nien Cheng: Courage in China	Chinese
Fox, Possum Magic	Australian
Fraser, On Top of the World	Tibetan
Ten Mile Day	Multicultural
Friedman, How My Parents Learned to Eat	Japanese
Fritz, Homesick: My Own Story	Chinese
Fujimura, Ho-Limlim: a Rabbit Tale from Japan	Japanese
Fujiwara, Baachan! Geechan! Arigato: a Story of Japanese Canadians	Chinese
Fyson, Family in China, A	Chinese
Gajadin, Amal and the Letter from the King	Asian Indian
Galdone, Turtle and the Monkey: a Philippine Tale, The	Filipino
Garland, Lotus Seed, The	Vietnamese
Song of the Buffalo Boy	Vietnamese
Why Ducks Sleep on One Leg	Vietnamese
Garrett, Australia	Australian
Garrigue, Eternal Spring of Mr Ito, The	Japanese
Garrison, Dream Eater, The	Japanese
Georges, Asia	Asian
Australia	Australian
Gerstein, Mountains of Tibet	Tibetan

Culture

Giff, Mother Teresa: Sister to the Poor	Asian Indian
Gilbreath, Great Barrier Reef: a Treasure in the Sea, The	Australian
Ginsburg, Chinese Mirror, The	Korean
Girard, We Adopted You, Benjamin Koo	Korean
Godden, Fu-dog	Chinese
Valiant Chatti-Maker	Asian Indian
Goff, Early China	Chinese
Goldfarb, Fighters, Refugees, Immigrants: a Story of the Hmong	Laotian
Goldin, Red Means Good Fortune	Chinese
Goom, Family in Singapore, A	Singaporean
Gordon, Asian Indians	Asian Indian
Graff, Where a River Runs: a Portrait of a Refugee Family	Cambodian
Greene, Indira Nehru Gandhi: Ruler of India	Asian Indian
Japan	Japanese
Gregory, Yellow River, The	Chinese
Gunner, Family in Australia, A	Australian
Hamanaka, Journey: Japanese Americans, Racism, and Renewal	Japanese
Screen of Frogs: an old tale	Japanese
Han, Sir Whong and the Golden Pig	Korean
Harkonen, Children of China, The	Chinese
Children of Nepal, The	Nepalese
Haskins, Count Your Way Through China	Chinese
Count Your Way Through India	Asian Indian
Count Your Way Through Japan	Japanese
Count Your Way Through Korea	Korean
Haugaard, Boy and the Samurai	Japanese
Hayashi, Aki and the Fox	Japanese
Heyer, Weaving of a Dream: a Chinese Folktale, The	Chinese
Hidaka, Girl from the Snow Country	Chinese
Higa, Girl with the White Flag	Japanese
Higham, Maoris, The	New Zealand
Hillman, Min-Yo and the Moon Dragon	Chinese
Ho, Clay Marble	Cambodian
Hodges, Voice of the Great Bell, The	Chinese
Hong, How the Ox Star Fell from Heaven	Chinese
Two of Everything	Chinese
Hoobler, Aloha Means Come Back: the story of a World War II Girl	Japanese
Vietnam: Why We Fought	Vietnamese
Hooks, Peach Boy	Japanese
Horton, What Comes in Spring	Asian
Howard, Her Own Song	Chinese
Hoyt-Goldsmith, Hoang Anh: a Vietnamese American Boy	Vietnamese

                                                  Culture

Hughes, Little Fingerling: a Japanese Folktale	Japanese
Hunter, Gandhi	Asian Indian
Huynh, Land I Lost: Adventures of a boy in Vietnam, The	Vietnamese
Ike, Japanese Fairytale, A	Japanese
Ikeda, Cherry Tree, The	Japanese
Over the Deep Blue Sea	Japanese
Princess and the Moon, The	Japanese
Snow Country Prince, The	Japanese
Ishii, Tongue-cut Sparrow, The	Japanese
Jacobsen, Family in India, A	Asian Indian
Jaffrey, Seasons of Splendor: Tales, Myths, and Legends of India	Asian Indian
Jagendorf, Magic Boat and Other Chinese Folk Stories, The	Chinese
James, Australia	Australian
Johnson, Great Barrier Reef: a Living Laboratory, The	Australian
Kenji and the Magic Geese	Japanese
Step into China	Chinese
Johnston, Badger and the Magic Fan: A Japanese Folk Tale, The	Japanese
Kamal, Bird Who Was an Elephant, The	Asian Indian
Kamen, Ringdoves, The	Asian Indian
Kapoor, Sikh Festivals	Asian Indian
Kasper, Street of Three Directions	Chinese
Kendall, Sweet and Sour: Tales from China	Chinese
Wedding of the Rat Family, The	Chinese
Kimmel, Greatest of All: A Japanese Folktale, The	Japanese
Klein, Hating Allison Ashley	Australian
Kline, Horrible Harry's Secret	Korean
Knowlton, Burma	Burmese
India	Asian Indian
Kogawa, Naomi's Road	Japanese
Kraus, Tall Boy's Journey	Korean
Krensky, Iron Dragon Never Sleeps	Chinese
Krull, City Within a City: How Kids Live in New York's Chinatown	Chinese
Kuklin, When I See My Doctor	Asian
Kwon, Moles and the Mireuk: a Korean Folktale, The	Korean
Lattimore, Little Pear and His Friends	Chinese
Leaf, Eyes of the Dragon	Chinese
Lee, Ba-nam	Vietnamese
Finding My Voice	Korean
Legend of the Li River: an Ancient Chinese Tale	Chinese
Legend of the Milky Way	Chinese
Silent Lotus	Vietnamese
Toad is the Uncle of Heaven	Vietnamese

                                                                    Culture

Lepthien, Corazon Aquino: President of the   Filipino
    Philippines
Levine, Boy Who Drew Cats, The   Japanese
        I Hate English!   Chinese
Levinson, Our Home is the Sea   Hong Kong
Levitin, Golem and the Dragon Girl   Chinese
Lewis, In the Night, Still Dark   Pacific Islands
        Young Fu of the Upper Yangtze   Chinese
Lifton, Joji and the Dragon   Japanese
Lightfoot, Mekong, The   Asian
Lim, West Coast Chinese Boy   Chinese
Liyi, Spring of Butterflies and Other Folktales of   Chinese
    China's Minority Peoples
Lobel, Ming Lo Moves the Mountain   Chinese
Loh, Tucking Mommy In   Asian
Lord, In the Year of the Boar and Jackie Robinson   Chinese
Louie, Yeh-shen: a Cinderella story from China   Chinese
Luenn, Dragon Kite, The   Japanese
Lye, Take a Trip to Indonesia   Indonesian
        Take a Trip to Nepal   Nepalese
MacDougall, Beyond Dreamtime: the Life and Lore of   Australian
    the Aboriginal Australian
MacMillan, My Best Friend Duc Tran: Meeting a   Vietnamese
        Vietnamese American Family
        My Best Friend Mee-yung Kim: Meeting   Korean
        a Korean-American Family
Mahy, Good Fortunes Gang   Australian
Margolies, Kanu of Kathmandu: a Journey in Nepal   Nepalese
Marriott, Letters to Lesley   Australian
Martin, Foolish Rabbit's Big Mistake   Asian Indian
        Yours Truly, Shirley   Vietnamese
Maruki, Hiroshima No Pika   Japanese
Mason, Take a Trip to China   Chinese
Mathieson, Very Special Sari: a Story Set in India, The Asian Indian
Mattingley, Miracle Tree, The   Japanese
Mayberry, Chinese   Chinese
        Filipinos   Filipino
McClung, Lili: a Giant Panda of Sichuan   Chinese
McCoy, Tale of Two Tengu, A   Japanese
McDearmon, Giant Pandas   Chinese
McDermott, Stone Cutter: a Japanese Folktale, The   Japanese
McDonald, Mail-order Kid   Korean
McGuire, Southeast Asians   Asian
McKenna, Family in Hong Kong, A   Hong Kong
McMahon, Chi-hoon: a Korean Girl   Korean
McNair, Indonesia   Indonesian
Medicott, Tales for Telling: from Around the World   Multicultural

Culture

Melmed, First Song Ever Sung	Japanese
Merrill, Girl Who Loved Caterpillars: A Twelfth Century Tale from Japan, The	Japanese
Miller, Moon Dragon, The	Chinese
Mochizuki, Baseball Saved Us	Japanese
Morey, Famous Asian Americans	Chinese
Mori, Shizuko's Daughter	Japanese
Morimoto, Inch Boy, The	Japanese
Mouse's Marriage, The	Japanese
My Hiroshima	Japanese
Morris, Magic Leaf, The	Chinese
Monkey and the White Bone Demon	Chinese
Mosel, Funny Little Woman, The	Japanese
Nakano, Easy Origami	Japanese
Nakawatari, Sea And I	Japanese
Namioka, Coming of the Bear	Japanese
Yang the Youngest and His Terrible Ear	Chinese
Narahashi, I Have a Friend	Asian
Newton, Five Sparrows: a Japanese Folktale, The	Japanese
Nhuong, Land I Lost, The	Vietnamese
Nomura, Grandfather's Town	Japanese
Norman, Paddock: a Story in Praise of the Earth, The	Australian
O'Brien, Princess and the Beggar: a Korean Folktale	Korean
Otsuka, Suho and the White Horse: a Legend of Mongolia	Mongolian
Paek, Aekyung's Dream	Korean
Palecek, Magic Grove, The	Asian
Park, Playing Beatie Bow	Australian
Patent, Shanghai Passage	Chinese
Paterson, Park's Quest	Vietnamese
Tale of the Mandarin Ducks, The	Japanese
Pattison, River Dragon	Chinese
Peng, Fun With Chinese Festivals	Chinese
Pepper, Australia	Australian
Perkins, Sunita Experiment, The	Asian Indian
Phipson, Tide Flowing, The	Australian
Pinkwater, Wingman, The	Chinese
Pittman, Gift of the Willows, The	Japanese
Grain of Rice, A	Chinese
Ram, Rama and Sita: an Indian Folk Tale	Asian Indian
Rana, Roller Birds of Rampur, The	Asian Indian
Rappaport, Journey of Meng: a Chinese Legend	Chinese
Rau, Red Earth, Blue Sky: The Australian Outback	Australian
Reddix, Dragon Kite of the Autumn Moon	Taiwanese
Reuter, Princess, and the Sun, Moon, and Stars, The	Chinese
Reynolds, Down Under	Australian
Himalaya	Tibetan

Culture

Rhee, Magic Spring: a Korean Folktale	Korean
Rodanas, Story of Wali Dad, The	Asian Indian
Rosen, Conquest of Everest, The	Nepalese
Roughsey, Giant Devil-dingo, The	Australian
Roy, Thousand Pails of Water, A	Japanese
Sadler, Heaven's Reward: Fairy Tales from China	Chinese
Two Chinese Families	Chinese
Sakai, Sachiko Means Happiness	Japanese
San Souci, Enchanted Tapestry, The	Chinese
Samurai's Daughter: a Japanese Legend	Japanese
Snow Wife	Japanese
Sasaki, Snow	Asian
Sato, I Wish I Had a Big, Big Tree	Japanese
Savin, Moon Bridge	Japanese
Say, Bicycle Man, The	Japanese
El Chino	Chinese
Feast of Lanterns, The	Japanese
Grandfather's Journey	Japanese
Lost Lake	Asian American
River Dream, A	Asian
Tree of Cranes	Japanese
Scarboro, Secret Language of the Sb, The	Taiwanese
Scariano, Picture Life of Corazon Aquino, The	Filipino
Scarsbrook, Family in Pakistan, A	Pakistani
Schecter, Sim Chung and the River Dragon: a Folktale from Korea	Korean
Schlein, Year of the Panda, The	Chinese
Serfozo, Who Said Red?	Asian
Seros, Sun and Moon: Fairy Tales from Korea	Korean
Shalant, Look What We've Brought You from Vietnam	Vietnamese
Sharma, Blue Jackal, The	Asian Indian
Shepard, Savitri: A Tale of Ancient India	Asian Indian
Shigekawa, Blue Jay in the Desert	Japanese
Shui, Chinese Food and Drink	Chinese
Shute, Momotaro: the Peach Boy	Japanese
Simon, Seiji Ozawa: Symphony Conductor	Japanese
Singh, Fat Gopal	Asian Indian
Sis, Komodo!	Indonesian
Snyder, Boy of the Three-year Nap, The	Japanese
Sobol, We Don't Look Like Our Mom and Dad	Korean
Soto, Pacific Crossing	Japanese
Soya, House of Leaves, A	Asian
Spagnoli, Judge Rabbit and the Tree Spirit: Folktale from Cambodia	Cambodian
Spence, Devil's Hole, The	Australian
Stamm, Three Strong Women: a Tall Tale from Japan	Japanese
Stanek, We Came from Vietnam	Vietnamese

ALPHABETICAL LISTING BY AUTHOR

Culture

Stanley, Last Princess: the story of Princess Ka'iulani of Hawaii, The	Pacific Islands
Stock, Emma's Dragon Hunt	Chinese
Surat, Angel Child, Dragon Child	Vietnamese
Svend, Children of the Yangtze River	Chinese
Tagore, Paper Boats	Asian Indian
Takashima, Child in Prison Camp, A	Japanese
Takeshita, Park Bench, The	Japanese
Talan, China	Chinese
Terada, Under the Starfruit Tree: Folktales from Vietnam	Vietnamese
Thiele, Fire in the Stone	Australian
Shadow Shark	Australian
Thompson, Hawaiian Myths of Earth, Sea, and Sky	Pacific Islands
Hawaiian Tales of Heroes and Champions	Pacific Islands
Story of Prince Rama, The	Asian Indian
Thomson, City Kids in China	Chinese
Family in Thailand, A	Thai
Timpanelli, Tales from the Roof of the World: Folktales of Tibet	Tibetan
Tompert, Bamboo Hats and a Rice Cake	Japanese
Grandfather Tang's Story	Chinese
Torre, Luminous Pearl	Chinese
Tran, Little Weaver of Thai-yen Village, The	Vietnamese
Tresize, Peopling of Australia, The	Australian
Trinca, One Woolly Wombat	Australian
Tsuchiya, Faithful Elephants: a True Story of Animals, People and War	Japanese
Tsutsui, Anna in Charge	Japanese
Anna's Secret Friend	Japanese
Anna's Special Present	Japanese
Before the Picnic	Japanese
Tune, How Maui Slowed the Sun	Pacific Islands
Tung, One Small Dog	Chinese
Turner, Through Moon and Stars and Night Skies	Asian American
Uchida, Best Bad Thing, The	Japanese
Birthday Visitor, The	Japanese
Bracelet, The	Japanese
Happiest Ending, The	Japanese
Invisible Thread: An Autobiography, The	Japanese
Jar of Dreams, A	Japanese
Journey Home, The	Japanese
Journey to Topaz	Japanese
Magic Listening Cap: More Folk Tales from Japan	Japanese
Magic Purse, The	Japanese
Rooster Who Understood Japanese, The	Japanese

Culture

Two Foolish Cats, The	Japanese
Villanueva, Nene and the Horrible Math Monster	Filipino
Vuong, Brocaded Slipper and Other Vietnamese Tales, The	Vietnamese
Waters, Lion Dancer: Ernie Wan's Chinese New Year	Chinese
Watkins, Tales from the Bamboo Grove	Japanese
Wettasinghe, Umbrella Thief, The	Sri Lankan
Wetzel, Christmas Box, The	Japanese
Wheatley, My Place	Australian
Whelan, Goodbye, Vietnam	Vietnamese
Whittle, Fisherman's Tale	Asian
Williams, And the Birds Appeared	Pacific Islands
Wilson, Acacia Terrace	Australian
Winthrop, Journey to the Bright Kingdom	Japanese
Wisniewski, Warrior and the Wise Man, The	Japanese
Wolkstein, Magic Wings, The	Chinese
White Wave: a Chinese Tale	Chinese
Wright, Hong Kong	Hong Kong
Wrightson, Ice is Coming	Australian
Wu, Chinese-American Experience	Chinese
Wyndham, Chinese Mother Goose Rhymes	Chinese
Yacowitz, Jade Stone: a Chinese Folktale	Chinese
Yagawa, Crane Wife	Japanese
Yanagi, Australia	Australian
Yashinsky, Storyteller at Fault, The	Multicultural
Ye, Bawshou Rescues the Sun: a Han Folktale	Chinese
Yee, Roses Sing on New Snow: a Delicious Tale	Chinese
Tales from Gold Mountain: Stories of the Chinese in the New World	Chinese
Yen, Why Rat Comes First: a Story of the Chinese Zodiac	Chinese
Yep, Child of the Owl	Chinese
Lost Garden, The	Chinese
Man Who Tricked a Ghost, The	Chinese
Rainbow People, The	Chinese
Sea Glass	Chinese
Shell Woman and the King: a Chinese Folktale	Chinese
Star Fisher	Chinese
Tongues of Jade	Chinese
Ying, Monkey Creates Havoc in Heaven	Chinese
Yolen, Emperor and the Kite, The	Chinese
Girl Who Loved the Wind, The	Asian
Seeing Stick, The	Chinese
Seventh Mandarin, The	Asian
Young, Lon Po Po	Chinese
Red Thread	Chinese
Yu, Family in Taiwan, A	Taiwanese

Culture

Zhensun, Young Painter: the Life and Paintings of Wang Yani, A   Chinese
Zimelman, I Will Tell You of Peach Stone   Chinese

Alphabetical listing by title

                                                                                 Culture

Title	Culture
A is for Aloha, Feeney	Pacific Islands
Aboriginal Family, An, Browne	Australian
Acacia Terrace, Wilson	Australian
Adventures of Rama, The, Beach	Asian Indian
Aekyung's Dream, Paek	Korean
Aki and the Fox, Hayashi	Japanese
Aloha Means Come Back: the Story of a World War II Girl, Hoobler	Japanese
Amal and the Letter from the King, Gajadin	Asian Indian
And the Birds Appeared, Williams	Pacific Islands
Angel Child, Dragon Child, Surat	Vietnamese
Anna in Charge, Tsutsui	Japanese
Anna's Goodbye Apron, Brillhart	Multicultural
Anna's Secret Friend, Tsutsui	Japanese
Anna's Special Present, Tsutsui	Japanese
Aquino, Chua-Eoan	Filipino
Artist and the Architect, The, Demi	Chinese
Asia, Georges	Asian
Asian Crafts, Corwin	Japanese
Asian Indians, Gordon	Asian Indian
Australia, Bailey	Australian
Australia, Garrett	Australian
Australia, Georges	Australian
Australia, James	Australian
Australia, Pepper	Australian
Australia, Yanagi	Australian
Australia Today, Arnold	Australian
Ba-nam, Lee	Vietnamese
Baachan! Geechan! Arigato: a Story of Japanese Canadians, Fujiwara	Chinese
Badger and the Magic Fan: a Japanese Folk Tale, The, Johnston	Japanese
Bamboo Hats and a Rice Cake, Tompert	Japanese
Baseball Saved Us, Mochizuki	Japanese
Bawshou Rescues the Sun: a Han Folktale, Ye	Chinese

ALPHABETICAL LISTING BY TITLE 193

Culture

Before the Picnic, Tsutsui	Japanese
Best Bad Thing, The, Uchida	Japanese
Beyond Dreamtime: the Life and Lore of the Aboriginal Australian, MacDougall	Australian
Bicycle Man, The, Say	Japanese
Bird Who Was an Elephant, The, Kamal	Asian Indian
Birthday Visitor, The, Uchida	Japanese
Blue Jackal, The, Sharma	Asian Indian
Blue Jay in the Desert, Shigekawa	Japanese
Bombers' Moon, The, Els	Chinese
Born in the Year of Courage, Crofford	Japanese
Boy and the Samurai, Haugaard	Japanese
Boy of the Three-year Nap, The, Snyder	Japanese
Boy Who Drew Cats, The, Levine	Japanese
Bracelet, The, Uchida	Japanese
Breakfast With the Birds, Evans	Chinese
Brocaded Slipper and Other Vietnamese Tales, The, Vuong	Vietnamese
Buddhist Festivals	Asian Indian
Burma, Knowlton	Burmese
Cambodian Folk Stories from the Gatiloke, Carrison	Cambodian
Chang's Paper Pony, Coerr	Chinese
Chen Ping and His Magic Axe, Demi	Chinese
Cherry Tree, The, Ikeda	Japanese
Chi-hoon: a Korean Girl, McMahon	Korean
Child in Prison Camp, A, Takashima	Japanese
Child of the Owl, Yep	Chinese
Children of China, The, Harkonen	Chinese
Children of Nepal, The, Harkonen	Nepalese
Children of the River, Crew	Cambodian
Children of the Yangtze River, Svend	Chinese
Children's Sports in China	Asian
Chin Yu Min and the Ginger Cat, Armstrong	Chinese
China, Talan	Chinese
Chinese, Mayberry	Chinese
Chinese Food and Drink, Shui	Chinese
Chinese Mirror, The, Ginsburg	Korean
Chinese Mother Goose Rhymes, Wyndham	Chinese
Chinese New Year, Brown	Chinese
Chinese Zoo: Fables and Proverbs, A, Demi	Chinese
Chinese-American Experience, Wu	Chinese
Chingis Khan, Demi	Chinese
Christmas Box, The, Wetzel	Japanese
City Kids in China, Thomson	Chinese
City Within a City: How Kids Live in New York's Chinatown, Krull	Chinese
Clay Marble, Ho	Cambodian

Culture

Cleversticks, Ashley	Chinese
Clues in the Desert, Davis	Pakistani
Coming of the Bear, Namioka	Japanese
Conquest of Everest, The, Rosen	Nepalese
Corazon Aquino: President of the Philippines, Lepthien	Filipino
Count Your Way Through China, Haskins	Chinese
Count Your Way Through India, Haskins	Asian Indian
Count Your Way Through Japan, Haskins	Japanese
Count Your Way Through Korea, Haskins	Korean
Crane Wife, Yagawa	Japanese
Crocodile's Tale: a Philippine Folk Story, A, Aruego	Filipino
Dancer, The, Burstein	Multicultural
Dawn, Bang	Japanese
Dear Mr Sprouts, Broome	Australian
Demi's Dragons and Fantastic Creatures, Demi	Chinese
Demi's Reflective Fables, Demi	Chinese
Demons of Rajpur; Five Tales from Bengal, Bang	Asian Indian
Devil's Hole, The, Spence	Australian
Down Under, Reynolds	Australian
Dragon Kite, The, Luenn	Japanese
Dragon Kite of the Autumn Moon, Reddix	Taiwanese
Dragon Kites and Dragonflies, Demi	Chinese
Dream Eater, The, Garrison	Japanese
Early China, Goff	Chinese
Easy Origami, Nakano	Japanese
El Chino, Say,	Chinese
Elaine and the Flying Frog, Chang	Chinese
Elaine, Mary Lewis and the Frogs, Chang	Chinese
Emma's Dragon Hunt, Stock	Chinese
Emperor and the Kite, The, Yolen	Chinese
Empty Pot, The, Demi	Chinese
Enchanted Tapestry, The, San Souci	Chinese
Eternal Spring of Mr Ito, The, Garrigue	Japanese
Everybody Cooks Rice, Dooley	Multicultural
Eyes of the Dragon, Leaf	Chinese
Faithful Elephants: a True Story of Animals, People and War, Tsuchiya	Japanese
Family in Australia, A, Browne	Australian
Family in Australia, A, Gunner	Australian
Family in China, A, Fyson	Chinese
Family in Hong Kong, A, McKenna	Hong Kong
Family in India, A, Jacobsen	Asian Indian
Family in Japan, A, Elkin	Japanese
Family in Pakistan, A, Scarsbrook	Pakistani
Family in Singapore, A, Goom	Singaporean
Family in South Korea, A, Ashby	Korean

Culture

Family in Sri Lanka, A, Bennett	Sri Lankan
Family in Taiwan, A, Yu	Taiwanese
Family in Thailand, A, Thomson	Thai
Famous Asian Americans, Morey	Chinese
Fat Gopal, Singh	Asian Indian
Feast of Lanterns, The, Say	Japanese
Festival, The, Bonnici	Asian Indian
Fighters, Refugees, Immigrants: a Story of the Hmong, Goldfarb	Laotian
Filipinos, Mayberry	Filipino
Finding My Voice, Lee	Korean
Fire in the Stone, Thiele	Australian
First Snow, Coutant	Vietnamese
First Song Ever Sung, Melmed	Japanese
Fisherman's Tale, Whittle	Asian
Five Sparrows: a Japanese Folktale, The, Newton	Japanese
Folk Tales from Asia for Children Everywhere: Book Three, Asian Cultural Centre	Asian
Foolish Rabbit's Big Mistake, Martin	Asian Indian
Fu-dog, Godden	Chinese
Fun With Chinese Festivals, Peng	Chinese
Funny Little Woman, The, Mosel	Japanese
Gandhi, Hunter	Asian Indian
Giant Devil-dingo, The, Roughsey	Australian
Giant Pandas, McDearmon	Chinese
Gift of the Willows, The, Pittman	Japanese
Girl from the Snow Country, Hidaka	Chinese
Girl Who Loved Caterpillars: a Twelfth Century Tale from Japan, The, Merrill	Japanese
Girl Who Loved the Wind, The, Yolen	Asian
Girl With the White Flag, Higa	Japanese
Golem and the Dragon Girl, Levitin	Chinese
Good Fortunes Gang, Mahy	Australian
Goodbye, Vietnam, Whelan	Vietnamese
Grain of Rice, A, Pittman	Chinese
Grandfather Tang's Story, Tompert	Chinese
Grandfather's Journey, Say	Japanese
Grandfather's Town, Nomura	Japanese
Great Barrier Reef: a Living Laboratory, The, Johnson	Australian
Great Barrier Reef: a Treasure in the Sea, The, Gilbreath	Australian
Great Wall of China, The, Fisher	Chinese
Greatest of All: a Japanese Folktale, The, Kimmel	Japanese
Hallowed Horse: a Folktale from India, The, Demi	Asian Indian
Happiest Ending, The, Uchida	Japanese
Happy Funeral, The, Bunting	Chinese
Hating Allison Ashley, Klein	Australian

ALPHABETICAL LISTING BY TITLE

Culture

Hawaii is a Rainbow, Feeney	Pacific Islands
Hawaiian Myths of Earth, Sea, and Sky, Thompson	Pacific Islands
Hawaiian Tales of Heroes and Champions, Thompson	Pacific Islands
Heaven's Reward: Fairy Tales from China, Sadler	Chinese
Her Own Song, Howard	Chinese
Himalaya, Reynolds	Tibetan
Hindu Festivals	Asian Indian
Hindu World, The, Bahree	Asian Indian
Hiroshima No Pika, Maruki	Japanese
Hmong Textile Designs, Chan	Laotian
Ho-Limlim: a Rabbit Tale from Japan, Fujimura	Japanese
Hoang Anh: a Vietnamese American Boy, Hoyt-Goldsmith	Vietnamese
Homesick: My Own Story, Fritz	Chinese
Hong Kong, Bailey	Hong Kong
Hong Kong, Wright	Hong Kong
Horrible Harry's Secret, Kline	Korean
House of Leaves, A, Soya	Asian
How Maui Slowed the Sun, Tune	Pacific Islands
How My Parents Learned to Eat, Friedman	Japanese
How the Ox Star Fell from Heaven, Hong	Chinese
I Hate English!, Levine	Chinese
I Have a Friend, Narahashi	Asian
I Will Tell You of Peach Stone, Zimelman	Chinese
I Wish I Had a Big, Big Tree, Sato	Japanese
I. M. Pei, Dell	Chinese
Ice is Coming, Wrightson	Australian
In the Eye of War, Chang	Chinese
In the Eyes of the Cat: Japanese Poetry for all Seasons, Demi	Japanese
In the Land of Small Dragon: a Vietnamese Folktale, Clark	Vietnamese
In the Night, Still Dark, Lewis	Pacific Islands
In the Year of the Boar and Jackie Robinson, Lord	Chinese
Inch Boy, The, Morimoto	Japanese
India, Bailey	Asian Indian
India, Cumming	Asian Indian
India, Knowlton	Asian Indian
Indira Nehru Gandhi: Ruler of India, Greene	Asian Indian
Indonesia, McNair	Indonesian
Inside India, Das	Asian Indian
Invisible Thread: an Autobiography, The, Uchida	Japanese
Iron Dragon Never Sleeps, Krensky	Chinese
Jade Stone: a Chinese Folktale, Yacowitz	Chinese
Japan, Bailey	Japanese
Japan, Greene	Japanese
Japanese Fairytale, A, Ike	Japanese

ALPHABETICAL LISTING BY TITLE

Culture

Jar of Dreams, A, Uchida	Japanese
Joji and the Dragon, Lifton	Japanese
Journey Home, The, Uchida	Japanese
Journey of Meng: a Chinese Legend, Rappaport	Chinese
Journey to the Bright Kingdom, Winthrop	Japanese
Journey to Topaz, Uchida	Japanese
Journey: Japanese Americans, Racism, and Renewal, Hamanaka	Japanese
Judge Rabbit and the Tree Spirit: a Folktale from Cambodia, Spagnoli	Cambodian
Kanu of Kathmandu: a Journey in Nepal, Margolies	Nepalese
Kenji and the Magic Geese, Johnson	Japanese
King's Chessboard, The, Birch	Asian Indian
Komodo!, Sis	Indonesian
Korean Cinderella, The, Climo	Korean
Land I Lost, The, Nhuong	Vietnamese
Land I Lost: Adventures of a Boy in Vietnam, The, Huynh	Vietnamese
Land of Yesterday, Land of Tomorrow: Discovering Chinese Central Asia, Ashabranner	Chinese
Last Princess: the Story of Princess Ka'iulani of Hawaii, The, Stanley	Pacific Islands
Lee Ann: the Story of a Vietnamese American Girl, Brown	Vietnamese
Legend of the Li River: an Ancient Chinese Tale, Lee	Chinese
Legend of the Milky Way, Lee	Chinese
Letters to Lesley, Marriott	Australian
Liang and the Magic Paintbrush, Demi	Chinese
Lili: a Giant Panda of Sichuan, McClung	Chinese
Lion Dancer: Ernie Wan's Chinese New Year, Waters	Chinese
Little Brother, Baillie	Cambodian
Little Fingerling: a Japanese Folktale, Hughes	Japanese
Little Pear and His Friends, Lattimore	Chinese
Little Weaver of Thai-yen Village, The, Tran	Vietnamese
Lon Po Po, Young	Chinese
Look What We've Brought You from Vietnam, Shalant	Vietnamese
Lost Garden, The, Yep	Chinese
Lost Lake, Say	Asian American
Lotus Seed, The, Garland	Vietnamese
Luminous Pearl, Torre	Chinese
Magic Boat, The, Demi	Chinese
Magic Boat and Other Chinese Folk Stories, The, Jagendorf	Chinese
Magic Fan, The, Baker	Japanese
Magic Grove, The, Palecek	Asian
Magic Leaf, The, Morris	Chinese

ALPHABETICAL LISTING BY TITLE

Culture

Magic Listening Cap: More Folk Tales from Japan, Uchida	Japanese
Magic Purse, The, Uchida	Japanese
Magic Spring: a Korean Folktale, Rhee	Korean
Magic Wings, The, Wolkstein	Chinese
Mail-order Kid, McDonald	Korean
Making Chinese Papercuts, Borja	Chinese
Man Who Tricked a Ghost, The, Yep	Chinese
Maoris, The, Higham	New Zealand
Mekong, The, Lightfoot	Asian
Michael Chang: Tennis Champion, Dell	Chinese
Mieko and the Fifth Treasure, Coerr	Japanese
Min-Yo and the Moon Dragon, Hillman	Chinese
Ming Lo Moves the Mountain, Lobel	Chinese
Miracle Tree, The, Mattingley	Japanese
Moles and the Mireuk: a Korean Folktale, The, Kwon	Korean
Momotaro: the Peach Boy, Shute	Japanese
Monkey and the White Bone Demon, Morris	Chinese
Monkey Creates Havoc in Heaven, Ying	Chinese
Moon Bridge, Savin	Japanese
Moon Dragon, The, Miller	Chinese
Mother Teresa: Sister to the Poor, Giff	Asian Indian
Mountains of Tibet, Gerstein	Tibetan
Mouse's Marriage, The, Morimoto	Japanese
Muslim Festivals,	Asian Indian
My Best Friend Duc Tran: Meeting a Vietnamese American Family, MacMillan	Vietnamese
My Best Friend, Mee-yung Kim: Meeting a Korean-American Family, MacMillan	Korean
My Hiroshima, Morimoto	Japanese
My Place, Wheatley	Australian
Naomi's Road, Kogawa	Japanese
Nene and the Horrible Math Monster, Villanueva	Filipino
New Zealand, Armitage	New Zealand
Next-door Neighbors, Ellis	Chinese
Nien Cheng: Courage in China, Foster	Chinese
Nine-in-one Grr! Grr! a Folktale from the Hmong People of Laos, Blia	Laotian
On Top of the World, Fraser	Tibetan
One Small Dog, Tung	Chinese
One Woolly Wombat, Trinca	Australian
Our Home is the Sea, Levinson	Hong Kong
Over the Deep Blue Sea, Ikeda	Japanese
Pacific Crossing, Soto	Japanese
Paddock: a Story in Praise of the Earth, The, Norman	Australian
Painter and the Wild Swans, The, Clement	Japanese
Panda, Allen	Chinese

  Culture

Paper Boats, Tagore   Asian Indian
Paper Crane, The, Bang   Japanese
Park Bench, The, Takeshita   Japanese
Park's Quest, Paterson   Vietnamese
Peach Boy, Hooks   Japanese
Peopling of Australia, The, Tresize   Australian
Philippines, Bailey   Filipino
Pianist's Debut: Preparing for the Concert Stage, A,   Korean
  Beirne
Picture Life of Corazon Aquino, The, Scariano   Filipino
Playing Beatie Bow, Park   Australian
Possum Magic, Fox   Australian
Princess and the Beggar: a Korean Folktale, O'Brien   Korean
Princess and the Moon, The, Ikeda   Japanese
Princess, and the Sun, Moon, and Stars, The, Reuter   Chinese
Rainbow People, The, Yep   Chinese
Rains, The, Bonnici   Asian Indian
Rama and Sita: an Indian Folk Tale, Ram   Asian Indian
Red Dragonfly on My Shoulder, Cassedy   Japanese
Red Earth, Blue Sky: the Australian Outback, Rau   Australian
Red Means Good Fortune, Goldin   Chinese
Red Thread, Young   Chinese
Remarkable Journey of Prince Jen, The, Alexander   Chinese
Ringdoves, The, Kamen   Asian Indian
River Dragon, Pattison   Chinese
River Dream, A, Say   Asian
Roller Birds of Rampur, The, Rana   Asian Indian
Rooster Who Understood Japanese, The, Uchida   Japanese
Roses Sing on New Snow: a Delicious Tale, Yee   Chinese
Sachiko Means Happiness, Sakai   Japanese
Sadako and the Thousand Paper Cranes, Coerr   Japanese
Samurai's Daughter: a Japanese Legend, San Souci   Japanese
Savitri: a Tale of Ancient India, Shepard   Asian Indian
Screen of Frogs: an Old Tale, Hamanaka   Japanese
Sea and I, Nakawatari   Japanese
Sea Glass, Yep,   Chinese
Seasons of Splendor: Tales, Myths, and Legends of   Asian Indian
  India, Jaffrey
Sebastian Lives in a Hat, Catterwell   Australian
Secret in the Dorm Attic, The, Andrews   Pakistani
Secret Language of the Sb, The, Scarboro   Taiwanese
Seeing Stick, The, Yolen   Chinese
Seiji Ozawa: Symphony Conductor, Simon   Japanese
Seventh Mandarin, The, Yolen   Asian
Sh-ko and His Eight Wicked Brothers, Bryan   Japanese
Shadow Shark, Thiele   Australian
Shanghai Passage, Patent   Chinese

Culture

Shell Woman and the King: a Chinese Folktale, Yep	Chinese
Shizuko's Daughter, Mori	Japanese
Shortstop from Tokyo, Christopher	Japanese
Sikh Festivals, Kapoor	Asian Indian
Silent Lotus, Lee	Vietnamese
Sim Chung and the River Dragon: a Folktale from Korea, Schecter	Korean
Singing Snake, Czernecki	Australian
Sir Whong and the Golden Pig, Han	Korean
Snow, Sasaki	Asian
Snow Country Prince, The, Ikeda	Japanese
Snow Wife, San Souci	Japanese
Song of Stars, A, Birdseye	Chinese
Song of the Buffalo Boy, Garland	Vietnamese
Southeast Asians, McGuire	Asian
Spring of Butterflies and Other Folktales of China's Minority Peoples, Liyi	Chinese
Star Fisher, Yep	Chinese
Step Into China, Johnson	Chinese
Stone Cutter: a Japanese Folktale, The, McDermott	Japanese
Story of Prince Rama, The, Thompson	Asian Indian
Story of Wali Dad, The, Rodanas	Asian Indian
Storyteller at Fault, The, Yashinsky	Multicultural
Street of Three Directions, Kasper	Chinese
Suho and the White Horse: a Legend of Mongolia, Otsuka	Mongolian
Sun and Moon: Fairy Tales from Korea, Seros	Korean
Sunita Experiment, The, Perkins	Asian Indian
Sweet and Sour: Tales from China, Kendall	Chinese
Take a Trip to China, Mason	Chinese
Take a Trip to Indonesia, Lye	Indonesian
Take a Trip to Nepal, Lye	Nepalese
Take a Trip to New Zealand, Burns	New Zealand
Tale of the Mandarin Ducks, The, Paterson	Japanese
Tale of Two Tengu, A, McCoy	Japanese
Tales for Telling: from Around the World, Medicott	Multicultural
Tales from the Bamboo Grove, Watkins	Japanese
Tales from Gold Mountain: Stories of the Chinese in the New World, Yee	Chinese
Tales from the Roof of the World: Folktales of Tibet, Timpanelli	Tibetan
Tales of a Chinese Grandmother, Carpenter	Chinese
Tall Boy's Journey, Kraus	Korean
Ten Mile Day, Fraser	Multicultural
Thailand, Bailey	Thai
This Place is Crowded: Japan, Cobb	Japanese
Thousand Pails of Water, A, Roy	Japanese

Culture

Three Strong Women: a Tall Tale from Japan, Stamm	Japanese
Through Moon and Stars and Night Skies, Turner	Asian American
Tide Flowing, The, Phipson	Australian
Toad is the Uncle of Heaven, Lee	Vietnamese
Tongue-cut Sparrow, The, Ishii	Japanese
Tongues of Jade, Yep	Chinese
Tree of Cranes, Say	Japanese
Tuan, Boholm-Olsson	Vietnamese
Tucking Mommy In, Loh	Asian
Turtle and the Monkey: a Philippine Tale, The, Galdone	Filipino
Two Chinese Families, Sadler	Chinese
Two Foolish Cats, The, Uchida	Japanese
Two of Everything, Hong	Chinese
Tye May and the Magic Brush, Bang	Chinese
Umbrella Thief, The, Wettasinghe	Sri Lankan
Under the Starfruit Tree: Folktales from Vietnam, Terada	Vietnamese
Valiant Chatti-maker, Godden	Asian Indian
Very Special Sari: a Story Set in India, The, Mathieson	Asian Indian
Vietnam: Why We Fought, Hoobler	Vietnamese
Voice of the Great Bell, The, Hodges	Chinese
Walk on the Great Barrier Reef, A, Arnold	Australian
Wall of Names: the Story of the Vietnam Veterans Memorial, A, Donnelly	Vietnamese
Warrior and the Wise Man, The, Wisniewski	Japanese
We Adopted You, Benjamin Koo, Girard	Korean
We Came from Vietnam, Stanek	Vietnamese
We Don't Look Like Our Mom and Dad, Sobol	Korean
Weaving of a Dream: a Chinese Folktale, The, Heyer	Chinese
Wedding of the Rat Family, The, Kendall	Chinese
West Coast Chinese Boy, Lim	Chinese
What Comes in Spring, Horton	Asian
When I See My Doctor, Kuklin	Asian
Where a River Runs: a Portrait of a Refugee Family, Graff	Cambodian
Where the Forest Meets the Sea, Baker	Australian
White Wave: a Chinese Tale, Wolkstein	Chinese
Who Killed Cockatoo?, Cawthorne	Australian
Who Said Red?, Serfozo	Asian
Why Ducks Sleep on One Leg, Garland	Vietnamese
Why Rat Comes First: a Story of the Chinese Zodiac, Yen	Chinese
Wingman, The, Pinkwater	Chinese
Yang the Youngest and His Terrible Ear, Namioka	Chinese
Year of Impossible Goodbyes, Choi	Korean
Year of the Panda, The, Schlein	Chinese

Culture

Yeh-shen: a Cinderella Story from China, Louie	Chinese
Yellow River, The, Gregory	Chinese
Young Fu of the Upper Yangtze, Lewis	Chinese
Young Painter: the Life and Paintings of Wang Yani, A, Zhensun	Chinese
Yours Truly, Shirley, Martin	Vietnamese

Listings by culture, category and grade

Fiction – Preschool through third grade

Asian

	Title
Asian Cultural Centre of Unesco	Folk Tales from Asia for Children Everywhere: Book Three
Horton, Barbara	What Comes in Spring
Loh, Morag	Tucking Mommy In
Narahashi, Keiko	I Have a Friend
Palecek, Libuse	Magic Grove, The
Sasaki, Isao	Snow
Say, Allen	River Dream, A
Soya, Kiyoshi	House of Leaves, A
Whittle, Emily	Fisherman's Tale
Yolen, Jane	Girl Who Loved the Wind, The
	Seventh Mandarin, The

Asian American

	Title
Say, Allen	Lost Lake
Turner, Ann	Through Moon and Stars and Night Skies

Asian Indian

	Title
Birch, David	King's Chessboard, The
Bonnici, Peter	Festival, The
	Rains, The
Demi	Hallowed Horse: a Folktale from India, The
Gajadin, Chitra	Amal and the Letter from the King
Godden, Rumer	Valiant Chatti-maker, The
Kamen, Gloria	Ringdoves, The
Martin, Rafe	Foolish Rabbit's Big Mistake
Mathieson, Feroza	Very Special Sari: a Story Set in India, The
Ram, Govinder	Rama and Sita: an Indian Folk Tale
Rodanas, Kristina	Story of Wali Dad, The
Sharma, Rashmi	Blue Jackal, The
Shepard, Aaron	Savitri: a Tale of Ancient India

FICTION – PRESCHOOL THROUGH THIRD GRADE

Asian Indian

	Title
Singh, Jacquelin	Fat Gopal
Tagore, Rabindranath	Paper Boats

Australian

	Title
Baker, Jeannie	Where the Forest Meets the Sea
Cawthorne, W.	Who Killed Cockatoo?
Czernecki, Stefan	Singing Snake
Fox, Mem	Possum Magic
Norman, Lilith	Paddock: a Story in Praise of the Earth, The
Roughsey, Dick	Giant Devil-dingo, The
Trinca, Rod	One Woolly Wombat
Wheatley, Nadia	My Place
Wilson, Barbara	Acacia Terrace

Cambodian

	Title
Spagnoli, Cathy	Judge Rabbit and the Tree Spirit: a Folktale from Cambodia

Chinese

	Title
Armstrong, Jennifer	Chin Yu Min and the Ginger Cat
Allen, Judy	Panda
Ashley, Bernard	Cleversticks
Bang, Molly	Tye May and the Magic Brush
Birdseye, Tom	Song of Stars, A
Chang, Heidi	Elaine and the Flying Frog
	Elaine, Mary Lewis and the Frogs
Coerr, Eleanor	Chang's Paper Pony
Demi	Artist and the Architect, The
	Chen Ping and His Magic Axe
	Chinese Zoo: Fables and Proverbs, A
	Chingis Khan
	Demi's Dragons and Fantastic Creatures
	Demi's Reflective Fables
	Dragon Kites and Dragonflies
	Empty Pot, The
	Liang and the Magic Paintbrush
	Magic Boat, The
Evans, Doris	Breakfast with the Birds
Godden, Rumer	Fu-dog
Heyer, Marilee	Weaving of a Dream: a Chinese Folktale, The
Hidaka, Masako	Girl from the Snow Country

FICTION – PRESCHOOL THROUGH THIRD GRADE

Chinese

Author	Title
Hillman, Elizabeth	Min-Yo and the Moon Dragon
Hodges, Margaret	Voice of the Great Bell, The
Hong, Lily	How the Ox Star Fell from Heaven
	Two of Everything
Kendall, Carol	Wedding of the Rat Family, The
Leaf, Margaret	Eyes of the Dragon
Lee, Jeanne	Legend of the Li River: an Ancient Chinese Tale
	Legend of the Milky Way
Levine, Ellen	I Hate English!
Lobel, Arnold	Ming Lo Moves the Mountain
Louie, Ai-Ling	Yeh-shen: a Cinderella Story from China
Miller, Moira	Moon Dragon, The
Morris, Jill	Monkey and the White Bone Demon
Morris, Winifred	Magic Leaf, The
Pattison, Darcy	River Dragon
Pinkwater, Manus	Wingman, The
Pittman, Helena	Grain of Rice, A
Rappaport, Doreen	Journey of Meng: a Chinese Legend
Reuter, Bjarne	Princess, and the Sun, Moon, and Stars, The
San Souci, Robert	Enchanted Tapestry, The
Stock, Catherine	Emma's Dragon Hunt
Svend, Otto	Children of the Yangtze River
Tompert, Ann	Grandfather Tang's Story
Torre, L.	Luminous Pearl
Wolkstein, Diane	Magic Wings, The
Wyndham, Robert	Chinese Mother Goose Rhymes
Yacowitz, Caryn	Jade Stone: a Chinese Folktale
Ye, Chun-Chan	Bawshou Rescues the Sun: a Han Folktale
Yee, Paul	Roses Sing on New Snow: a Delicious Tale
Yep, Laurence	Man Who Tricked a Ghost, The
	Shell Woman and the King: a Chinese Folktale
	Tongues of Jade
Ying, Pen	Monkey Creates Havoc in Heaven
Yolen, Jane	Emperor and the Kite, The
	Seeing Stick, The
Young, Ed	Lon Po Po
	Red Thread
Zimelman, Nathan	I Will Tell You of Peach Stone

Filipino

Author	Title
Aruego, Jose	Crocodile's Tale: a Philippine Folk Story, A
Galdone, Paul	Turtle and the Monkey: a Philippine Tale, The
Villanueva, Marie	Nene and the Horrible Math Monster

FICTION – PRESCHOOL THROUGH THIRD GRADE

Hong Kong	*Title*
Levinson, Riki	Our Home is the Sea

Indonesian	*Title*
Sis, Peter	Komodo!

Japanese	*Title*
Baker, Keith	Magic Fan, The
Bang, Molly	Paper Crane, The
Bryan, Ashley	Sh-ko and His Eight Wicked Brothers
Friedman, Ina	How My Parents Learned to Eat
Fujimura, Hisakazu	Ho-Limlim: a Rabbit Tale from Japan
Garrison, Christian	Dream Eater, The
Hamanaka, Sheila	Screen of Frogs: an Old Tale
Hayashi, Akiko	Aki and the Fox
Hooks, William	Peach Boy
Hughes, Monica	Little Fingerling: a Japanese Folktale
Ike, Jane	Japanese Fairytale, A
Ikeda, Daisaku	Cherry Tree, The
	Over the Deep Blue Sea
	Princess and the Moon, The
	Snow Country Prince, The
Ishii, Momoko	Tongue-cut Sparrow, The
Johnson, Ryerson	Kenji and the Magic Geese
Johnston, Tony	Badger and the Magic Fan: a Japanese Folk Tale, The
Kimmel, Eric	Greatest of All: a Japanese Folktale, The
Levine, Arthur	Boy Who Drew Cats, The
Lifton, Betty	Joji and the Dragon
Luenn, Nancy	Dragon Kite, The
McCoy, Karen	Tale of Two Tengu, A
McDermott, Gerald	Stone Cutter: a Japanese Folktale, The
Melmed, Laura	First Song Ever Sung
Merrill, Jean	Girl Who Loved Caterpillars: a Twelfth Century Tale from Japan, The
Mochizuki, Ken	Baseball Saved Us
Morimoto, Junko	Inch Boy, The
	Mouse's Marriage, The
Mosel, Arlene	Funny Little Woman, The
Nakawatari, Harutaka	Sea and I
Newton, Patricia	Five Sparrows: a Japanese Folktale, The
Nomura, Takaaki	Grandfather's Town
Paterson, Katherine	Tale of the Mandarin Ducks, The
Pittman, Helena	Gift of the Willows, The

FICTION – PRESCHOOL THROUGH THIRD GRADE

Japanese	*Title*
Roy, Ronald	Thousand Pails of Water, A
Sakai, Kimiko	Sachiko Means Happiness
San Souci, Robert	Samurai's Daughter: a Japanese Legend
	Snow Wife
Sato, Satoru	I Wish I Had a Big, Big Tree
Say, Allen	Bicycle Man, The
	Tree of Cranes
Shigekawa, Marlene	Blue Jay in the Desert
Shute, Linda	Momotaro: the Peach Boy
Snyder, Dianne	Boy of the Three-year Nap, The
Stamm, Claus	Three Strong Women: a Tall Tale from Japan
Takeshita, Fuiko	Park Bench, The
Tompert, Ann	Bamboo Hats and a Rice Cake
Tsutsui, Yoriko	Anna in Charge
	Anna's Secret Friend
	Anna's Special Present
	Before the Picnic
Uchida, Yoshiko	Birthday Visitor, The
	Bracelet, The
	Magic Purse, The
	Rooster Who Understood Japanese, The
	Two Foolish Cats, The
Winthrop, Elizabeth	Journey to the Bright Kingdom
Wisniewski, David	Warrior and the Wise Man, The
Yagawa, Sumiko	Crane Wife

Korean	*Title*
Climo, Shirley	Korean Cinderella, The
Ginsburg, Mirra	Chinese Mirror, The
Han, Oki	Sir Whong and the Golden Pig
Kline, Suzy	Horrible Harry's Secret
Kraus, Joanna	Tall Boy's Journey
Kwon, Holly	Moles and the Mireuk: a Korean Folktale, The
O'Brien, Anna	Princess and the Beggar: a Korean Folktale
Paek, Min	Aekyung's Dream
Rhee, Nami	Magic Spring: a Korean Folktale
Schecter, Ellen	Sim Chung and the River Dragon: a Folktale from Korea
Seros, Kathleen	Sun and Moon: Fairy Tales from Korea

Mongolian	*Title*
Otsuka, Yuzo	Suho and the White Horse: a Legend of Mongolia

FICTION – PRESCHOOL THROUGH THIRD GRADE

Multicultural	Title
Brillhart, Julie	Anna's Goodbye Apron
Burstein, Fred	Dancer, The
Dooley, Norah	Everybody Cooks Rice
Medicott, Mary	Tales for Telling: from Around the World
Yashinsky, Dan	Storyteller at Fault, The

Pakistani	Title
Davis, Emmett	Clues in the Desert

Pacific Islands	Title
Lewis, Richard	In the Night, Still Dark
Williams, Julie	And the Birds Appeared

Sri Lankan	Title
Wettasinghe, Sybil	Umbrella Thief, The

Taiwanese	Title
Reddix, Valerie	Dragon Kite of the Autumn Moon

Tibetan	Title
Gerstein, Mordicai	Mountains of Tibet

Vietnamese	Title
Boholm-Olsson, Eva	Tuan
Clark, Ann	In the Land of Small Dragon: a Vietnamese Folktale
Coutant, Helen	First Snow
Garland, Sherry	Lotus Seed, The
	Why Ducks Sleep on One Leg
Lee, Jeanne	Ba-nam
	Silent Lotus
	Toad is the Uncle of Heaven
Surat, Michele	Angel Child, Dragon Child
Tran, Khanh	Little Weaver of Thai-yen Village, The

Listings by culture, category and grade

Fiction – Fourth through sixth grade

Asian

	Title
Asian Cultural Centre Unesco (eds)	Folk Tales from Asia for Children Everywhere: Book Three

Asian Indian

	Title
Bang, Betsy	Demons of Rajpur; Five Tales from Bengal
Beach, Milo	Adventures of Rama, The
Birch, David	King's Chessboard, The
Godden, Rumer	Valiant Chatti-maker, The
Perkins, Mitali	Sunita Experiment, The
Ram, Govinder	Rama and Sita: an Indian Folk Tale
Shepard, Aaron	Savitri: a Tale of Ancient India
Thompson, Brian	Story of Prince Rama, The

Australian

	Title
Broome, Errol	Dear Mr Sprouts
Klein, Robin	Hating Allison Ashley
Mahy, Margaret	Good Fortunes Gang
Marriott, Janice	Letters to Lesley
Park, Ruth	Playing Beatie Bow
Phipson, Joan	Tide Flowing, The
Spence, Eleanor	Devil's Hole, The
Thiele, Colin	Fire in the Stone
	Shadow Shark
Wrightson, Patricia	Ice is Coming

Cambodian

	Title
Baillie, Allan	Little Brother
Crew, Linda	Children of the River
Graff, Nancy	Where a River Runs: a Portrait of a Refugee Family

FICTION – FOURTH THROUGH SIXTH GRADE

Cambodian	*Title*
Ho, Minfong	Clay Marble
Spagnoli, Cathy	Judge Rabbit and the Tree Spirit: a Folktale from Cambodia

Chinese	*Title*
Alexander, Lloyd	Remarkable Journey of Prince Jen, The
Bunting, Eve	Happy Funeral, The
Carpenter, F.	Tales of a Chinese Grandmother
Chang, Margaret	In the Eye of War
Ellis, Sarah	Next-door Neighbors
Els, Betty	Bombers' Moon, The
Goldin, Barbara	Red Means Good Fortune
Heyer, Marilee	Weaving of a Dream: a Chinese Folktale, The
Hodges, Margaret	Voice of the Great Bell, The
Howard, Ellen	Her Own Song
Jagendorf, M.	Magic Boat and Other Chinese Folk Stories, The
Kasper, Vancy	Street of Three Directions
Kendall, Carol	Sweet and Sour: Tales from China
Krensky, Stephen	Iron Dragon Never Sleeps
Lattimore, Eleanor	Little Pear and His Friends
Levitin, Sonia	Golem and the Dragon Girl
Lewis, Elizabeth	Young Fu of the Upper Yangtze
Liyi, He	Spring of Butterflies and Other Folktales of China's Minority Peoples
Lord, Bette	In the Year of the Boar and Jackie Robinson
Namioka, Lensey	Yang the Youngest and His Terrible Ear
Patent, Gregory	Shanghai Passage
Sadler, Catherine	Heaven's Reward: Fairy Tales from China
Schlein, Miriam	Year of the Panda, The
Tung, S.	One Small Dog
Wolkstein, Diane	White Wave: a Chinese Tale
Yee, Paul	Tales from Gold Mountain: Stories of the Chinese in the New World
Yep, Laurence	Sea Glass
	Star Fisher
	Tongues of Jade

Japanese	*Title*
Bang, Molly	Dawn
Christopher, Matt	Shortstop from Tokyo
Clement, Claude	Painter and the Wild Swans, The
Coerr, Eleanor	Mieko and the Fifth Treasure

FICTION – FOURTH THROUGH SIXTH GRADE

Japanese	*Title*
Crofford, Emily	Born in the Year of Courage
Fujiwara, Alan	Baachan! Geechan! Arigato: a Story of Japanese Canadians
Garrigue, Sheila	Eternal Spring of Mr Ito, The
Haugaard, Erik	Boy and the Samurai
Hoobler, Dorothy	Aloha Means Come Back: the Story of a World War II Girl
Ishii, Momoko	Tongue-cut Sparrow, The
Kogawa, Joy	Naomi's Road
Maruki, Toshi	Hiroshima No Pika
Mattingley, Christobel	Miracle Tree, The
Mori, Kyoko	Shizuko's Daughter
Namioka, Lensey	Coming of the Bear
Pittman, Helena	Gift of the Willows, The
Savin, Marcia	Moon Bridge
Say, Allen	Feast of Lanterns, The
Soto, Gary	Pacific Crossing
Uchida, Yoshiko	Best Bad Thing, The
	Happiest Ending, The
	Journey Home, The
	Journey to Topaz
	Magic Listening Cap: More Folk Tales from Japan
Watkins, Yoko	Tales from the Bamboo Grove

Korean	*Title*
Choi, Sook	Year of Impossible Goodbyes
Kraus, Joanna	Tall Boy's Journey
Lee, Marie	Finding My Voice
MacMillan, Dianne	My Best Friend Mee-yung Kim: Meeting a Korean-American Family
McDonald, Joyce	Mail-order Kid

Pakistani	*Title*
Andrews, Jean	Secret in the Dorm Attic, The

Taiwanese	*Title*
Scarboro, Elizabeth	Secret Language of the Sb, The

FICTION – FOURTH THROUGH SIXTH GRADE

Vietnamese *Title*

Garland, Sherry — Lotus Seed, The
Song of the Buffalo Boy
MacMillan, Dianne — My Best Friend Duc Tran: Meeting a Vietnamese American Family
Martin, Ann — Yours Truly, Shirley
Paterson, Katherine — Park's Quest
Vuong, Lynette — Brocaded Slipper and Other Vietnamese Tales, The

Listings by culture, category and grade

Nonfiction – Preschool through third grade

Asian	Title
Kuklin, Susan	When I See My Doctor

Asian Indian	Title
Bailey, Donna	India
Haskins, Jim	Count Your Way Through India

Australian	Title
Bailey, Donna	Australia
Catterwell, Thelma	Sebastian Lives in a Hat
Tresize, Percy	Peopling of Australia, The

Chinese	Title
Dell, Pamela	I.M. Pei
	Michael Chang: Tennis Champion
Fisher, Leonard	Great Wall of China, The
Fyson, Nance	Family in China, A
Harkonen, Reijo	Children of China, The
Haskins, Jim	Count Your Way Through China
Mason, Sally	Take a Trip to China
Peng, Ta	Fun With Chinese Festivals
Say, Allen	El Chino
Waters, Kate	Lion Dancer: Ernie Wan's Chinese New Year
Yen, Clara	Why Rat Comes First: a Story of the Chinese Zodiac
Zhensun, Zheng	Young Painter: the Life and Paintings of Wang Yani, A

Filipino

	Title
Bailey, Donna	Philippines

Hong Kong

	Title
Bailey, Donna	Hong Kong

Indonesian

	Title
Lye, Keith	Take a Trip to Indonesia

Japanese

	Title
Bailey, Donna	Japan
Corwin, Judith	Asian Crafts
Haskins, Jim	Count Your Way Through Japan
Morimoto, Junko	My Hiroshima
Nakano, Dokuohtei	Easy Origami
Say, Allen	Grandfather's Journey
Simon, Charnan	Seiji Ozawa: Symphony Conductor
Tsuchiya, Yukio	Faithful Elephants: a True Story of Animals, People and War
Wetzel, Joanne	Christmas Box, The

Korean

	Title
Beirne, Barbara	Pianist's Debut: Preparing for the Concert Stage, A
Girard, Linda	We Adopted You, Benjamin Koo
Haskins, Jim	Count Your Way Through Korea
Sobol, Harriet	We Don't Look Like Our Mom and Dad

Laotian

	Title
Blia, Xiong	Nine-in-one Grr! Grr! a Folktale from the Hmong People of Laos

Multicultural

	Title
Fraser, Mary	Ten Mile Day

NONFICTION – PRESCHOOL THROUGH THIRD GRADE

Nepalese	*Title*
Harkonen, Reijo	Children of Nepal, The
Lye, Keith	Take a Trip to Nepal
Margolies, Barbara	Kanu of Kathmandu: a Journey in Nepal

New Zealand	*Title*
Burns, Geoff	Take a Trip to New Zealand

Pacific Islands	*Title*
Feeney, Stephanie	A is For Aloha
	Hawaii is a Rainbow

Taiwanese	*Title*
Yu, Ling	Family in Taiwan, A

Thai	*Title*
Bailey, Donna	Thailand
Thomson, Ruth	Family in Thailand, A

Tibetan	*Title*
Fraser, Mary	On Top of the World
Reynolds, Jan	Himalaya

Vietnamese	*Title*
Donnelly, Judy	Wall of Names: the Story of the Vietnam Veterans Memorial, A
Shalant, Phyllis	Look What We've Brought You from Vietnam

SCOLAR PRESS

A Guide to Children's Books about Asian Americans

Owing to a printing error the final sections of this book were not printed. This booklet contains the missing material.

We apologise to readers for this oversight.

Listings by culture, category and grade

Nonfiction – Fourth through sixth grade

Asian	Title
Georges, D	Asia
Lightfoot, Paul	Mekong, The
McGuire, William	Southeast Asians

Asian Indian	Title
	Buddhist Festivals
	Hindu Festivals
	Muslim Festivals
Bahree, Patricia	Hindu World, The
Cumming, David	India
Das, Prodeepta	Inside India
Giff, Patricia	Mother Teresa: Sisters to the Poor
Gordon, Susan	Asian Indians
Greene, Carol	Indira Nehru Gandhi: Ruler of India
Hunter, Nigel	Gandhi
Jacobsen, Peter	Family in India, A
Jaffrey, Madhur	Seasons of Splendor: Tales, Myths, and Legends of India
Kapoor, Sukhbir	Sikh Festivals
Knowlton, Marylee	India

Australian	Title
Arnold, Caroline	Australia Today
	Walk on the Great Barrier Reef, A
Browne, Rollo	Aboriginal Family, An
	Family in Australia, A
Garrett, Dan	Australia
Georges, D.	Australia
Gilbreath, Alice	Great Barrier Reef: a Treasure in the Sea, The
Gunner, Emily	Family in Australia, A
James, Ian	Australia

NONFICTION – FOURTH THROUGH SIXTH GRADE

Australian

	Title
Johnson, Rebecca	Great Barrier Reef: a Living Laboratory, The
MacDougall, Trudie	Beyond Dreamtime: the Life and Lore of the Aboriginal Australian
Pepper, Susan	Australia
Rau, Margaret	Red Earth, Blue Sky: the Australian Outback
Reynolds, Jan	Down Under
Yanagi, Akinobu	Australia

Burmese

	Title
Knowlton, Marylee	Burma

Cambodian

	Title
Carrison, Muriel	Cambodian Folk Stories from the Gatiloke

Chinese

	Title
Ashabranner, Brent	Land of Yesterday, Land of Tomorrow: Discovering Chinese Central Asia
Borja, Robert	Making Chinese Papercuts
Brown, Tricia	Chinese New Year
Foster, Leila	Nien Cheng: Courage in China
Fritz, Jean	Homesick: My Own Story
Goff, Denise	Early China
Gregory, K.	Yellow River, The
Harkonen, Reijo	Children of China, The
Johnson, Neil	Step into China
Krull, Kathleen	City Within a City: How Kids Live in New York's Chinatown
Lim, Sing	West Coast Chinese Boy
Mayberry, Jodine	Chinese
McClung, Robert	Lili: a Giant Panda of Sichuan
McDearmon, Kay	Giant Pandas
Morey, Janet	Famous Asian Americans
Peng, Ta	Fun With Chinese Festivals
Sadler, Catherine	Two Chinese Families
Shui, Amy	Chinese Food and Drink
Talan, Sally	China
Thomson, Peggy	City Kids in China
Wu, Dana	Chinese-American Experience
Yen, Clara	Why Rat Comes First: a Story of the Chinese Zodiac
Yep, Laurence	Lost Garden, The

NONFICTION – FOURTH THROUGH SIXTH GRADE

Chinese	Title
Zhensun, Zheng	Rainbow People, The Young Painter: the Life and Paintings of Wang Yani, A

Filipino	Title
Chua-Eoan, Howard	Aquino
Lepthien, Emilie	Corazon Aquino: President of the Philippines
Mayberry, Jodine	Filipinos
Scariano, Margaret	Picture Life of Corazon Aquino, The

Hong Kong	Title
McKenna, Nancy	Family in Hong Kong, A
Wright, David	Hong Kong

Indonesian	Title
McNair, Sylvia	Indonesia

Japanese	Title
Cassedy, Sylvia	Red Dragonfly on My Shoulder
Cobb, Vicki	This Place is Crowded: Japan
Coerr, Eleanor	Sadako and the Thousand Paper Cranes
Elkin, Judith	Family in Japan, A
Greene, Carol	Japan
Hamanaka, Sheila	Journey: Japanese Americans, Racism, and Renewal
Higa, Tomike	Girl With the White Flag
Takashima, Shizuye	Child in Prison Camp, A
Uchida, Yoshiko	Invisible Thread: an Autobiography, The

Korean	Title
Ashby, Gwynneth	Family in South Korea, A
Beirne, Barbara	Pianist's Debut: Preparing for the Concert Stage, A

NONFICTION – FOURTH THROUGH SIXTH GRADE

Laotian

	Title
Chan, Anthony	Hmong Textile Designs
Goldfarb, Mace	Fighters, Refugees, Immigrants: a Story of the Hmong

Multicultural

	Title
Fraser, Mary	Ten Mile Day

Nepalese

	Title
Harkonen, Reijo	Children of Nepal, The
Rosen, Mike	Conquest of Everest, The

New Zealand

	Title
Armitage, Ronda	New Zealand
Higham, Charles	Maoris, The

Pacific Islands

	Title
Stanley, Fay	Last Princess: the Story of Princess Ka'iulani of Hawaii, The
Thompson, Vivian	Hawaiian Tales of Heroes and Champions
	Hawaiian Myths of Earth, Sea, and Sky
Tune, Suelyn	How Maui Slowed the Sun

Pakistani

	Title
Scarsbrook, Alisa	Family in Pakistan, A

Singaporean

	Title
Goom, Bridget	Family in Singapore, A

Sri Lankan

	Title
Bennett, Gay	Family in Sri Lanka, A

NONFICTION – FOURTH THROUGH SIXTH GRADE

Tibetan	Title
Fraser, Mary	On Top of the World
Timpanelli, Gioia	Tales from the Roof of the World: Folktales of Tibet

Vietnamese	Title
Donnelly, Judy	Wall of Names: the Story of the Vietnam Veterans Memorial, A
Hoobler, Dorothy	Vietnam: Why We Fought
Hoyt-Goldsmith, Diane	Hoang Anh: a Vietnamese American Boy
Huynh, Quang	Land I Lost: Adventures of a Boy in Vietnam, The
Krull, Kathleen	Lee Ann: the Story of a Vietnamese American Girl
Nhuong, Huynh	Land I Lost, The
Terada, Alice	Under the Starfruit Tree: Folktales from Vietnam

Select list of sources of Asian children's books

ARC Associates, Inc.
310 Eighth Street, Suite 220
Oakland, CA 94607

Asahlya Bookstores
Little Tokyo Square
333 S. Alameda Street, Suite 108
Los Angeles, CA 90746

Asahlya Bookstores
2324 S. Elmhurst Road
Mt. Prospect, IL 60056

Asia Resource Center
Box 15275
Washington, DC 20003

Bantam Books
666 Fifth Avenue
New York, NY 10019

Barnaby Books
3290 Pacific Heights Road
Honolulu, Hawaii, 96813

Bess Press
P.O. Box 22388
Honolulu, Hawaii, 96823

Booklines Hawaii
P.O. Box 2170
Pearl City, Hawaii, 96782–9170

Carolrhoda Books
241 First Avenue N.
Minneapolis, MN 55401

Children's Press
5440 N. Cumberland
Chicago, IL 60656

China Books & Periodicals
2929 24 Street
San Francisco, CA 94110

China International Book Trading Corp.
P.O. Box 399
Beijing, China

Council on Interracial Books for Children
1841 Broadway
New York, NY 10023

Crown Publishers
225 Park Avenue S.
New York, NY 10003

Dell Publishing Company
One Dag Hammarskjold Plaza
245 E. 47 Street
New York, NY 10017

Dial Books for Young Readers
Two Park Avenue
New York, NY 10016

Doubleday & Company
Books for Young Readers
245 Park Avenue
New York, NY 10017

Farrar, Straus & Giroux
Children's Books
19 Union Square W.
New York, NY 10003

Four Winds Press
866 Third Avenue
New York, NY 10022

SOURCES OF ASIAN CHILDREN'S BOOKS

Greenwillow Books
105 Madison Avenue
New York, NY 10016

Hakusendo Bookstore
3904 Convoy Street, Suite 106
San Diego, CA 92111

Harcourt Brace Jovanovich
1250 Sixth Avenue
San Diego, CA 92101

HarperCollins
Children's Books
10 East 53rd Street
New York, NY 10022

Hawaiian Island Concepts
P.O. Box 1069
Wailuku, Maui, Hawaii, 96793

Hawaiian Resources
203 Kilea Place
Wahiawa, Hawaii, 96786

Houghton Mifflin Company
Children's Book Division
Two Park Street
Boston, MA 02107

Island Heritage
99–880 Iwaena Street
Aiea, Hawaii, 96701

Iwase Books Atlanta
Around Lenox Shopping Center
3400 Wooddale Drive Unit C510
Atlanta, GA 30326

Joy Street Books
34 Beacon Street
Boston, MA 02106

Julian Messner
1230 Avenue of the Americas
New York, NY 10020

Jung Ku Book and Stationery Co.
8 Pell Street
New York, NY 10013

Kamehameha Schools Press
Kapalama Heights
Honolulu, Hawaii, 96817

Kane/Miller Book Publishers
Box 529
Brooklyn, NY 11231
or
Box 12374
La Jolla, CA 92037

Kinokuniya Bookstores
10 W. 49th Street
New York, NY 10020

Kinokuniya Bookstores
675 Saratoga Avenue
San Jose, CA 95129

Kinokuniya Bookstores
2141 W. 182d Street
Torrance, CA 90504

Lerner Publications Company
241 First Avenue N.
Minneapolis, MN 55401

Lothrop, Lee & Shepard Books
105 Madison Avenue
New York, NY 10016

Margaret K. McElderry Books
866 Third Avenue
New York, NY 10022

Native Books
P.O. Box 37095
Honolulu, Hawaii, 96837

Pan Asian Publication (USA) Inc.
29564 Union City Blvd.
Union City, CA 94587

Puffin Books
40 W. 23 Street
New York, NY 10010

Random House
201 E. 50 Street
New York, NY 10022

Sakura Book Store
15809 S. Frederick Road
Rockville, MD 20855

Tokyo-do Shoten
18924 Brookhurst Street
Fountain Valley, CA 92708

SOURCES OF ASIAN CHILDREN'S BOOKS 223

University of Hawaii Press
2840 Kolowalu Street
Honolulu, Hawaii, 96822

Viking Kestrel
40 W. 23 Street
New York, NY 10010

World Journal Book Store, Inc.
377 Broadway
New York, NY 10013

WITHDRAWN
STAFFORD LIBRARY
COLUMBIA COLLEGE
COLUMBIA, MO 65216